INTERNATIONAL MARKETING

STRATEGY AND MANAGEMENT

Colin Gilligan and Martin Hird

ROUTLEDGE

First published 1986 by Croom Helm
Reprinted by Routledge 1989
11 New Fetter Lane, London EC4P 4EE

© 1986 Colin Gilligan and Martin Hird

Typeset in Times Roman by Leaper & Gard Ltd, Bristol
Printed and bound in Great Britain by Mackays of Chatham Ltd, Kent

British Library Cataloguing in Publication Data

International marketing: strategy and
  management.
  1. Export marketing
  I. Title   II. Hird, Martin
  658.8'48   HF1009.5

ISBN 0-415-04609-2

CONTENTS

LIST OF TABLES

LIST OF FIGURES

ACKNOWLEDGEMENTS

In writing this book we wish to acknowledge the help and co-operation that we have received from a variety of people, including Gordon Heald and Elizabeth Stodel of Gallup Poll who gave us permission to reproduce their work on British exporters' use of market research; Barclays Bank which provided the diagram that we have used to illustrate approaches to counter trade; McCann-Erickson, whose table on the criteria for global advertising appears in Chapter 8; and the various publishers who have allowed us to reproduce diagrams and tables throughout the text. Our particular thanks go to Ruth Barker, Barbara Colledge and Liz Burrows who typed the manuscript.

Colin Gilligan
Martin Hird

Colin Gilligan is a Principal Lecturer and the Subject Leader in Marketing in the Department of Business Studies and Economics, Sheffield City Polytechnic. His previous books include *Advertising Management* (Philip Allan, 1976) and *Business Decision Making* (Philip Allan, 1983).

Martin Hird is Head of the Faculty of Business, Humberside College of Higher Education. His course responsibilities include a BA European Business Studies programme which is run in conjunction with Fachhochschule Münster, West Germany.

*For
Rosie and Ben,
Eleanor, Colin, Iain and Nicholas.*

PREFACE

International business is currently going through the most fundamental and far-reaching process of change of the post-war period.
The implications of this change pose a significant challenge both to
industry and government throughout the world and promise to
alter not only the nature and structure of competition, but also the
balance of economic power. Prominent amongst the causes of this
change are shifting demographic profiles, ever-greater levels of
political intervention in the market mechanism, and, perhaps most
importantly of all, an increasingly competitive and malevolent
market environment in which only the fast-moving and proactive
organisation is likely to prosper. Arguably the single most dramatic
cause of change during the past twenty years has, however, been
the rise of Japan as a world economic power and the subsequent
domination by Japanese firms of many European and North
American markets. The consequences of the growth of Japan Inc.
have been felt in a wide variety of ways and reflected in the
dramatic and remarkably rapid collapse of many traditionally
strong industries throughout the Western world including televisions, motorcycles, cameras, and machine tools. The pressures of
this new and aggressive competition are, in turn, being exacerbated
by the emergence and growth of the newly industrialised countries
(NICs) such as Taiwan, Singapore, South Korea, India, Brazil and
Malaysia, all of which have begun to recognise and exploit their
economic strengths.

These changes in the balance of economic power, the growth of
new market opportunities, and the development of new technologies face businessmen with a deceptively straightforward and
stark choice: they must either respond to the challenges posed by
this new environment or recognise and accept the long-term
consequences of failing to do so. This need to respond should not,
however, be thought to be limited to firms of either a certain size
or to those that operate in particular industries. It is a change
which to a greater or lesser extent will ultimately affect companies
of all sizes in virtually all markets. The pressures of the international environment are now so great that the opportunity to
survive with a broadly reactive strategy no longer exists. The long

1

accepted models both of the international and the multinational corporation are becoming increasingly outdated with the future resting in the hands of the global corporation which recognises not only the greater commonality and convergence of markets, but also the need to pursue the notion of production sharing in the most cost-efficient parts of the world. Recognition of the significance of these pressures is reflected in the rapid growth in recent years of the number of strategic alliances between firms in various parts of the world in a desperate attempt to gain the economies of scale in production, distribution and marketing that are needed if a viable competitive profile is to be maintained.

The Japanese have, as we have observed, been instrumental in creating this change and subsequently have been successful in capitalising upon it. Elsewhere, evidence suggests that American firms are increasingly coming to terms with it, as indeed are the Germans and some of the NICs. By way of contrast, the majority of British firms appear reluctant either to accept the reality of the new competition or to respond to it. The long-term consequences of this are, quite obviously, significant and seem likely to worsen Britain's position in the world economic league and to aggravate its post-war economic performance which has been little short of catastrophic with its share of the major industrial countries' total exports having shown a consistent and significant decline, whilst levels of import penetration of finished goods have risen dramatically. These failings are particularly apparent when compared with the performance of our major European competitors and are reflected in the British Overseas Trade Board (BOTB) observation that the massive exporting opportunities that exist are quite simply not being exploited. It is the case that for a majority of British companies the challenge of international marketing is one that is either ignored or only partially recognised.

In attempting to explain the reasons for this poor performance, commentators have pointed to a wide variety of possible contributory factors, but particularly to our apparent lack of price competitiveness in international markets. Our inability to compete on price, it is argued, is due largely to our own making and attributable to a combination of poor manufacturing productivity, low levels of investment, the slow adoption of new technology and processes, restrictive labour practice, relatively high levels of inflation, and unfavourable exchange rates, all of which have contributed to higher prices than those of our major overseas competitors. Others, however, argue that there is a danger of over-emphasising the role of price and that our inability to compete effectively is attributable to a series of far more fundamental factors. Baker, for example, in focusing upon the export problems of medium-sized firms, suggests that many of the difficulties that they typically experience in international markets are due to the fact that:

(a) Many companies do not have the resources to develop a sophisticated marketing process.
(b) Most companies seek a market for an existing product with which they have had considerable domestic experience — i.e. the company is seeking to match needs with their products rather than develop a product to satisfy identified but unfulfilled needs.
(c) Few companies have a natural feel for a foreign market. As a result, their experience will be limited and takes time to develop.
(d) Few companies possess the wealth of published data available in domestic markets making the quantification and prediction of export markets more difficult.[1]

A broadly similar theme emerges from a number of other studies (see, e.g., Tessler (1981) and Turnbull and Cunningham (1981)) and point to the same general conclusion that 'it is a failure in exporting practice rather than exogenous variables such as the state of the economy, that are primarily to blame'.[2] This notion of an export myopia has been pursued by Baker who in an award winning article on the ills of British exporting claims that:

Perhaps the single most pervading finding of research into export performance is the fact that many companies simply fail to carry forward any marketing orientation they may have developed in their domestic market to overseas markets. While many companies have now adopted and embraced the marketing philosophy at home, they still follow a product orientation abroad.[3]

In support of this, he cites a considerable body of evidence to suggest that many firms view exports as a way of dealing with seasonal fluctuations in demand in the domestic market, or as an outlet for excess production, a theme which has, in turn, been developed by Turnbull and Cunningham:

> Commitment by a company to exporting, as expressed in its operations, is one of the most crucial issues we have encountered in our research ... We have encountered companies with a lack of full commitment to exporting even though they are involved in selling abroad. Many previous studies have shown that export sales are regarded by many companies as a way of utilising surplus capacity. This lack of commitment leads to such companies taking a half-hearted attitude to export sales and they have failed to adapt to foreign market requirements. These new requirements are seen as unreasonable and impose difficulties which are impediments and interruptions to the company's normal operations.[4]

A further barrier to export success that has been increasingly evident in recent years is the inability of many export salesmen to speak to the customer in his own language. Suntook, for example, points to the fact that less than 30 per cent of companies he interviewed saw foreign language capability as the major criterion for the selection of export sales staff.[5] By way of contrast, the French and German respondents in an ITI study suggested that language proficiency is the single most important factor of effective export staff, since: 'It improves the flow of communication, enhances one's ability to grasp the ethos and mentality of an overseas market, and is an important psychological tool in the art of selling.'[6] This lack of total commitment to export marketing has also been pointed to by Hooley and Newcomb who put much of the blame upon top management. This manifests itself, they suggest, 'in the low status and importance attached to the exporting department (where this even exists) and a lack of resource allocation to exporting'.[7] To support this argument, they point to a considerable body of evidence, including the work of the British Overseas Trade Board which concluded that too many British companies simply treat exporting as a marginal activity rather than integrating it fully into corporate operations;[8] Industrial Market Research Ltd (IMRL) which found that even in companies which had been exporting for a considerable time, responsibility for export activity was rarely at board level and that in only one firm out of five were the export sales staff engaged full time on exports;[9] Tessler who found that, size for size, not only do British firms typically have fewer export salesmen than their German or French counterparts, but also attempt to cover a far larger part of the world;[10] and McFarlane who pointed to the fact that only a small minority of Scottish Queen's Award to Industry winners have a market research specialist and that fewer than a third subscribed to the BOTB Export Intelligence Service.[11]

However, even where British firms are engaged in exporting, significant differences emerge between the strategies pursued and those of our major competitors. Prominent amongst these is the way in which many British companies tend to spread their effort across a variety of markets rather than concentrating the marketing effort upon a more limited number of key markets. An ITI study of more than 120 companies, for example, concluded that:

> The purposeful selection of a relatively few markets is perceived to present such benefits as limiting the resources required to establish export business, gaining greater market knowledge and permitting greater manpower specialisation giving the company more opportunity to compete on non-price factors rather than relying on price competition.[12]

Similar comments have emerged from a variety of other studies, including one by Barclays Bank which suggested that 40 per cent of British exporters sold in more than 100 markets compared with 32 French firms and only 20 per cent of German firms. These results are, in turn, supported by Turnbull and Cunningham,[13] who point to the consequent difficulty of developing a detailed understanding of each market and its requirements.[14]

A final major reason for poor British export performance appears to be a lack of willingness on the part of many firms to adapt their product to meet specific market requirements. Michell, for example, found that the most common product strategy involved offering the domestic product to all export markets.[15] The problems caused by such an unsophisticated strategy are for the most part self-evident, but are, in turn, exacerbated by the apparent lack of attention paid to after-sales service (see, e.g. McFarlane 1978), and to an emphasis upon straightforward cost-plus pricing rather than to market-oriented approaches.

The net effect of these sorts of failings, most of which are attributable to the attitudes of senior management, have proved to be significant and are reflected not just in a decline in our standards of living compared with those of our major trading partners, but also in the way in which Britain's reputation within the international business community has suffered in recent years. In an attempt to reverse this, a number of solutions have been proposed, including:

(i) the adoption of an international marketing orientation,
(ii) the more effective use of marketing research, and
(iii) a concentration of marketing effort.[16]

Underlying these suggestions is the need for a fundamental change in attitude on the part of many managers, together with a far greater recognition of the fact that success is international markets is unlikely to be achieved unless there is a total commitment throughout the organisation to the exporting function. The implications of such a change are, of course, significant and need to be reflected not just in the product itself, but throughout the marketing mix so that full recognition is given to the differing demands of each market.

It is against this background that this book has been written. It highlights many of the problems encountered by firms operating internationally and attempts to show how a formalised process of analysis, planning and control can contribute to their resolution. The book consists of three sections. Following the introduction, we examine the nature of the international marketing environment, the role of market research and the need for formal approaches to opportunity analysis. We then move on to consider market entry strategies and the particular problems of international marketing planning. From here, we go on to consider the major elements of the international marketing mix and the nature of the constraints within which these decisions are taken. We conclude by focusing upon one of the perennial problems of international business, how best to co-ordinate and control subsidiaries, some of which may be located on the other side of the world or in countries which have a very different cultural and political climate. A constant theme throughout the book is the increasing globalisation of markets and an ever more aggressive international environment in which companies face greater threats and higher levels of competition than ever before.

Quite deliberately, we have taken as our focus medium- and

large-sized organisations. The international marketing process for a small firm often differs considerably both in its nature and in the severity of the financial constraints within which decisions are made with the result that far greater emphasis is often placed upon market nicher strategies and on operating at arm's length through foreign intermediaries. Thus, although occasional reference is made within the text to a small firm's example, our primary concern is the decision-making processes of larger organisations.

Throughout the text we assume that the reader is familiar, in broad terms at least, with the basic principles of marketing. Our concern is therefore to show how these principles can be applied within the international environment and to illustrate the particular problems that are faced by many firms when moving out of their domestic market. To help in this, a case study designed to highlight a particular aspect of the discussion appears at the end of a number of the chapters.

References and Further Reading

1. M.J. Baker, *Marketing: An Introductory Text* (Macmillan, 1985).

2. G.J. Hooley and J.R. Newcomb, 'Ailing British Exports: Symptoms, Causes and Cures', *The Quarterly Review of Marketing*, vol. 8, no. 4 (1983), p. 16.

3. M.J. Baker, 'Export Myopia', *The Quarterly Review of Marketing*, vol. 4, no. 3, (Spring 1979).

4. P.W. Turnbull and M.T. Cunningham, *International Marketing and Purchasing* (Macmillan, 1981).

5. F. Suntook, 'How British Industry Exports', *Marketing*, June (1978).

6. ITI, 'Factors of International Success', *Barclays Bank International* (1979).

7. Hooley and Newcomb, 'Ailing British Exports', pp. 18-19.

8. British Overseas Trade Board (BOTB), 'Selling to Western Europe', BOTB (1981).

9. Industrial Market Research Ltd, 'How British Industry Exports', Report no. 4 (1978).

10. A. Tessler, 'The Loneliness of the Long Distance Salesman', *Export Direction*, March (1981).

11. G. McFarlane, 'Scots Queens Award Winners Don't Excel', *Marketing*, April (1978).

12. ITI, 'Concentration on Key Markets: A Development Plan for Exports', ITI Research Ltd (1975).

13. Barclays Bank Review, 'UK Economic Survey', 26 March 1982.

14. Turnbull and Cunningham, *International Marketing and Purchasing*.

15. P.C.N. Michell, 'Infrastructures and International Marketing Effectiveness', *Columbia Journal of World Business*, vol. 14, Spring (1979).

16. Hooley and Newcombe, 'Ailing British Exports', pp. 20-1.

INTRODUCTION

1 THE GROWTH OF INTERNATIONAL BUSINESS

The immediate post-World War II period saw a new commitment to international trade from the major industrial countries of the world. Not only was there an increasingly widespread acceptance of the principles of comparative advantage and its implication that it is in the economic interests of all nations that international trade should take place, but there was also recognition of the undesirable consequences that protectionism had produced in the 1930s. This commitment was most clearly manifest in a series of institutional agreements, including the creation of the International Monetary Fund (IMF) in 1944 following the Bretton Woods Agreement. The creation of the IMF was designed to achieve a number of objectives, including the expansion of international trade by ensuring the provision of sufficient international liquidity to finance the trade. A secondary objective in setting up the IMF was to provide funds for the short-term support of countries with a balance of trade deficit: this previously had acted as a major obstacle to their getting fully involved in reciprocal international arrangements.

An additional development designed to encourage multilateral trading was the General Agreement on Tariffs and Trade (GATT) in 1947. The basic premise of GATT was that if nations could come together and jointly agree upon multilateral reductions in barriers to trade, international trade would be stimulated and benefit all concerned. As we will see at a later stage in this chapter, GATT has subsequently been the forum for the successful reductions in tariff barriers for a wide variety of product groups which have, in turn, contributed to a significant growth in trade. Nevertheless, substantial barriers to trade still remain and are most evident in specific product areas and between some of the major trading blocs.

But despite these barriers, the period between 1948 and 1973 witnessed an unprecedented growth in world trade which was only brought to a halt by the first major oil crisis. The subsequent period has seen a marked slowdown throughout the world both in output and trade which has, in turn, brought renewed calls for protectionism and restrictions on the freedom of international trade from many quarters. In the UK, for example, the Cambridge

Economic Policy Group have argued that some degree of control over the flow of imports should be an essential element in any future overall economic strategy.

Nevertheless, despite the slower rates of growth since 1973 and calls for protectionist measures, international trade is a far more significant element in the economic activity of most industrialised countries than at any point in the post-war period. This growing dependence on international trade at the macroeconomic level is, of course, mirrored at the microeconomic level of the individual firm where exporting has become a more significant feature of activity than ever before for many businesses. This concern with exporting has manifested itself in an estimated 25-30 per cent of all post-war investment in the industrial world being related to production for export. Moreover, there has been an increasing tendency for firms to establish or acquire overseas production facilities which, in turn, is reflected in the rapid growth in the number and size of multinational companies.

Within this chapter, we begin by examining the nature and rationale of international marketing and discuss the ways in which multinational corporations have developed to meet the demands of world markets. We then turn our attention to the barriers to trade that still exist and comment upon their significance to the international marketer.

The Nature of International Marketing

In the Preface we stated that throughout the text we assume that the reader is broadly familiar with the basic principles of marketing and that our primary concern is to illustrate the particular problems that many firms face when moving out of their domestic market. In taking this approach, perhaps the most obvious starting point is to explain what is meant by international marketing and how it differs from domestic marketing. At its simplest level it involves the firm in making one or more marketing-mix decisions across national boundaries. At its most complex, it involves the firm in establishing manufacturing facilities overseas and making what are perhaps very different mix decisions in a variety of markets. These differences can be illustrated by considering two examples. At the one extreme are companies that opt for 'international marketing' simply by signing a distributive agreement with a foreign agent who then takes on the responsibility for pricing, promotion, distribution, and so on. At the other extreme, there are companies such as Ford which, with a worldwide turnover in excess of $55 billion in 1985, operates in some 120 countries via a combination of manufacturing plants, assembly operations and sales subsidiaries with a product range which includes cars and lorries, farm and industrial tractors, industrial engines, construction machinery, steel, glass and plastics, automotive replacement parts, electronics, communications and space technology.

Domestic marketing is often explained in terms of a company manipulating a series of controllable variables such as price, advertising, distribution and the product, in a largely uncontrollable external environment made up of competitors, cultural values, a legal infrastructure, and so on. The unique dimension of *international marketing* is that in many cases not only do the uncontrollable variables differ significantly between one market and another, but the controllable factors in the form of cost and price structures, opportunities for advertising, and distributive infrastructure are also likely to differ significantly between markets. It is these sorts of differences that lead to the complexities of international marketing.

A further dimension of the larger and more complex international operation is that of *multinational marketing management*; in other words, how the company might most effectively co-ordinate, integrate and control a whole series of national marketing programmes into a worthwhile multinational marketing effort. A primary objective of international marketing is to achieve a degree of synergy in the overall operation so that by taking advantage of different exchange rates, tax rates, labour rates, skill levels and market opportunities, the organisation as a whole will be greater than the sum of its parts. This can be illustrated by considering how multinational firms make use of production-sharing techniques, a practice that we discuss in greater detail at a later stage in this chapter:

> The hand-held calculator may carry the nameplate of a Japanese company — but this is the only thing on it that is 'Made in Japan'. The electronic chips came from the United States. They were assembled in Singapore, in Malaya, in Indonesia, perhaps in Nigeria. The steel for the housing may be the product of an Indian steel mill. And then, in some free-port

zone in Kobe or Yokohama, the label 'Made in Japan' was put on. The calculator is then sold all over the world — the bulk, of course, in developed countries. The design, the quality control, and the marketing of the calculator were handled by a Japanese company located in a highly developed country. The stages of production that require high technology, tight quality control, high capital investment — that is the design and manufacture of the chips — were also handled in a developed country, the United States. But the labor-intensive work was done in developing countries.[1]

These sorts of production and sales arrangements have a number of significant managerial implications and call for managers who are capable of operating as international managers, a task which is far broader than that of operating either in a specific foreign country or in the domestic market. In discussing this, Terpstra comments that 'the international marketing manager has a threefold responsibility: *international marketing* (marketing across national boundaries); *foreign marketing* (marketing within foreign countries); and *multinational marketing management* (co-ordinating marketing in multiple markets).'[2]

However, before we focus upon each of these areas, we need to consider why firms move out of their domestic markets and go international. Empirical studies over a number of years have pointed to a wide variety of reasons, including saturation of the domestic market whilst opportunities for further growth still exist overseas; foreign competition in the domestic market which leads firms either to seek other less competitive markets or take on the competitor in its home markets; the emergence of new markets, particularly in the developing world; government incentives to export; tax incentives offered by foreign governments to establish manufacturing plants in their countries in order to create jobs; the availability of cheaper or more skilled labour; an attempt to minimise the risks of a recession or political instability in one country; and, as in Polaroid's case, a desire to achieve the greater economies of scale which were only possible by moving into foreign markets.[3]

Because international marketing has become so important for many firms in recent years, its impact upon domestic marketing programmes is becoming increasingly significant. This can be illustrated by considering its effect upon just one aspect of the marketing mix, the product itself. Increasingly, companies are adapting product development programmes so that the final product can be marketed in as many countries as possible with few, if any, modifications. Both Ford and General Motors, for example, have in recent years pursued the development of 'world cars' which are targeted at an identifiable world market segment and modified only slightly for individual market requirements. A similar approach has also been adopted by Toyota with the Corolla, and Caterpillar with a range of construction and earth-moving equipment.

The ultimate objective for many companies in pursuing such a strategy is the development of the truly global brand, one which is acceptable throughout the world. The synergistic benefits, particularly in terms of the potential for economies of scale, are considerable and for this reason the global brand has been referred to as the international marketer's holy grail.

The Theory of Comparative Advantage

The rationale for world trade is based largely upon the theory of comparative advantage that was developed mainly by the classical economist David Ricardo. At its simplest level, the theory suggests that trade between countries takes place because one country is able to produce a product at a lower price than is possible elsewhere. An illustration of this is provided by the way in which Japanese companies such as Sony and Hitachi came to dominate the British television market in the 1970s. Their strategy was based upon higher product quality, better design and, more importantly for our purposes here, the lower prices that were made possible by far greater economies of scale and better manufacturing technology than was currently being achieved by the domestic producers.

It is this notion of relative cost that underpins world trade; in other words, countries should concentrate upon producing products that have a *comparative advantage* over those of other countries, and then export them in exchange for those for which their foreign competitor has a comparative advantage.

A comparative advantage can be achieved in a variety of ways. A sustained period of investment, for example, may well lead to significantly lower operating costs. Alternatively, a firm operating internationally might quite deliberately locate a manufacturing or assembly plant in one of the less developed countries (LDCs) such as Taiwan to take advantage of lower labour costs; a substantial proportion of the televisions, radios, calculators and jeans sold in European markets by the multinationals in the 1980s, for example, are manufactured in the LDCs in order to take advantage of their far more favourable labour costs. Equally, a comparative advantage may be based upon managerial ability, an abundance of a raw material, or indeed by a government providing subsidies to help its native industries. This was illustrated quite dramatically in 1984 when a British company appeared to have won a contract from the Turkish government to build a new bridge across the Bosphorus. At almost the last moment, the Japanese government stepped in to provide a subsidy to one of their companies, with the result that the British lost the comparative advantage they had previously enjoyed and subsequently the contract.

The International Product Life Cycle

The theory of comparative advantage is often seen as the classic explanation of world trade. In the late 1960s, however, Raymond Vernon, who was then working at the Harvard Business School, proposed a new explanation of world trade and investment patterns that was based upon the product life cycle concept.[4] Writing from an American perspective, he suggested that on an international level products move through four distinct phases:

Phase I   US firms manufacture for the home market and begin exporting.
Phase II   Foreign production starts.
Phase III Foreign products become increasingly competitive in world markets.
Phase IV   Imports to the USA begin and provide significant competition.

This cycle, which is illustrated in Figure 1.1, begins with the product being developed and manufactured in the United States for high income markets, and subsequently being introduced into other markets in the form of exports. The second phase begins to emerge as the technology is developed further and becomes more

Figure 1.1: The Product Life Cycle in International Trade

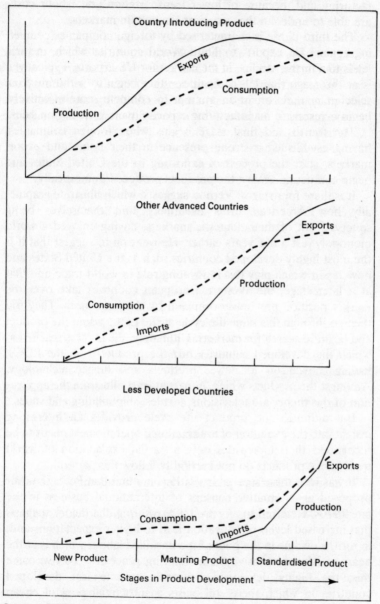

Source: L.T. Wells, 'A Product Life Cycle for International Trade?', *Journal of Marketing*, July (1968), pp. 1-6.

easily transferable. Companies in other countries then begin manufacturing and, because of lower transportation and labour costs, are able to undercut the Americans in certain markets.

The third phase is characterised by foreign companies competing against US exports to Third World countries which, in turn, leads to a further decline in the market for US exports. Typically, it is at this stage that US companies either begin to withdraw from selected markets or, in an attempt to compete more effectively, begin investing in manufacturing capacity overseas to regain sales.

The fourth and final stage begins when foreign companies, having established a strong presence in their home and export markets, start the process of exporting to the United States and begin competing against the products produced domestically.

It is these four stages, Vernon suggests, which illustrate graphically how American firms eventually find themselves being squeezed out of their domestic markets, having enjoyed a world monopoly just a few years earlier. He went on to suggest that it is the most highly developed countries such as the United States and now Japan which play this innovating role in world trade and that at a later stage, the Western European countries take over the market position previously occupied by the innovators. They too then go through this same life cycle as the LDCs adopt the product and begin to search for markets. Ultimately, the point is reached at which the developed countries buy the product from the LDCs, having moved on to newer products and higher technology. Amongst the products which, in part at least, illustrate the application of this theory are televisions, textiles, shipbuilding and shoes.

But although the product life cycle provides an interesting insight into the evolution of multinational operations, it needs to be recognised that it provides only a partial explanation of world trade, since products do not inevitably follow this pattern.

It was with these sorts of limitations in mind that Peter Drucker proposed an alternative concept of international business in the late 1970s. Referred to as *production-sharing*, the theory suggests that increased levels of education lead to higher expectations and, in turn, a decline in the pool of the unskilled labour which is at the heart of labour-intensive manufacturing processes. To overcome this, the highly developed countries turn to less developed countries in which there still exists a substantial pool of cheap labour. This labour is then used either to make the entire product or to assemble it partially with the final manufacturing stages being

performed either in the home country or in a country in which the
level of skill, and hence the labour costs, fall between the two. The
way in which this works was illustrated in our earlier example of
the manufacturing process for hand-held calculators, and is also
shown by the ways in which many shoes are now made:

> Men's shoes sold in the United States usually start out as the
> hide on the American cow. As a rule the hide is not tanned,
> however, in the United States, but shipped to a place like Brazil
> for tanning — highly labor-intensive work. The leather is then
> shipped — perhaps through the intermediary of a Japanese trad-
> ing company — to the Caribbean. Part of it may be worked up
> into uppers in the British Virgin Islands, part into soles in Haiti.
> And then uppers and soles are shipped to islands like Barbados
> or Jamaica, the products of which have access to Britain, to the
> European Common Market, and to Puerto Rico, where they are
> worked up into shoes that enter the United States under the
> American tariff umbrella. Surely these are truly transnational
> shoes. The hide, though it's the largest single-cost element, still
> constitutes no more than one quarter of the manufacturer's cost
> of the shoe. By labor content these are 'imported shoes'. By skill
> content they are 'American-made'. Raising the cow, which is
> capital-intensive, heavily automated, and requires the greatest
> skill and advanced management, is done in a developed
> country, which has the skill, the knowledge and the equipment.
> The management of the entire process, the design of the shoes,
> their quality control and their marketing are also done entirely
> in developed countries where the manpower and the skills
> needed for these tasks are available.[5]

Because of the quite obvious advantages of production sharing,
its use has grown enormously over the past decade. It is, as one
commentator has observed, a new phenomenon for which there
are no classic or neo-classic explanatory theories. Strictly speaking,
production sharing is different from the traditional idea of international trade. It is a transnational business integration — a new
relationship made possible by technological and business forces.
Production sharing offers both the developed and developing
countries of the world a chance to share their resources and
strengths for their mutual benefit.[6]

More recently, Drucker's arguments have been developed by

Kenichi Ohmae. In his book *Triad Power*,[7] he points to the emergence of the three major trading blocs — the United States, Japan and Europe — and to the implications for the bases of competition amongst the multinationals. Together, the Triad accounts for 54 per cent of world trade and provides a market of 600 million people. In order to survive and compete effectively within this market, he argues that the old model of a multinational is out of date. The high costs of R & D, the swiftness with which the competition now reacts to new products particularly in the high-technology area, and the similarities of public taste across the developed world, all compel large companies to adopt a new strategy. The markets of the Triad have to be attacked simultaneously and products have to be designed from the start for world markets.

An additional implication of this is that alliances between companies have become increasingly necessary to enable them to keep up with rapid technological change. Faced with this, firms that think only of regional or national markets are increasingly likely to lose their competitive advantage. The implications of this changed approach are reflected in the marketing strategies of a wide variety of companies, including Sony which now pursues a philosophy in which products such as the Walkman are launched throughout the world simultaneously. Both the feasibility and the necessity for such a strategy have been brought about by the development of capital-intensive techniques that produce the product in such large quantities that only the Triad is a large enough market for an adequate return. It was the early recognition of this need for a global perspective that provided the basis for the Japanese attack upon many of the European and Japanese consumer goods markets in the 1960s and 1970s. In the case of motorcycles, for example, the Japanese were surprised by the ease with which they captured the British market and the lack of resistance from established manufacturers. The British companies failed to recognise the need for a counter-attack, or indeed for alliances between companies. Instead, they fell into a vicious cycle in which they gave up their main segments, concentrated upon relatively peaceful niches, confined their activities to the domestic markets, and repeated the cost reduction and removal of overhead cycle.

The lessons learned from this have subsequently been used by other Japanese manufacturers, including Nissan and Toyota who claim to be almost twice as productive as their nearest rivals, whilst the entire Japanese motor industry employs less people than General Motors. Equally, labour now accounts for only 5 per cent of the production costs of many Japanese electronics products. Jamazaki, the machine tools firm, and Fujitsu Fanuc, the robot manufacturers, for example, are capable of breaking even at only 10 per cent capacity utilisation.

The problems that these levels of efficiency have caused for firms in other parts of the world have, quite obviously, been considerable and have resulted in a variety of calls for protectionist measures. This, in turn, has led a number of Japanese companies to begin production overseas and to forge strategic alliances both with European and American firms. This trend for competitors to merge and share R & D and production facilities has proved to be particularly popular amongst manufacturers of cars, robotics, bio-technology, computers and aero-engines. The consortia, joint ventures and technical tie-ups that have emerged are designed to achieve three major objectives: (i) to stay abreast of technological developments; (ii) to become 'insiders' throughout the Triad; and (iii) to increase the ability to attack all of the constituent markets simultaneously.

Although it is the Japanese that have led this move, a number of American and European firms including IBM, Coca-Cola, Pepsi Cola, Unilever, Nestlé, Ford, General Motors, Olivetti and Philips, have also begun making significant moves in this direction in recent years. It is recognition of the benefits of such alliances that is also at the heart of the BL-Honda deal. (For a discussion of the growth of joint ventures amongst car manufacturers, the reader should refer to the motor industry case study that appears at the end of Chapter 4.)

The Role of the Multinational Corporations

Over the past three decades, multinational corporations (MNCs) have become the most significant single factor in patterns of world trade and investment. The significance of their role stems from their allocation and use of world resources through the development of new products and services, the creation of patterns of demand, and by their development of methods of manufacturing and distribution. Indeed, it is now the case that the pattern and pace of industrialisation both in the developed and the developing world are determined to a very large extent by the MNCs. Their significance in this sense can perhaps be illustrated by considering that there are currently some 7,500 firms throughout the world which may be considered as MNCs; that almost 450 of these have annual sales in excess of $1 billion; and that many MNCs have an annual turnover which exceeds the gross national product (GNP) of many highly developed nations such as Belgium, Switzerland and, indeed, the United Kingdom. Their significance can also be appreciated by recognising that in 1985 the 20 largest MNCs *each* had gross sales that were greater in value than the GNP of 73 of the World Bank's 101 member countries. General Motors alone, for example, with some $70 billion of sales in 1984, superseded the GNP of around 130 world nations. It is power of this magnitude that has led to many smaller countries feeling threatened by the operations of MNCs.

The crucial feature of a multinational's operation is the pursuit of a global strategy of investment, production and distribution. This, in turn, leads to many MNCs deriving more than 50 per cent of their annual sales from overseas operations. Included amongst the companies in this position are Nestlé, IBM, Ford, Coca-Cola, BP, Black & Decker, Massey-Ferguson and H.J. Heinz. An additional feature of many MNCs is that they operate predominantly in oligopolistic markets where their technological advantages and financial resources can be used to reinforce the market's oligopolistic character. It is this, above all else, which has led in recent years to increasingly widespread criticism of the multinational's method of operation and to the argument that many MNCs use their power both to limit emerging competition and to influence government policy in their favour. These criticisms are levelled particularly at those MNCs which operate in the developing world where their relative strength is far greater than in their domestic market of, say, the United States, Japan or the United Kingdom.

The Rise of the Multinationals

The growth of MNCs within international business can be traced back to the 1950s and 1960s when the notion of producing, as well as selling, in overseas markets was welcomed by many governments. As we observed at an earlier stage in this chapter, it was the system of fixed exchange rates, a reduction in tariff barriers, and an expanding world economy that led to a transfer of financial, technological and managerial resources across national boundaries and which contributed enormously to the creation of jobs and the growth of many world economies.

In the late 1960s, however, this substantial upsurge in the level of international business led to a number of commentators raising questions about the economic, political and social implications of the changes that were following. An important milestone in this was the publication in 1968 of Servan-Schreiber's book, *The American Challenge*, in which he suggested that the spread of American MNCs through Europe represented a fundamental challenge both to European corporations and to European societies.[8] The concern that this engendered was, in turn, heightened by the subsequent United Nations Conference on Trade and Development (UNCTAD) which began to argue more strongly for better terms of trade between the developed and the developing worlds and, following from this, a redistribution of wealth on an international scale. In arguing for this, UNCTAD did however state explicitly that they saw the MNCs and their power as a major obstacle to achieving this changed economic order.

This increased questioning of the role of the MNCs led, in turn, to a further move at the beginning of the 1970s in the form of the United Nations Charter on Economic Rights and Duties of States. The Charter represented an attempt to change the international economic environment and led ultimately to the United Nations Commission on Transnational Corporations and to the emergence of the first code of conduct for international and multinational business dealings.

It is movements such as these, together with the extensive publicity given in recent years to the transgressions of the MNCs, that has led to many governments questioning the nature of their contribution and whether they have simply become too powerful.

Despite this, it needs to be recognised that the role played by the MNCs in developing patterns of international trade, stimulating local economies, and increasing standards of living is immeasurable. It was, however, in recognition of the increasingly vociferous criticisms made of their methods of operation that led in the early 1980s to a number of MNCs, particularly in the United States, issuing codes of ethical conduct governing overseas business transactions. It was this changed climate which also resulted in the American government taking measures to regulate US-based MNCs by means of the Foreign Corrupt Practices Act which, amongst other measures, prohibited MNCs from bribing foreign officials.

It is pressures such as these, together with a far greater expressed willingness on the part of host countries to control MNCs by means of a variety of political and economic measures, that has forced MNCs to rethink their marketing strategies. It is now the case, for example, that many of the less developed countries are pursuing policies which, amongst other things, call for closer government and private sector co-operation; a greater use of social cost-benefit analysis; increased pressure to employ a higher proportion of nationals; and far greater levels of local ownership and participation. This has, in some cases, led to a position in which MNCs are tolerated only to the extent that they are able to demonstrate their value to the host economy.

The implications for multinationals of these sorts of changes are quite obviously significant and call for marketing strategies which are far more responsive to local needs than was originally necessary in the past. It also requires far more sophisticated techniques for identifying and monitoring levels of risk in the international environment so that if withdrawal from a particular market becomes necessary, it can be done at the minimum cost to the organisation.

Barriers to Trade

Although, as we have observed, world trade has grown enormously in the post-war period, numerous obstacles to trade still exist, both in the form of tariff barriers and non-tariff barriers. Tariffs are the taxes that are imposed upon goods as they move from one country to another and, most typically, take the form of customs duties, export tariffs and transit tariffs. Non-tariff barriers (NTBs), by way of contrast, are the less visible obstacles to trade such as quotas, laws giving priority to domestic suppliers, customs documentation requirements, marks of origin and labelling regulations that are used by nearly all governments to limit trade and provide a form of protection for the home market. In Great Britain, for example, Japanese car importers are required to adhere to a 'voluntary' limit of 11 per cent penetration of the market. In an attempt to circumvent such moves, the Japanese have in recent years adopted a number of different strategies, including joint ventures and, in the case of Nissan, establishing a British manufacturing plant.

Non-tariff barriers have also been used against the Japanese by the French government. Alarmed by a sudden and dramatic leap in the number of Japanese-made video recorders being imported into the country in 1983, the government imposed a non-tariff barrier in the form of a declaration requiring all video recorder imports to be processed through an inland customs post with only limited transport access. In this case, however, the outcry both from the Japanese manufacturers and the video-recorder-starved French market led to a diplomatic withdrawal several weeks later.

In an attempt to remove trade barriers as far as possible, a variety of tariff reduction programmes have been pursued by the major trading nations. The most important of these was the 1947 General Agreement on Tariffs and Trade (GATT) which acted as the starting point for many of the tariff reduction programmes that have subsequently taken place. Although GATT's initial membership was made up of only 23 nations, it now has more than 100 members and associates who between them account for more than 80 per cent of world trade.

The objectives pursued by GATT have been broadened considerably since its formation so that, in addition to tariff reduction, it now also provides a framework for multilateral trade negotiations designed to increase world trade. But although GATT has been extremely successful in achieving this, not all countries have benefited equally. The LDCs, for example, became increasingly dissatisfied in the 1960s as their share of world trade began to show a progressive decline and the gap between the prices they received for their raw material exports and the prices they paid for the finished goods imported began to increase alarmingly. These feelings of dissatisfaction led to the belief that GATT worked to the greater benefit of the developed nations. In an attempt to come to terms with this, the United Nations established a Conference on Trade and Development (UNCTAD) in 1964 which, with 147 members, has subsequently become a permanent agency of the UN General Assembly.

UNCTAD's primary objective is to further the development of the emerging nations by expanding trade and establishing commodity agreements which are designed to raise prices by controlling supplies. Unfortunately, however, apart from the International Coffee Agreement (ICA), few commodity agreements have worked well in practice, largely because the individual member countries, tempted by the higher market prices, have often broken ranks by releasing further supplies onto the market. This, in turn, has then led to a drop in price which affects all members.

More recently, UNCTAD has attempted to establish a tariff preference system designed to favour the export of manufactured goods from the LDCs. The scheme works by the developed nations agreeing to impose low or zero tariffs on LDC exports, while at the same time allowing these countries to maintain high protectionist tariffs themselves. Although such a concept is alien to GATT's stated objectives, some progress has been made in that Western nations have agreed in principle to accept these preferential tariffs. In practice, however, obstacles still exist, since the Western nations have insisted upon excluding certain industries, including textiles, from the list of preferential tax concessions on the grounds that their own low-technology industries will be damaged.

It is largely because of these sorts of problems that UNCTAD's achievements have been relatively limited. Insofar as it can be said to have been successful, it is in terms of the publicity that it has given to the major problems of trade between the developed world and the developing world, problems which were highlighted by the publication of the Brandt Commission Report.[9]

Nevertheless, despite UNCTAD's relative lack of success, a variety of marketing implications stem both from UNCTAD and GATT. Perhaps the most important of these is that the reduced, and reducing, barriers to trade mean that global logistics can be developed on an ever more rational and international basis than would otherwise be the case. A further implication is that firms have access, via their governments, to a mechanism that should enable them to protect their interests in advance of trade negotiations taking place.

References

1. Peter F. Drucker, 'Economics Erase National Boundaries', in Peter Drucker, *Managing in Turbulent Times* (Harper & Row, 1979), repr. in *Industry Week*, 28 April 1980, pp. 63-4.

2. Vern Terpstra, *International Marketing* (The Dryden Press, 1978), p. 5.

3. See, for example, Douglass Norvell and Sion Raveed, 'Eleven Reasons for

Firms to go International', *Marketing News*, 17 October 1980, p. 1.
    4. Raymond Vernon, 'International Trade & International Investment in the Product Life Cycle', *Quarterly Journal of Economics*, May 1966, pp. 190-207.
    5. Drucker, 'Economics Erase National Boundaries', p. 63.
    6. Subhash C. Jain, *International Marketing Management* (Kent Publishing Co, 1984), p. 50.
    7. K. Ohmae, *Triad Power* (Collier Macmillan, 1985).
    8. Jean Jacques Servan-Schreiber, *Le Defi Americaine*, (Paris, Editions de Noel, 1967).
    9. *North–South, a programme for survival: A Report of the Independent Commission on International Development Issues* (Pan, 1980).
    For a detailed discussion on the role of the multinationals, see Christopher Tugendhat, *The Multinationals* (Eyre & Spottishwoode, 1971); Lawrence Franko, *The European Multinationals: A Renewed Challenge to American and British Big Business* (Harper & Row, 1976); Michael Taylor and Nigel Thrift (eds), *The Geography of Multinationals* (Croom Helm, 1982); and John Stopford and John Dunning, *Multinational Company Performance and Global Trends* (Macmillan, 1983).

Appendix 1.1: Regional Agreements

Market agreements affect international marketing programmes in a wide variety of ways. The first and perhaps the most important of these is that the scope of the 'domestic' market is broadened. Thus, the entry of Great Britain to the European Economic Community meant that access to other European markets was made far easier and the 'home' market expanded accordingly. This, in turn, meant that it was simpler for products to be moved between countries and allowed economies of scale to be achieved in such areas as production and distribution. Ford, for example, took advantage of this to make changes to their British and German operations:

A new management organization was created to make all the critical decisions for both the British and German companies. There were obvious operating economies in the arrangement — the duplicate dealer organizations in third markets could be eliminated and responsibility went where the skill was: body development work was concentrated in Germany, power train development concentrated in Britain. The pooling cut the engineering bill in half for each company, provided economies of scale with double the volume in terms of purchase — commonization of purchase, common components — provided the financial resources for a good product programme at a really good price.[1]

A second consequence of regional agreements is that the nature and basis of competition often changes. In the European Community, for example, a succession of mergers and joint ventures across national boundaries in the 1970s and early 1980s led to the emergence of MNCs of sufficient size to begin competing effectively for the first time with the American multi-nationals. Previously, the Americans had faced only limited competition from the far smaller European firms. One example of such a change in the computer field was the joint venture between Philips (Dutch), Cie Internationale Pour L'Informatique (French) and Siemens (German) in an attempt to compete more effectively with IBM. Similarly, the development of the Tornado multi-role combat aircraft was the result of a joint venture on the part of British Aerospace, Aer Italia (Italian) and Messerschmidt Bolkow Blohm (German); without such a venture, it is likely that European governments would have been obliged to buy from one of the American multinationals such as Lockheed.

But although regional market agreements have a number of obvious and significant benefits for the member countries, it needs to be remembered equally that tensions can arise. Spain's entry to the EEC, for example, not only added a major new source of supply for such products as wine, of which there had long been a surplus, but also led to many of their nationals looking to countries such as Germany for work. At a more general level, the com-munity's Common Agricultural Policy has led to bitter accusations of individual governments acting selfishly to promote their own interests.

Appendix 1.2: Forms of Market Agreement

There are, in essence, five main forms of market agreement: free trade areas, customs unions, common markets, economic unions, and political unions. The essential characteristics of each of these appear in Table 1.1.

Table 1.1: The Major Characteristics of Regional Market Agreements

	Free Trade Area	Customs Union	Common Market	Economic Union	Political Union
Common internal tariffs	Yes	Yes	Yes	Yes	Yes
Common external tariffs	No	Yes	Yes	Yes	Yes
Free flow of factors of production (capital, labour, technology)	No	No	Yes	Yes	Yes
Harmonised fiscal and monetary policy	No	No	No	Yes	Yes
Supranational authority with the power to develop and impose policy	No	No	No	Yes	Yes
Political harmony between members	No	No	No	No	Yes

Appendix 1.3: Current Market Agreements

The majority of market agreements currently in existence are based upon geographical links. In Europe, the three major agreements in existence are the European Community, the European Free Trade Association, and the Council for Mutual Economic Assistance.

Of these, the *European Community* is by far the most signficant in that it is now the world's largest exporter and, under the terms of the 1957 Treaty of Rome, has as its ultimate objective the development of economic and political union. Although progress has been made towards achieving the former, the EC still has a considerable way to go before achieving any real degree of political union.

Membership of *EFTA* is made up of those European countries such as Austria, Finland, Iceland, Norway, Sweden and Switzerland which, for one reason or another, decided not to join the EEC. Although EFTA has a far lower profile than the EC, it has resulted in a significant increase in trade between the member countries.

More frequently referred to as the *COMECON* countries (Council of Mutual Economic Co-operation), CMEA was established in 1949 to co-ordinate and promote trade between the communist countries of Bulgaria, Czechoslovakia, East Germany, Hungary, Mongolia, Poland, Romania, Russia, Cuba and Vietnam. In many ways, CMEA is more akin to a political than an economic group, and is dominated by the Soviet Union. The extent to which it has encouraged trade and economic integration is difficult to assess, largely because of the way in which in many centrally planned economies foreign trade is used as a means of balancing domestic shortages and surpluses.

The African nations have had considerably less success than their European counterparts in achieving any real degree of economic co-operation, although a variety of market agreements are in existence. These include the *Afro-Malagasy Economic Union*, the *East Africa Customs Union*, the *West African Economic Community*, the *Maghreb Economic Community*, and *the Economic Community of West African States*. The major reason for their relative lack of success is that the majority of member nations have only a limited economic infrastructure for trading between themselves and rely instead upon exporting natural resources to the developed world and importing finished goods.

By way of contrast, Latin America — helped by the United States — has a number of relatively successful and long-standing market agreements, although these are periodically disrupted by outbursts of political instability. The four principal agreements are the *Latin American Integration Association*, the *Andean Common Market*, the *Caribbean Community and Common Market*, and the *Central American Common Market*. The major objective in each case is to encourage a degree of specialisation within member countries in an attempt to achieve economies of scale and the benefits of experience.

Currently the fastest growing region in the world, Asia and the Pacific Basin have several market agreements including the *Association of South East Asian Nations* (ASEAN) and the *Arab Common Market* (ACM). In addition, Japan, Australia, New Zealand, the United States and Canada established the Pacific Basin Economic Council at the end of the 1970s to encourage trade within the region and, in recognition of the area's rapid and sustained economic growth, may ultimately develop this into a formal market agreement.

In addition to market agreements based upon geographical proximity, a variety of other links exist between countries which have implications for international marketing. These include the *Commonwealth* within which member nations import from one another on a selective basis; commodity agreements for products such as coffee, sugar, tin, olive oil and cocoa that are designed to stabilise prices and prevent severe fluctuations; and producer cartels such as *OPEC* in which the suppliers of a commodity or resource agree to deal as a group with the buyers of the commodity.

Reference

1. 'Common Marketing for the Common Market', *Forbes Magazine*, 1 July 1972, p. 23.

PART ONE

THE INTERNATIONAL MARKETING ENVIRONMENT AND APPROACHES TO OPPORTUNITY ANALYSIS

The essential elements of effective international marketing are the ability to interpret the business environment, recognise foreign market opportunities, and appreciate how the firm's resources can best be used to match and develop patterns of market demand. Within the two chapters that make up this section of the book, we focus upon the major dimensions of the international environment and consider how market research and techniques of opportunity analysis can be used as a basis for developing a marketing strategy.

2 THE INTERNATIONAL MARKETING ENVIRONMENT

Environmental analysis is a necessary element in the development of any marketing programme. For the international marketer, it is an activity which takes on an added importance both because of the large number of different countries in which the firm may operate, and because of the very great differences that can exist between the market environments even of neighbouring countries. Within this chapter, we focus upon four of the major dimensions of the international business environment — the economic, cultural, political and legal environments — and examine the ways in which they influence decisions on market entry and marketing strategy.

The Economic Environment

The economic environment influences demand in a number of ways and its potential effect upon an international marketing programme needs to be examined from two separate but inter-related viewpoints. At the macro level the marketer needs to consider people's wants and needs, the country's economic policy, its state of development and the economic outlook. At the micro level he needs to focus upon the firm's ability to satisfy market demand and compete effectively with firms already in the market. It is, therefore, the economic environment that to a large extent defines the marketing opportunities for international operations and it is only by means of a detailed analysis of this aspect of the environment that the marketer is able to answer two fundamental questions: firstly, how big is the market, and secondly, what is the market like? It is the answers to these questions which then help to determine the firm's market potentials and priorities, and subsequently the nature of the marketing task that is to be performed. We therefore begin this chapter by considering a number of the elements that make up the macro and micro economic environments, and then move on to discuss how they influence marketing strategy.

The Macroeconomic Environment

The starting point for any analysis of a market involves identifying the level and nature of economic activity. Because the economies of different nations can vary quite enormously (consider, for example, the implications of the differences between the United States and Somalia with populations of 230 millions and 4.5 millions, and per capita incomes of $14,000 and $350 respectively),* the international marketer needs to develop a clear idea of the economic situation and how it will influence the marketing mix. The most fundamental elements of such an analysis are the size and structure of the population, together with the level and distribution of income and wealth. However, having obtained this information and arrived at an initial measure of market attractiveness, care needs to be taken in its interpretation since the level of economic development can change significantly in a relatively short period. This is illustrated quite dramatically in the case of some of the Gulf States which, by virtue of their oil revenues over the past twenty years, have moved from being near the bottom of a league table of economic prosperity to a position very near the top. (In the mid 1980s, for example, the United Arab Emirates, Kuwait, and Saudi Arabia occupied positions 1, 2 and 8 respectively in the World Bank table of GNP per capita.)

Less dramatically, but perhaps equally significantly in the long term, the need to focus upon international market life cycles is illustrated by the ways in which the newly industrialised countries (NICs) such as Taiwan and Korea have leaped to prosperity over the past decade, and subsequently how some less developed nations are rapidly becoming markets which offer considerable potential. Any analysis needs therefore to take account not only of a country's current position, but also of the ways in which the economy, and hence the market, is likely to develop in the foreseeable future.

The ways in which the stage of economic development reached influences patterns of consumption is reflected in Engel's laws of consumption which state that poorer families will tend to spend a higher proportion of their incomes on food than more prosperous societies, and that rural populations will spend a larger percentage of their incomes on food than urban dwellers. These laws are, in turn, borne out by the Household Income and Expenditure Statis-

*Source: World Bank, 1984.

tics produced by the International Labour Organisation in Geneva and have quite obvious and significant implications for market attractiveness.

Returning, however, to our earlier comment that the starting point for any economic analysis is the size and structure of the population, together with the level and distribution of income, the marketer should attempt to build up a market profile which includes information on the size of the current population, population trends, the distribution of the population, the gross national product, patterns of income distribution, and income per capita. Having got this information he can then begin the process of market evaluation and selection.

The Size and Structure of the Market

Although the size of a country's current population is an important determinant of its potential, straightforward population data by itself provides only a limited and unidimensional view of the market. For a more detailed and useful picture, information is also needed on population trends and its distribution by age.

With regard to the first of these, population growth rates throughout the world currently vary enormously with countries such as Mexico, India and Brazil experiencing annual growth of 4 per cent or more, whilst the European nations, Japan, Canada and the United States average less than 1 per cent. These trends affect companies in a variety of ways. On the positive side, population growth leads to a certain buoyancy in the economy in the sense that new households increase the demand for household goods. At the same time, however, it is increasingly being recognised that high rates of population growth can stifle economic development by virtue of the constraints it places upon per capita income, and hence reduces a market's attractiveness. It is for these reasons that many governments in the developing world are currently pursuing active birth control programmes. Nevertheless, even in those nations in which population growth rates are high, the market potential for manufacturing such products as medicines and certain foodstuffs may be considerable.

A further dimension which the marketer needs to take into account in his population analysis is its distribution by demographic variables such as age and social grouping. The significance of the social group is discussed at a later stage in this chapter; here we will concentrate upon changing age profiles.

It has long been recognised that age profiles throughout the western world in particular are changing in a dramatic and far-reaching way. Many of the highly industrialised nations in Western Europe have now reached a position in which birth rates are low and the average age of death has increased. By way of contrast, many of the developing nations are faced with a population explosion as rates of infant mortality decline. At the same time, however, life expectancy in many of these countries is still far below that of people in Western Europe with the result that a disproportionate part of the population is in the economically inactive 0-14 age group. These differences are reflected in Table 2.1.

The final factor to which the marketer should pay attention in considering the distribution of the population is its geographical concentration or dispersion. All other things being equal, there are obvious advantages in operating in markets which are geographically concentrated, since transportation and communication costs are minimised. Typically, the starting point for measuring the degree of concentration within a country is the number of people per square mile. In many countries, however, there are quite significant regional variations around the national average. In Egypt in 1984, for example, the approximate population density was listed as 97 persons per square mile. This compares with Asia's 230 and Europe's 258 persons per square mile. In practice, however, Egypt's population is far more concentrated than that of most other nations since it lives almost exclusively in a narrow strip along the River Nile.

The significance of these concentration figures needs to be

Table 2.1: Age Structure of the Population in Selected Regions (%)

	Age Group		
	0–14	15–64	65+
South-East Asia	40	57	3
Africa	42	54	4
Latin America	41	56	3
Europe	26	63	11
North America	31	63	6
USSR	31	64	5

Source: 'Population Trends in Developing Countries', *Finance and Development*, December 1969, p. 51.

viewed, however, not just in terms of the implications for communication and transportation, but also for production since it may well be possible for regional markets to be supplied from a common production unit, possibly located in a neighbouring country.

The Level and Distribution of Income and Wealth

Although the size and structure of a market's population is an important part of economic analysis, an equally important dimension is that of income levels throughout the country. The most commonly used basis for a comparison between countries is that of per capita income, since not only is it easily calculated and widely accepted, but it also provides a reasonably accurate indication of a market's worth. Having said this, however, it needs to be remembered that, despite their value, per capita income figures do suffer from certain limitations. The most prominent of these stems from the way in which they are calculated. For a meaningful income comparison to be made, the per capita figures need to be expressed in a common currency — typically the United States dollar — and this is done by means of a simple exchange rate conversion. This figure is then used as the basis for comparison. The extent to which these figures reflect accurately the relative domestic purchasing power of the two countries can, however, be questioned, since the exchange rate used to arrive at the comparative figures may well vary significantly over a relatively short period as patterns of demand and supply on the foreign exchanges alter. This problem can, in turn, be exacerbated both by currency speculation and devaluation.

Other factors which tend to detract from the real value of per capita income comparisons include the way in which the sales of many products correlate only partially with per capita income. Many consumer goods, for example, have a far closer correlation with population figures, whilst sales of industrial products tend to be a reflection of overall national income or industrial structure.

Nevertheless, despite these problems, per capita income figures do represent a useful starting point for comparisons between markets, particularly for companies selling goods requiring high disposable incomes. An alternative measure which also provides a basis for comparison is that of gross national product. For certain types of good, and particularly those in the industrial sector, GNP has proved to be a more meaningful indication of market potential than per capita income and where this is the case, a straightforward ranking of countries by GNP is a more realistic measure of market value.

Recognising these problems of comparison, the United Nations International Comparison Project (ICP) was established in 1968. Conducted jointly by the United Nations Statistical Office and the University of Pennsylvania with the support of the World Bank and a number of other international, national and private institutions, the ICP has concentrated upon developing a more sophisticated method for measuring total expenditure, which can then be used to derive more reliable and directly comparable estimates of per capita income.

Other Elements of the Economic System

Having examined the size and value of the market, the marketer needs then to consider a number of other elements of the economy before making a final judgement on its potential. Amongst these is the nature of the economic system itself, since this affects the political/regulatory control of the economy and, in certain cases, may well lead to marketing problems. Some Moslem countries, for example, are increasingly adopting an economic perspective based upon fundamental Islamic principles. This trend, led by Iran, is still in its formative stages and it is difficult to predict either how far it will go or what long-term effect it will have upon firms doing business in Moslem countries. Nevertheless, as firms operating in Iran since the overthrow of the Shah, as well as in many other fiercely Moslem countries such as Pakistan and Saudi Arabia have found, the constraints placed upon business practice can be significant and can alter in a quite dramatic way the attractiveness of the market.

The marketer also needs to take account of trade agreements between countries and regions, as well as the degree of mutual economic dependence that exists. Their importance can perhaps be illustrated by considering the interrelationships that exist between the Western Europe and United States economies; a slump or boom in one will almost always be felt shortly afterwards in the other. It is because of these sorts of interrelationships that 'the international marketer needs to consider the economic perspectives of the overall world economy, particularly those of its major trading partners and the host country'.[1]

The Microeconomic Environment

Having identified the markets of interest to the company, the focus of attention switches to the microeconomic environment and an assessment of whether the firm is able to enter the market and compete effectively.

Sources of Competition

Any firm entering a new market is likely to face competition from two quite distinct sources: local companies, and other foreign organisations. The nature of this competition can vary enormously and will be influenced firstly by the types of demand currently being satisfied, and secondly, by the characteristics of the products being sold.

With regard to the first of these, it is possible to identify three different types of demand: existing demand, latent demand, and incipient demand. Existing demand relates to products that are being bought to satisfy existing specific needs. Latent demand refers to the situation in which new needs have been identified but which currently are not being met. Incipient demand is the sort of need that will emerge when the market becomes aware of a new product at some time in the future.

The nature of competition can be analysed in a broadly similar way with three distinct product types: competitive products, improved products, and breakthrough products. A competitive product is one that has no significant advantages over those already on offer. An improved product is one which whilst not unique, represents an improvement upon those currently available. A breakthrough product, by way of contrast, represents an innovation and, as such, is likely to have a significant competitive advantage.

The level and nature of competition that a firm will encounter can therefore be analysed by relating the three types of demand to the three types of product. This is illustrated in Figure 2.1, and can be used as a basis for determining firstly whether market entry is likely to succeed, and secondly whether the company possesses any degree of competitive advantage. This, in turn, provides an insight to the nature of the marketing task needed. In saying this, however, it needs to be emphasised that this sort of analysis provides an initial framework for analysis and nothing more. What is then needed is a far more detailed assessment of the degree of

Figure 2.1: Product/Market Combinations and the Scope for Competitive Advantage on Market Entry

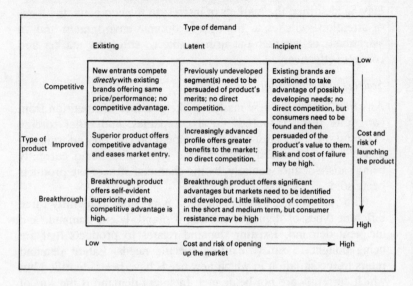

competitive advantage that the company possesses. One way of doing this is by means of the sort of checklist which appears as Figure 2.2.

By adopting this sort of approach, a detailed profile of the market can be developed and the marketing implications more fully explored. Markets which are characterised by small-scale, single-industry national companies, for example, differ considerably from those that are dominated by large-scale national companies, and these in turn differ from those which are controlled by a series of multinationals. The implications for competition in each case do, of course, vary enormously. Before entering any market it is therefore essential that the marketer is fully aware of the competitive environment he is entering and the implications both for methods of competition and the scope for development.

It needs to be emphasised, however, that although large multi-national corporations undoubtedly have a great many advantages in terms of size, resources and managerial expertise, it is dangerous and short-sighted to underestimate local competitors. Many local firms, whilst not being able to compete directly in terms of sheer size and power, often have inbuilt advantages stemming from a

Figure 2.2: Assessing Competitive Strengths

- What is the structure of competition?
- Who are the competitors today, and who are they likely to be in the future? Are they locally owned or foreign companies?
- What objectives are firms currently in the market pursuing?
- What sorts of co-operative relationships exist within the market? How do they manifest themselves? How effective have they proved to be? How durable are they likely to be?
- What are the key features of the strategies currently being pursued? Do firms emphasise price or non-price competition?
- What particular strengths, weaknesses, skills and resources does each company possess?
- What unique selling propositions exist? How significant are they?
- Are there any major weaknesses which can be exploited?
- How important is each market sector to each firm?
- How is each company likely to retaliate when faced by competitive action? How significant are these responses?
- What marketing and financial resources does each firm have? Are they likely to invest heavily to match a competitive threat?
- Could competitors possibly block access to distribution channels?
- Does any firm have a significant level of political influence?
- Who has leadership in terms of
    market share
    product quality
    product innovation and design
    manufacturing efficiency
    distribution and logistical efficiency
    sales force effectiveness
    advertising effectiveness?
- Are competitors' strategies likely to change in the foreseeable future?
- What relative strengths do we possess?
- How effective are our strategies likely to be?
- How well developed and entrenched are patterns of custom loyalty?
- What scope exists for innovatory strategies?
- What lessons can be learned from competitors' past strategies?
- What experience gained in other markets can be applied here?

more detailed local knowledge, and possibly government support if the industry is threatened by foreign competition.

The Influence of the Economic Environment upon Marketing Strategies

We suggested at an earlier stage that the need for a detailed economic analysis stems from the way in which this environment defines the marketing opportunities for international operations. In part, this can be seen by the way in which marketing opportunities generally increase in a time of economic boom and decrease in a time of economic decline. More specifically, it can be illustrated by considering the impact of shifting exchange rates, differences in tax systems, levels of inflation, import restrictions and changes in agricultural outputs. The overall state of the economy is therefore a major influence upon the nature of the decisions faced by the international marketer.

In the case of the microeconomic environment, its influence upon marketing strategy can perhaps be seen by the way in which the choice of market has a direct bearing upon the nature and degree of competition the firm faces, the speed with which the product moves through the product life cycle, and the overall level of marketing investment that is needed.

Assessing the Implications of the Economic Environment

Having identified the various dimensions of a market's economic environment, the marketer eventually reaches a point at which he can begin to decide whether market entry is likely to be worthwhile. The two sets of criteria used for this are cost–benefit analysis and risk/reward analysis.

Cost Benefit Analysis. By giving consideration to cost-benefit criteria, the marketer is posing a series of questions designed to identify the costs of operating in a particular market, and the possible financial returns. The three major elements of this are therefore consumers, competitors, and the level of financial commitment. Thus:

Consumers: Will they want the product? Will they be willing to pay an economic price? Is the market sufficiently large to justify entry?

Competitors: What is the likely level and nature of competition? Will the competition stem from national, or international companies? Are national companies likely to benefit from government subsidies or participation?

Financial commitments: What level of commitment is needed? What returns are likely? How long will the period of investment recovery be? Will constraints upon repatriating capital and profits be applied?

There are, of course many other elements that can be introduced into this sort of analysis, including the availability of a skilled workforce and perhaps the wisdom of using local managers. Nevertheless, the framework outlined is a starting point for such an exercise.

The second part of the analysis focuses upon risk/reward criteria in which emphasis is placed upon the social and political issues that are capable of influencing the economics of business operations. These include the nature of the monetary and fiscal policies being pursued, the strength of the currency, inflation rates, standards of living, levels of education, whether the society is progressive and receptive to new ideas, and the general degree of social and political stability. It is the answers to these questions which provide a picture of the overall business environment, the extent to which the business community might have to cope with political and social upheavals, and hence whether investment is likely to be subject to unpredictable government action.

The Cultural Environment

The second aspect of the environment that has a direct effect upon the nature of the international marketing programme is that of culture. Conducting business across national boundaries inevitably leads to interaction with people and their organisations who have been brought up in a different cultural environment and who as a consequence have a different set of values and expectations. These differences in attitudes, beliefs and perception, together with the many other cultural characteristics, are of fundamental importance to the international marketer and have a direct and pervasive influence upon the nature of the marketing programme.

The Importance of Cultural Analysis

Over time, culture has been defined in many different ways. In essence, however, it is the set of values and the patterns of learned behaviour that develop as a result of living within a particular society. The concept is, therefore, a broad one since it embraces every part of a person's life and has a direct effect upon patterns of behaviour.

For the international marketer, a detailed understanding of the cultural environment is of crucial importance as many businessmen have found to their cost. It is only too easy to enter a market with certain preconceived notions of behaviour only to find that the reality is significantly different. Cultural analysis is, therefore, a fundamental part of the marketing task, although in some countries it is made particularly difficult by the existence of two quite distinct cultures. In Canada, for instance, the marketer has to cope with the dual culture of the English-speaking and French-speaking Canadians. Similarly, Belgium has a Flemish culture in the north of the country and a very different Walloon or predominantly French culture in the south. In Israel, there is what is frequently referred to as the Western group made up of European and United States immigrants whose culture reflects their background, and the oriental group made up of immigrants from the African and Asian countries.

An added problem for the international businessman is that cultures change over time as the result of a wide variety of environmental forces, including advertising. This can be seen in the case of Japan which has moved from being a closed society to a highly industrialised nation in the comparatively short period of forty years. Western influences upon Japanese culture have been significant and, particularly over the past decade, have led to the far wider acceptance of Western values and, indirectly, to a partial rejection by the young of more traditional Japanese values and culture.

Approaches to Cultural Analysis

Because culture is such a broad and pervasive concept, cultural analysis can prove to be a difficult and time-consuming task. Murdock, for example, has identified more than seventy different aspects of culture and suggests that in order to understand a particular society, an in-depth analysis of each is necessary.[2] For the marketer, such a task is quite obviously unrealistic both in terms of the cost and the time involved. Instead, he needs to focus upon those aspects of culture which are most likely to have an influence upon the marketing programme. These include *patterns of social interaction* such as the role of women and the importance of social class; *language* and the scope that exists for mistakes and ambiguity when translating (Jain, for example, recounts how the literal translation into Spanish of 'Let Hertz put you in the driver's seat' is 'Let Hertz make you a chauffeur'[3]); *religion* and its influence upon the acceptability of certain products; *ethics* and how they influence certain behaviour patterns such as bribery (in the Western world, bribery is an illegal act; in many Arab countries, bribery is, by way of contrast, a commonly accepted part of the business process); *aesthetics*, such as colours and symbols and how they influence the design and marketing of many products (in many Eastern countries, including Japan, white is the colour of mourning, whilst in Western Europe it is a symbol of purity and innocence); and *prejudices*, including reactions to marks of origin such as 'Made in Great Britain'. The 'Made in Great Britain' label can operate either positively or negatively depending upon the nature of the product and the region of the world in which the product is being sold. In the United States, for example, the label represents a positive marketing advantage when applied to clothing and foodstuffs. When applied to cars, however, it has proved to be a distinct disadvantage because of the very poor reputation for quality and reliability that many British cars built up over a number of years. Indeed, it was this aspect which was at the heart of John Egan's changed marketing strategy for Jaguar; recognising that, along with most other British cars, Jaguar had a poor reputation, he set out to improve product quality and reliability and to communicate this to his most important single market, America.

The Influence of Culture Upon Marketing Strategies

In the light of these comments, it can be seen that culture has a direct influence upon patterns of behaviour and that cultural differences need to be reflected in the international marketing programme. Nevertheless, many companies still make the mistake of underestimating the significance of these differences by adopting a marketing strategy which is more appropriate to its domestic market. This *ethnocentric approach* to international marketing is based on the assumption that what works well in one country will work equally well in another. The alternative and more appropriate philosophy which emphasises the need for decisions to be made in the light of the host-country's cultural characteristics is referred to as *the primacy of host-country approach.* Based upon an analysis of perceptions, attitudes, motivations and learning processes, this approach is designed not simply to provide an insight into the patterns of social interaction, the language of the country, and so on, but more importantly to show *how* they influence marketing decisions. An outline of this approach to cross-cultural behavioural analysis appears in Figure 2.3.

There are several ways in which companies can go about the process of answering the questions raised by this sort of analysis, including market research. Alternatively, the information can be obtained by making use of local personnel and basing decisions upon their evaluation of the situation rather than by adopting the ethnocentric approach referred to above.

The Political Environment

The third major environmental variable of interest to the international marketer is the political environment and it is this that provides the focus of the three case studies at the end of this chapter. The politics of a country are inexorably linked with government attitudes to business and to the freedom with which they are allowed to operate. As a result, a seemingly valuable foreign market may not justify entry if the political climate is unstable, uncertain or anti-international business. Furthermore, it needs to be remembered that the political environment of a country rarely remains static for any length of time and major political changes can occur after substantial financial commitments have been made. The Iranian revolution in the 1970s, for example, is estimated to have cost American businesses some $1 billion, and British companies £900 million.

In arriving at a decision on whether to enter markets in certain parts of the world, it may well therefore be advisable to give consideration not only to the level of commitment involved, but also to the likelihood of political change and the scope that exists for withdrawing from the market should conditions change. Unstable

Figure 2.3: An Outline of Cross-cultural Analysis of Consumer Behavior

- Determine Relevant Motivations in the Culture:

  What needs are fulfilled with this product in the minds of members of the culture? How are these needs presently fulfilled? Do members of this culture readily recognize these needs?

- Determine Characteristic Behavior Patterns:

  What patterns are characteristic of purchasing behavior? What forms of division of labor exist within the family structure? How frequently are products of this type purchased? What size packages are normally purchased? Do any of these characteristic behaviours conflict with behavior expected for this product? How strongly ingrained are the behavior patterns that conflict with those needed for distribution of this product?

- Determine What Broad Cultural Values are Relevant to This Product:

  Are there strong values about work, morality, religion, family relations, and so on, that relate to this product? Does this product connote attributes that are in conflict with these cultural values? Can conflicts with values be avoided by changing the product? Are there positive values in this culture with which the product might be identified?

- Determine Characteristic Forms of Decision Making:

  Do members of the culture display a studied approach to decisions concerning innovations or an impulsive approach? What is the form of the decision process? Upon what information sources do members of the culture rely? Do members of the culture tend to be rigid or flexible in the acceptance of new ideas? What criteria do they use in evaluating alternatives?

- Evaluate Promotion Methods Appropriate to the Culture:

  What role does advertising occupy in the culture? What themes, words, or illustrations are taboo? What language problems exist in present markets that cannot be translated into this culture? What types of salesmen are accepted by members of the culture? Are such salesmen available?

- Determine Appropriate Institutions for This Product in the Minds of Consumers:

  What types of retailers and intermediary institutions are available? What services do these institutions offer that are expected by the consumer? What alternatives are available for obtaining services needed for the product but not offered by existing institutions? How are various types of retailers regarded by consumers? Will changes in the distribution structure be readily accepted?

(Reproduced with permission from J. Engel and R. Blackwell, *Consumer Behaviour* (The Dryden Press 1982), p. 97.

political regimes expose foreign businesses to a variety of risks, including physical violence to the firm's senior managers, as was seen in the 1960s and '70s with a long series of kidnappings and murders of foreign executives in Latin America. The other types of risk that unstable regimes pose are in the form of restrictions on repatriating capital and remitting profits, as well as more general restrictions upon business operations. Large multinationals have proved to be particularly vulnerable in this context and in the eyes of politicians in many parts of the world:

> can be blamed for everything from corrupting public officials and increasing social tensions to pursuing corporate policies that have negative impacts on host and source countries alike. Multinational companies are held to be irresponsible to host government and/or employees as they maximise their global profits while minimising their global liabilities, exporting host-country factors of production while helping to generate polarised societies, squeezing out local entrepreneurs and generating monopoly power while undermining national sovereignty and exacerbating international disparities in income distribution.[4]

It is often such a perception that is at the heart of political intervention in business and as American-based multinationals in particular have found to their cost, the implications of political intervention can be significant.

Types of Political Intervention

In essence, political intervention is any decision on the part of the host government that necessitates a change in the operating practices of a foreign firm. The forms of intervention vary enormously and range from expropriation at the one extreme to minor tax controls at the other.

Expropriation: This involves the 'official seizure of foreign property by a host country whose intention is to use the seized property in the public interest'[5] and may or may not lead to full or partial financial compensation. The history and patterns of expropriation vary greatly from one part of the world to another, as Bradley[6] has demonstrated. His work has revealed that between 1960 and 1976, Latin American countries were responsible for 49 per cent of all expropriations, followed by the Arab countries with

27 per cent, Black Africa with 13 per cent, and the Asian nations with 11 per cent. Further detail has subsequently been added by a United Nations Study which revealed that slightly less than 70 per cent of all expropriations in the period 1960-74 were accounted for by the actions of just ten countries including Cuba, Peru, Argentina, Algeria and Iraq.[7]

In an attempt to minimise the likelihood of expropriation, many firms have opted for joint ventures with host governments rather than operating wholly owned subsidiaries. Bradley's work suggests however that, if anything, such a strategy is even more likely to lead to takeovers. An even gloomier picture emerges where firms opt for a joint venture with another foreign multinational; in these circumstances, the likelihood of expropriation leaps by a factor of 8. A further major cause of expropriation has proved to be size; firms with total assets of more than $100 million were shown to be fifty times more likely to be taken over than firms with an asset value of $1 million or less.[8]

Insofar as obstacles to expropriation have been found to exist, they centre around technology and a high level of vertical integration. Thus, where the technology of the firm can only be duplicated by the host government with difficulty, governments have shown a somewhat greater reluctance to expropriate assets than in those circumstances in which the technology can be copied with relative ease. Similarly, if the degree of vertical integration between the parent company and the operating subsidiary is high in the sense that the parent is the only realistic source of product supply, there is little value to be gained from a government takeover of the firm's foreign operation.

A less extreme form of intervention is that of *domestication* in which the government gradually reduces the control of the foreign parent. This is typically achieved by means of a slow transfer of ownership from the foreign firm, whilst at the same time promoting nationals within the company to ensure their greater involvement in the decision process. Although, quite obviously, from the viewpoint of the multinational, domestication is to be preferred to outright expropriation, it also has a number of distinct benefits for the host government. Most prominent of these is that it is significantly less likely to have an adverse effect on the country's international credit rating, since the transfer of power and ownership is a gradual, less disruptive and generally much fairer process.

Other and rather milder forms of intervention that exist include *the imposition of exchange controls* in order to avoid too great a flow of capital and profits flowing back to the parent company; *restrictions on imports* so that, of necessity, the MNC makes use of local suppliers; *tax controls* so that MNCs are subject to additional taxes; *price controls* which limit the freedom to alter prices in line with world market conditions; *labour controls* which impose restrictions on employment policies; and *market controls* which are designed to prevent the firm operating in particular market sectors (restrictions of this nature are the focus of the case study on the banana market at the end of this chapter).

The use of market controls by governments as a means of exerting pressure upon foreign firms has been increasingly frequent in recent years and is illustrated by the ways in which the Arab States have attempted to boycott firms that have links with Israel, and by the restrictions imposed by President Reagan at the beginning of the 1980s in an attempt to prevent the construction of a gas pipe-line between Europe and the USSR. Broadly similar controls have also been imposed by many other Western governments in an attempt to prevent the sale of high technology to a wide variety of countries, including Iran and Cuba, as well as virtually all Iron Curtain countries.

Because of the potential political problems that can arise from operating in foreign markets, the need for a detailed political profile can be met by developing the sort of list illustrated in Figure 2.4 and then applying techniques of political risk assessment.

Approaches to Political Risk Assessment

Although techniques of political risk assessment (PRA) have existed for many years, they were the subject of a significant upsurge in interest only after the largely unexpected collapse of the Shah of Iran's regime and the overthrow of seemingly stable and secure governments in South Korea and Nicaragua. Techniques of PRA are therefore applied with two objectives in mind: firstly, to help identify those governments which are likely to pose an increased political risk so that multinational firms can take steps to reduce their level of commitment within the country, and secondly to highlight those countries which although currently seen to be too risky, might well offer substantial and secure opportunities in the future. In essence, therefore, it involves a continual monitoring of existing and potential markets so that corporate management is

Figure 2.4: A Political Profile Checklist

- What type of government is in power?
- How stable has the political system proved to be during the past 5 — 10 — 15 years?
- What role does the political opposition play?
- Is there a history of trades union and/or student unrest?
- What is the incidence of strikes?
- How effective have the government's economic policies been?
- How stable is the monetary system?
- Is there a sizeable anti-private sector lobby?
- How does the host government view foreign investment?
- Is there a history of expropriation?
- What sort of relationship exists between the government of the host country and that of the parent company?
- How are foreign personnel viewed?
- Is there a history of political or terrorist action against foreign nationals?
- How is the government viewed internationally?
- How does the banking community view the country?
- How fair and honest are government officials?

less likely to be caught unawares when political conditions change. The methods of doing this range from the highly qualitative to the supremely quantitative, although probably the two best known and most frequently used of these are the Delphic forecasting technique in which a group of experts is asked to rate certain political possibilities ranging from stability to a *coup d'état*, and mathematical modelling in order to develop a forecast of the likelihood of a particular event occurring. This latter technique is used particularly by the major banks before granting international loans.

As an alternative to the firm making the assessment itself, it is possible to call upon specialist agencies which provide summaries of political risk. The obvious attractions of using an outside agency are that the information is readily available, albeit at a fee, and, in the eyes of many commentators, it is more likely to be objective than if the work is carried out in-house by an analyst who is possibly pursuing a philosophy of risk-reduction as the basis of career enhancement. At the same time, however, it needs to be recognised that such studies tend to be general rather than specific and, as many critics have pointed out, different agencies tend to arrive at different and conflicting conclusions about the degree of political risk involved.

Strategic Responses to Intervention

When a company finds itself threatened by government action, it has two major strategic alternatives which it can pursue: withdrawal from the market, or adaptation to the new and changed conditions by the adoption of a substantially revised strategy in order to gain a new competitive advantage.

Withdrawal from the market is in many ways the most straightforward, although also possibly the most expensive of the two options and has been pursued by many multinationals over the years, including IBM and Coca Cola in India, when it has been felt that the new restrictions limit freedom of action to such an extent that the maket is no longer commercially viable. If, however, the company believes that the market still offers a worthwhile long-term return, the alternative is to maintain a presence and alter the strategy being pursued. It was this approach which was adopted in Iran by Chrysler after the overthrow of the Shah.

It should not be thought, however, that the international firm is always in an exposed position. Many countries rely heavily upon the large multinationals for their expertise, technology, employment, levels of investment and the access to other markets that they bring with them. The imposition by a government of overly restrictive controls can all too easily change a market from being one that MNCs find attractive, to one from which they would be only too willing to withdraw; it is a fact of commercial life that many governments throughout the world fully recognise.

The Legal Environment

The fourth and final element of the international environment that is of direct interest to the marketer is the legal infrastructure of each of the markets he is considering entering (See Figure 2.5). Throughout the world, legal systems vary greatly both in terms of their complexity and methods of interpretation and, of necessity, the multinational enterprise needs to be fully aware not only of the individual legal systems, but also of the ways in which the firm's methods of operation will be affected by the laws of the country in which it has its base. Thus, a British-based multinational is bound not only by the laws of the host country in which it is operating, but also by certain British laws. In addition, it is required to comply with a variety of international laws and conventions

Figure 2.5: Aspects of the Legislative Framework

The Foreign Legislative Framework

- What tariffs are imposed upon imports and exports?
- Are there are constraints upon exports to particular markets?
- Do any products attract subsidies?
- Does anti-dumping legislation exist?
- Is there price legislation?
- What restrictions are there on foreign investment?
- Are national companies likely to receive preferential treatment?
- What import/export licences are needed?
- Are there any restrictive trade agreements e.g. import quotas or customs entry procedures? (See note 1)
- Do any Friendship, Commerce and Navigation (FCN) treaties exist? (See note 2)
- What patterns of employment legislation exist?
- What powers and rights are trades unions given by legislation?
- Is there anti-monopoly or anti-trust legislation?
- What tax legislation exists and how is it likely to affect foreign companies?
- What patent protection exists?
- How effective is the legislative framework? Is the legislative framework based on Code Law or Civil Law?
- Is there legislation to prevent profits being repatriated?
- Is there anti-bribery legislation?

Parent Country Legislation

- What laws affect the operation of foreign trade?
- Do any tax treaties exist with the governments of the countries in which we intend operating?
- What laws are there to eliminate tax loopholes?
- What support for exporting is given by the parent country?
- Do restrictions exist on exporting certain products to particular markets (e.g. high technology equipment to proscribed nations)?
- Is there government support for boycotting particular markets?
- What laws exist to protect domestic industry?
- Is there anti-bribery legislation which affects operations overseas? (See note 3)

International Laws

- What regional treaties exist and how are any agreements likely to affect methods of operation?
- Do any United Nations Treaties and Conventions apply? (See note 4)
- What safeguards exist for the protection of property (including trademarks and patents)

Notes
   1. An import quota may be introduced to safeguard local industry or to give it a degree of extra protection. This is illustrated by the way in which a 'voluntary' quota is applied to the number of Japanese cars entering the British market each year.
   2. FCN treaties are bilateral agreements designed to cover certain aspects of commercial relations between the two signatory nations.
   3. The United States, for example, passed the Foreign Corrupt Practices Act in 1977 to prevent officials of American registered companies from making unauthorised and illegal payments to foreign nationals, political parties and companies in an attempt to influence business practices.
   4. Examples include the *International Labour Organisation* which protects and promotes workers' rights; the *International Civil Aviation Organisation* which regulates standards of airworthiness; and the *International Standards Organisation* which has responsibility for promoting the standardisation of different products and processes.

designed to regulate international business practice.

Because of the highly complex and specific nature of the international legal environment, it is not our intention within this chapter to discuss legal systems in depth, but rather to provide an overview of the areas to which attention needs to be paid, the constraints which apply, and the framework for arbitration which exists.

The Legal Environment and Marketing

The aspects of the legal environment that are of particular importance to the marketer are principally those laws which affect the individual elements of the marketing mix, together with those which determine patterns of competition. Thus, he needs to be aware of laws affecting the product (e.g. packaging, service and warranty, patents, trademarks, the product's suitability for its purpose), advertising (the provision of factual information, constraints upon using particular media for certain products), distribution (the rights and responsibilities of dealerships), pricing (price discrimination, resale price maintenance, price labelling), and of the existence of any law relating to methods of competition (in the case of Britain, these include the Sale of Goods Act, 1979; the Unfair Contract Terms Act, 1977; the Consumer Credit Act, 1974; and the Misrepresentation Act, 1967). In addition, of course, the marketer needs to be fully aware of the rights of the consumer and the scope that exists for action against the company in the event of complaints.

As a first step in this, the marketer needs to determine whether a particular country's legal system is based upon common law or code law. Common law is English in origin and rests on the notion of precedent and past practice. Code or civil law, by way of contrast, is based on the development of detailed and specific rules designed to cope with all possible circumstances. Amongst the countries which use common law are the United States and Great Britain, together with most of the Commonwealth countries. Followers of code law include France, Germany, Scandinavia, Italy and Switzerland.

The marketing implications of these different legal systems can be significant, since code law tends to be relatively less flexible and adaptable, and subject to a strict and literal interpretation of the law. This can be illustrated by considering the issue of trademark restriction regulations. Under common law the ownership of a trademark is determined by priority of *use*. In other words, the owner of a trademark is the person who is first to use it. In a code law country, however, the ownership is determined by priority in *registration*, even though the trademark may not subsequently have been used. One consequence of this is that a multinational firm with established brand names may well find that when it attempts to move into a new market subject to code laws these brands have already been registered by a less than scrupulous local citizen. The firm is then in the position of having to buy back its own brand names from the local owner in order to use them.

Foreign Laws and the Marketing Mix

Anyone who has been involved in marketing in the United Kingdom for any length of time will be aware of the myriad of laws affecting marketing practice. The position in other countries does, however, vary significantly with many of the Western nations having developed a great many legal constraints upon marketing behaviour, whilst most of the developing world still operates with a relatively loose legal framework. In examining how the legal environment of a particular market is likely to affect the nature of marketing strategy, the marketer needs to begin by examining the nature of any constraints upon the product, since these will, in turn, have a bearing upon patterns of distribution, pricing and advertising.

Typically, legislation regarding the product is designed to protect consumers by setting levels for safety, performance or purity. That the legislation can vary greatly in its severity is illustrated by a variety of tragic cases including the Thalidomide controversy which led to many deformed babies being born after the drug had been used by the mother during pregnancy. Although the drug was sold in Britain and Germany, the United States Food and Drug Administration had reservations about the product's safety and refused to issue a licence authorising its sale in the United States.

Similar differences in the severity of legislation are illustrated in the case of the car industry. Many European car manufacturers selling into the United States in the 1970s were severely affected by the threat of increased safety legislation. Amongst the British companies affected was MG which when faced with the need for substantial investment in order to meet the growing body of safety and exhaust emission legislation, eventually decided to withdraw from what had at one time been thought its largest and most profitable markets.

But although safety legislation has an important role to play in protecting consumers, it needs to be recognised, as Terpstra has observed, that it is also used by many governments as a form of protectionism:

> By maintaining different national standards, nations seem to be saying that consumers in other countries are not being adequately protected. The real reason nations often persist in their particular legal requirements is that they provide a way to protect their own producers.[9]

A further aspect of product legislation relates to packaging, labelling and the provision of guarantees. Packaging requirements are for the most part spelled out in only a general way, although by way of contrast, labelling legislation tends to be far stricter. The labelling items which are included most frequently in such legislation are the name of the product, the name of the manufacturer or distributor, a description of the ingredients, methods of usage, the weight, and the country of origin. With regard to the guarantees that are provided, the marketer very often has a reasonable degree of freedom within the general constraint of the product's being 'of merchantable quality' or 'suitable for its purpose'. In recent years, however, many governments have begun to pay far greater attention to the ideas of product liability. As a general rule, code law countries interpret product liability in a far stricter fashion than do common law countries which have traditionally relied upon the principle of *caveat emptor* — let the buyer beware. This situation is, however, changing rapidly with the United States in particular having introduced quite severe product liability legislation which, in turn, many European governments have begun to emulate.

The final major aspect of the product that needs to be taken into account is the way in which brand names and trademarks are used. We have already made reference to the differences between code law and common law and the implications for the legal ownership of a trademark, but it is perhaps worth emphasising that in certain parts of the world trademark piracy is a recurrent and ever more expensive problem for the multinationals. Amongst the many companies that have experienced piracy of this nature are Chanel, Raleigh and Girling. In the Western world it tends to be far less of a problem, since many of the larger countries are members of the Paris Union or signatories to other trademark conventions which specify how trademarks may be used and which monitor abuses.

Having identified the nature of any product legislation in existence, the international marketer can then go on to consider the legal constraints upon other aspects of the marketing mix. In the case of price, there are broadly two types of legislation that may be of importance. The first of these relates to the scope that exists for price control either by means of a Prices Commission, as in the United Kingdom in the 1970s, or by allowing resale price maintenance (rpm). Although many countries have some form of legal provision for rpm, the trend in recent years has been away from its use, largely because of the problems of enforcement. Price control on specific products has, however, proved to be a more popular and successful form of government action and, at various times, has been used as a means of controlling the price of petrol, foodstuffs, and luxury goods. The implications for the marketer can be significant in that, regardless of their nature, price controls can, by limiting freedom of action, make a market far less attractive.

The second major form of price legislation is less direct in the sense that it stems from the framework of tax legislation in existence. It can, however, have a major impact on a firm's price strategy in that changes in excise duty or value added tax will either be reflected in the price to the consumer, or, if a proportion of the tax is absorbed, in the firm's reduced profit margins.

The third area of legislation to influence the marketing

programme is that which is designed to control advertising. As the most prominent element of the marketing mix for many companies, advertising has often proved to be a contentious activity which in many countries has led to the development of a substantial body of legislation supported by self-regulatory codes of practice. The most common form of advertising legislation is designed to ensure the truthfulness of the advertising message and avoid potentially ambiguous or misleading statements. The second aspect of much legislation in this area is concerned with imposing controls upon where or when particular products can be advertised. An extreme example of this is seen in Finland where legislation prevents newspaper and television advertising of political organisations, alcohol, slimming drugs, religious messages, and many other products. Elsewhere, the constraints tend to be less extreme and focus most frequently upon such products as alcohol and cigarettes by limiting the media in which advertisements might appear.

The fourth and final marketing element influenced by legislation is distribution. On balance, there are relatively few, if any, constraints placed upon the choice of patterns of distribution, although care does need to be taken in ensuring that when appointing distributors, the parent company is aware of the consequences of trying to change or end the distributive agreement at a later stage.

Conflict and Its Consequences

It is almost inevitable that, over time, international firms will encounter difficulties with consumers, distributors, other business organisations, or the host government. These difficulties may arise for one or more of a variety of reasons such as conflicting interpretations of contractual terms, a fault in the product, or misleading advertising. When this happens there are three main courses of action open to the company: (i) the two parties arrive at a mutually acceptable way of settling their differences; (ii) one party sues the other; or (iii) the two parties go to arbitration. Of the three, it is the first which is by far the cheapest and least likely to lead to unfavourable publicity. If, however, an acceptable settlement cannot be arrived at in this way, a variety of other considerations come into play, including how the courts are likely to view the foreign company; the long-term marketing consequences of the disagreement; the likelihood of winning any action; and the scope that exists for going to arbitration rather than through the courts. It needs to be remembered, however, that the international marketer is not a lawyer and would therefore do well to take specialist legal advice from the moment the decision to enter a particular market is taken.

Summary

Within this chapter we have tried to illustrate the fundamental importance of environmental analysis before work begins on developing the international marketing programme. For a wide variety of reasons, multinational firms are vulnerable to changes in the economic, political, socio-cultural and legal environments, and their long-term success is therefore heavily dependent upon being constantly aware of their environment and the changes that take place within it. In part, this is illustrated in the appendix to this chapter, and many of the points covered here are developed further in the chapter on opportunity analysis that follows.

References

1. Subhash Jain, *International Marketing Management* (Kent Publishing Company, 1984), p. 169.
2. George P. Murdock, 'The Common Denominator of Cultures', in Ralph Linton (ed.), *The Science of Man in the World Crises* (Columbia University Press, 1945), pp. 123-42.
3. Jain, *International Marketing Management*, p. 194.
4. Ibid., pp. 221-2.
5. David K. Eitman and Arthur I. Stonehill, *Multinational Business Finance* (Addison-Wesley, 1979), p. 186.
6. David G. Bradley, 'Managing Against Expropriation', *Harvard Business Review*, July-August (1977), pp. 75-83.
7. *Transnational Corporations in World Development: a Re-examination* (United Nations, 1978).
8. Bradley, 'Managing against Expropriation', pp. 75-83.
9. Vern Terpstra, *International Marketing* (The Dryden Press, 1978), p. 141.

Appendix 2.1: Politics and the Multinationals

France, in 1968, saw students and workers take to the streets in what were to become the most violent riots seen in Europe in the post-war period. Amongst the international business community, there was a widespread feeling that a major social upheaval was inevitable, and a number of foreign-owned multinationals began reviewing their plans for either a partial or total withdrawal from the French market.

Amongst the French companies which viewed the situation with particular dismay was the tyre manufacturer Michelin. Faced with what appeared to be an ever more unstable environment in their home market, the decision was taken to spread the political risk by investing abroad. Despite the company's size, this was their first such venture in the Western Hemisphere, and their eventual choice of Nova Scotia in Eastern Canada was viewed with surprise.

Michelin's stated objective in setting up first one and then a second manufacturing plant in Canada, was to establish a base from which they could supply the United States' markets with their unique steel cord tyres. However, this in itself surprised many observers, since Nova Scotia is more than 1,000 miles away from the primary US markets for which 85 per cent of the company's output was destined. Furthermore, Nova Scotia had no comparable manufacturing base and Michelin therefore incurred higher costs by having to establish the base. Indeed, for Nova Scotia it was to be the first multinational to enter the province without being rooted in an indigenous resource such as timber, fish or minerals.

In the event, however, the rationale for the choice of location was shown to be the virtually unprecedented package of financial incentives offered by the federal and provincial governments; these ultimately amounted to more than $100 million (1973 values). In addition, the company was allowed to import tyres from France free of duty for a period of three years; plant and machinery was also imported duty free; and, to safeguard the secrecy of their manufacturing techniques, the firm was allowed to use its own French construction crews. At the same time, depreciation of the plant was to be an allowable tax exemption at the rate of 50 per cent per annum. Overall, this was a deal that few companies could afford to turn down, since the package of grants virtually paid for the total development of the plant and the financial risk to Michelin was, as a consequence, almost totally eliminated. The final major attraction of Nova Scotia to Michelin, particularly in view of their original reason for looking overseas, was that the workforce had a history of non-militancy and could be trained from scratch. In this way, the company avoided any problems that could arise from custom and practice.

In return for this almost idealised commercial package, Michelin provided the province with some 4,000 jobs.

Critics of the package negotiated by Michelin proved to be vociferous and argued that the government was inviting multi-national blackmail. For them, this was confirmed three years later when further investment by the company was made dependent upon certain conditions being met, conditions which eventually required the provincial government to pass new labour legislation which suited the company's no-union rule. This sort of development provided the critics with substantial ammunition and led to the argument that when faced with the possibility of further multi-national investment, the government should pay far more attention to the social costs involved. In the case of Michelin, these social costs were identified as the way in which Michelin acted as its own prime contractor in the construction phase, thereby minimising any benefits to local construction firms; the way in which in the operational phase the provincial government introduced legislation making union organisation more difficult; and, finally, the very limited amount of technology transfer that resulted from Michelin's secretive aproach. Workers, for example, were not allowed to move about the plant freely but were limited to specific areas so that they saw only part of the manufacturing process.

In its defence, Michelin pointed to the 4,000 jobs that had been created and the fact that it had become the largest single private sector employer in the province.

Canadian Government Attitudes to Multinationals

Canada has long had a history of free enterprise and has always welcomed foreign investment. This has, however, led to the position today where significantly more than 50 per cent of the country's manufacturing industry is foreign owned, a proportion that is far higher than that of any other developed nation. It is this which critics say has led to the country's immense economic vulnerability to withdrawal.

At the heart of the Canadian government's policy is the extreme willingness to 'buy' development off the shelf by offering packages to multinationals, such as the one offered to Michelin, rather than pursue the longer term and more difficult policy of building the fundamental economic infrastructure. The current policy, critics have suggested, leads to a variety of problems, including a loss of economic sovereignty and, on occasions, a possible trade-off of jobs between one province and another. Thus, Michelin's entry, it has been argued, led to the eventual loss of jobs in a Canadian-owned tyre plant in Ontario. But whatever the truth, the fact remains that Canada now has a highly distorted pattern of domestic versus foreign investment, with the result that in Nova Scotia alone, the five largest private sector employers are now foreign-owned multinationals.

India and the Multinationals

In India, by way of contrast, the government has long pursued a policy designed to build the country's fundamental economic strength by making full use of its own resources, and particularly the large pool of labour.

The sheer size of the Indian market with its still-growing population of some 800 million has obvious attractions for large multinationals. However, with the multinationals being viewed by many government officials as predators, numerous obstacles have been put in their way to prevent or limit the nature of their investment. Thus, in the case of the car manufacturing industry, Hindustan Motors enjoys a virtual monopoly, even though the large multinationals have consistently expressed an interest and willingness to invest in manufacturing capacity. The fact that Hindustan Motors' most popular model is based largely on the design of the 1954 Morris Oxford rather than anything more up to date, is not in itself seen as a reason for modifying the policy in any significant way, since the car is ideally suited to India's conditions and stage of development. Allowing significant and unconstrained foreign investment in the car industry would, it is believed, lead to a conflict between the aims of the investor and those of the Indian government.

Foreign investment is therefore strictly controlled and based upon the terms of the 1973 Foreign Exchange Regulations Act which limits the level of equity a foreign company can hold in India to 40 per cent. Within the Act, some dispensations exist for high technology companies, although for many multinationals such as IBM and Coca-Cola, the introduction of the Act was seen to be too significant a constraint upon their operations and they withdrew.

Coca-Cola's departure led, in turn, to the setting up of a wholly-owned Indian soft drinks firm, Campa Cola, which uses virtually identical graphics to its predecessor. The subsequent success of the firm is illustrated not only by the growth that it has enjoyed in a variety of markets and the way in which it has established subsidiaries in countries such as Holland and Britain, but also by the way in which it outsells Coca Cola in some of the Third World markets in which they both compete.

The protectionist measures pursued by India have meant that home-based companies have been given an opportunity to develop so that ultimately they will be able to compete more effectively in world markets. They have also helped India to reach its current position as the world's tenth most industrialised nation. This, in turn, has led to the gradual relaxation of some of the stricter measures and the development of a number of joint ventures between Indian companies and multinationals. Amongst these is the deal between the Xerox and Modi Corporations to build photocopiers for the Indian market. The arrangements between the two firms took almost a decade to finalise, largely because of Xerox's reluctance to engage in any venture in which they have less than total control. In the event, however, the company was faced with the choice of entering into a joint venture and gaining access to the Indian market, or coming to terms with the fact that entry would otherwise be barred. It is a decision that many other multinationals wanting to break into the Indian market will have to face within the next few years.

It was the stark reality of this that, in turn, led Gillette to begin negotiations with Poddar of Calcutta in 1984, with an agreement for a joint venture being signed in late 1985. Under the terms of the agreement, Gillette holds 24 per cent of the equity in the company, Indian Shaving Products, established with a capital base of $14 million. For Gillette the deal represented a significant marketing triumph not only because of the access that it had gained to the world's largest market with total demand of 1.8 billion blades a year, but also because it was one of the first to take advantage of the increasingly relaxed interpretations of India's trade mark policy and use its 7 o'clock mark.

Gillette did not, however, achieve all that it wanted. In line with the Foreign Exchange Regulations Act, the company had begun by arguing for 40 per cent of its joint venture equity. This was vetoed by the Government which had increasingly begun to look for greater investment from the Indian public. The result was that

Gillette received 24 per cent whilst Poddar was allowed 24.5 per cent. A further 3.5 per cent was reserved for employees, with the remaining 48 per cent being offered to the public including 10 per cent for non-resident Indians living abroad. It was in this way that the Indian government ensured that the power of yet one more multinational was curbed. An additional benefit to the Indian economy was that the company agreed to a government request that 25 per cent of its initial 200 million razor blades a year output was exported. Most of this was destined for the USSR and other East European countries, and provided a welcome addition to the country's balance of trade.

Appendix 2.2: The Banana Market and the Effects of a Trade Embargo

In May 1985, President Reagan announced economic sanctions against Nicaragua. The total embargo on trade that followed was the culmination of a series of steps by the Americans following an increasingly rapid deterioration in relationships between the two countries which, in turn, had significant implications not only for Nicaragua, but also for a number of American multinationals and the world banana market.

The background to the dispute is one that has been echoed in many parts of the world and resulted from American dissatisfaction with internal Nicaraguan politics. Nicaraguan guerrillas had, for many years, fought to overturn the pro-American government of President Somosa. When eventually they succeeded, the new Sandinista government under President Daniel Ortega pursued an active policy of reducing the level of US government intervention in the country's affairs, a course of action which led President Reagan to view the Sandinista government as a subversive threat in America's Caribbean backyard. The final split occurred in 1985 when American fears of subversion were heightened by Ortega's acceptance of $200 million of Russian aid.

The American multinationals that were operating in Nicaragua had built up considerable investments in the country, but anticipating trouble had begun the slow and often difficult process of divestment or withdrawal; Standard Fruit, for example, managed to withdraw completely from the market in 1982.

The earlier attraction of Nicaragua to the multinationals was based on the high quality of the bananas produced, low wages and the country's proximity to the American markets both on the eastern and western seaboards. It was the combination of these factors that had led to the situation in 1984 in which half of Nicaragua's $58 million trade with the US was accounted for by the sales of bananas.

Faced with the sudden and total disappearance of such a sizeable market, Bananic, the Nicaraguan government owned agency, began to look to Europe and its $300 million banana market. Meanwhile, in the US, Pandol Brothers, the American importers, lost one-quarter of their total sales overnight, including $110 million worth of sales of agro-chemicals, as the trade embargo took effect.

Having decided to enter the European market, the Nicaraguans selected Ghent in Belgium as their European operating base and, at a cost of $360,000 per ship, began shipping bananas. The longer journey — 14 days from Nicaragua to Ghent as opposed to just 4 days to California — together with less than ideal off-loading and warehousing facilities, led to a significant drop in product quality and an increase in the proportion of bananas that were unsuitable for the highly discriminating European market. These problems were exacerbated in August 1985 when the crown of the bananas began to be affected by a fungal growth.

In order to prevent the growth, Bananic needed supplies of Mertect, a fungicide manufactured by the American company Merck. Because of the total trade embargo, direct purchases were impossible and additional problems and delays were caused as the Nicaraguans searched for new suppliers. Having eventually obtained them at a premium from Costa Rica and Honduras, Bananic managed to slow down the fungal rot, but only after their reputation for quality had suffered yet further in Europe.

The European banana market has for many years been dominated by three large American multinationals selling under the Del Monte, Chiquita and Fyffes brand names. With the sudden influx of bananas from Nicaragua, prices began to fall and led to a price war in which prices dropped from an average of $11 per carton to around $8.50 per carton. The Nicaraguans, suffering from problems of poor quality and, they argued, the oligopolistic power of their competitors, saw their prices plummet even further to below what was commonly recognised as the breakeven price of $6 per carton.

Meanwhile, in Nicaragua, the trade embargo was being felt in a variety of other ways. American-made machines on the plantations, for example, needed spare parts that were easily and cheaply obtainable only from the American manufacturers. The Nicaraguans were forced to begin manufacturing the parts themselves, or to set up triangular trading relationships with other nations so that spare parts might be obtained in a less direct way. However, the Foreign Assets Control Department of the United States Treasury has the responsibility for stopping any actions designed to circumvent trade embargoes and acted quickly to prevent a number of these deals. In doing this, they were helped by a US law which requires US corporations to self-regulate their activities, and which carries a penalty of up to ten years' imprisonment plus a sizeable fine for deliberate transgressors.

Elsewhere in Nicaragua, other firms were also having problems. Coca-Cola, for example, is made and bottled under licence, and whilst supplies of the syrup could be obtained relatively easily from other bottlers, the bottling plant utilised American technology and hence needed American spare parts.

Similar effects were felt throughout the country's industrial infrastructure as the trade embargo took effect and managers began the difficult task of searching for new international markets and coming to terms with an aggressive international business environment.

Appendix 2.3: The Role of (Unsuccessful) Political Intervention in the Award of a Defence Contract

In the early 1980s, the American defence establishment announced that it intended to buy a new mobile battlefield communication system for the American Army. After initial skirmishing, the two main contenders for the contract emerged as Plessey of Great Britain and Thomson — CSF, the French state-owned electronics group. Both companies had forged alliances with US groups — General Telephone and Electronics for Thomson and Rockwell International with Plessey — in putting forward their bids. The contract, under which 25 divisions of the American Army were to be equipped with a coded computerised communications network, was estimated to be worth $4 billion (£2.79 billion). It quickly became apparent that the two competing systems differed in a number of fundamental ways. The French Rita system was claimed by its supporters to be an infinitely more attractive proportion than Plessey's Ptarmigan both because of its lower cost and because of the relatively lengthy experience that it had enjoyed with the French Army. Plessey, however, argued that Ptarmigan, although more expensive, was far more sophisticated and offered greater scope for further development than Rita.

Because of the size and long-term implications of the contract, the British government loaned its support to Plessey's application, with the Prime Minister, Margaret Thatcher, intervening in late summer 1985 by writing to President Reagan. In doing this, Mrs Thatcher referred to Britain's favourable response to the US Strategic Defence Initiative and to the Anglo-American 'special relationship', an approach which annoyed part of both the American media and, apparently, certain sections of the defence establishment for the publicity it attracted. For their part, the French government made few overt moves, although the newspaper *Liberation* wrote that 'there was a rumour that Paris would look more favourably on the purchase of three American radar planes (Awacs) if Rita was chosen by the Pentagon'. In making such moves both sides were fully aware that success in the American market would almost inevitably lead to further business as other armies followed the American initiative.

When the decision was announced in November 1985, the French emerged as the victors and immediately began to emphasise that they had won the contract fairly on the grounds of a lower price and superior product quality, without the need for the French Government to apply pressure as Mrs Thatcher had done. Plessey, however, tried to mitigate disappointment by suggesting that few jobs would have been created and that under the terms of the contract, the American partner would act as the prime contractor with only one-quarter of the total value of the contract being carried out in the victor's home country. They also pointed to their subsequent development of a more sophisticated and more compact second-generation Ptarmigan system that would undoubtedly find greater favour than Rita with other armies.

From a political point of view, the award of the contract to the

French represented an undeniable snub and in the eyes of many commentators reinforced the need for future political intervention in foreign business to be more circumspect and to receive less obvious media coverage.

3 INTERNATIONAL MARKET RESEARCH AND OPPORTUNITY ANALYSIS

In the previous chapter we explored the major elements of the international business environment and discussed their influence upon the international marketing programme. Here, we narrow the focus considerably by providing an *overview* of current approaches to identifying specific market opportunities and of the ways in which the international market research programme should be developed.

Identifying and Analysing Market Opportunity

Within a majority of companies operating either domestically or internationally, formal techniques of market opportunity analysis are still only poorly developed. Instead, many managers rely upon a mixture of guesswork and close observation of competitors in what is often a vain attempt to identify the most likely and profitable areas for market growth and company development. An alternative and radically different approach to which companies are, however, now paying increasing attention involves a far more formalised analysis in which the firm's strengths are matched much more directly to market opportunities. In doing this, specific account is taken both of the risk factors that we referred to in the previous chapter and to competitors' strengths and weaknesses. In this way, the marketer attempts to identify market areas with a high earnings potential for the company and in which, by virtue of the company's particular strengths, there is a moderate to high probability of marketing success.

The key determinants of any market opportunity can therefore be seen in terms of the size of the market and its scope for development; the activities of other companies currently operating in the market; and the ability of any new entrant either to match the market's current requirements more effectively or to develop them in such a way that competitors are put at a marketing disadvantage. It needs to be recognised, however, that barriers to realising the full potential of a market often exist either in the form

71

of the political climate which may, for example, be antimulti-national business, or because a series of rather more general tariff or non-tariff barriers to trade exist. In both cases, the implications for market opportunity analysis are quite obviously significant and can be illustrated by considering the Japanese and the Eastern bloc markets.

Although the Japanese market with its population of almost 125 million people has long been recognised by the multinationals as offering enormous potential, numerous practical difficulties have prevented the vast majority of firms achieving little more than a marginal penetration of the market. To a very large extent, this is due to the way in which the Japanese have erected a wide range of non-tariff barriers. The result of this was that in 1985, not only did Japan have a trade surplus of $45.6 billion — beating the previous world record trade surplus set by Saudi Arabia in 1980 — but imports were at a lower level than in 1980. Obstacles to trade also stem from aspects of Japanese culture:

> Tight medical coteries promote certain drugs and do their utmost to keep competitive medicines out of the market. This system is reinforced by the Japanese practice known as 'Amakuda-ri' — literally, descent from heaven. Health ministry bureaucrats can expect to 'retire' to compatible jobs with the drug companies — so long as their record of making matters awkward for foreign drug firms is judged satisfactory.

Market opportunities are also restricted by the way in which the Japanese make use of customs:

> It takes at least nine days for imports to clear Japanese customs — one day only for inspection, but a minimum of eight for safety and certification tests required by Japanese ministries. For electronic goods, such as telephone equipment, the Ministry of International Trade and Industry (Miti) insists on complex tests, ostensibly to ensure that foreign-made goods do not damage Japan's telephone system. Often, the suitability of the imports is finally certified when it comes from one particular factory, but if the seller switches production of the same goods to a different factory, he is forced to tackle the bureaucratic obstacle course again.

Goods are returned to their country of origin on the basis of tiny errors in customs documentation. Even aluminium baseball bats from America were turned down on alleged safety grounds.

American shipping lines were inhibited from doing business by the Transport Ministry's ban on carrying the 9.6 ft high cube containers favoured by US shippers on Japanese roads. Japanese shippers use the smaller 8.6 ft containers. Yet Japanese firms make the bigger containers, and are allowed to run them empty along the same roads that foreign shippers want to use them on.[1]

Although the obstacles to trade with Eastern bloc countries are often very different, the net effect can be the same. Typically, exporters experience difficulties in the initial stages when attempting to gain market entry, but having achieved this, often then face constraints upon opportunity either as a result of Western trade embargoes upon such products as high technology equipment, or because the customer is unable or reluctant to pay for the goods in a hard currency. Faced with this, the marketer has to decide whether to withdraw from the market or arrange a barter deal.

The amount of analysis that is therefore needed in order to arrive at a true measure of opportunity is considerable and on an international level is made more difficult both because of the large number of potential markets that need to be surveyed, and because of the problems involved in collecting accurate comparative data. It is for these reasons that if a company is to pursue a policy of formal market opportunity analysis, there is a need for a highly developed international marketing information system supported by a marketing research resource.

The nature and scope of marketing information and research at an international level is infinitely broader than in domestic marketing, with international researchers being far more likely, for example, to spend time analysing information on social and political issues than their domestic counterparts. However, the degree to which multinational companies do in practice allocate time and money to general background research compared to specific projects differs substantially and will be discussed in greater detail at a later stage. A major issue in international marketing that affects opportunity analysis, however, is the general level of intelligence activities undertaken by companies. There is evidence that small and medium-sized organisations undertake little or no market research when operating in international markets, and that even the larger multinationals may allocate research budgets in such a way that there is heavy concentration upon only the very largest markets. This may be understandable when total budgets are strictly delineated but it may well lead to market opportunities not being recognised.

The Scope of Opportunity Analysis

Although the range of tasks facing the international marketer in identifying and analysing opportunity is broad, it is possible to divide these tasks into three broad categories:

(i) scanning international markets to determine which countries have potential for entry or growth;

(ii) developing an effective international marketing information system; and

(iii) undertaking detailed marketing research projects in order to answer specific questions.

International Market Scanning

Techniques of business scanning provide the basis of information gathering in international markets and are designed both to provide macro-market data and highlight *broad* areas of market opportunity. This is reflected in Aguilar's definition of market scanning as 'The process that seeks information about events and relationships in a company's outside environment, the knowledge of which assists top management in its task of charting the company's future course of action.'[2] A scanning approach should, therefore, help the international marketer in three main ways:

(i) by identifying potentially relevant changes in the international environment (included within this are changes in a country's government and shifts in economic power);

(ii) by monitoring these changes, determining their nature, direction and rate of change; and

(iii) by providing a basis for forecasting the timing of these changes and assessing their likely eventual impact upon the company.

The approaches used for environmental scanning vary from undirected viewing, where the scanning unit simply exposes itself to general information with no particular purpose in mind, to a formal search in which a deliberate attempt is made to search out information relating to a specific issue. Quite clearly, therefore, the introduction of a scanning unit into a company's international market opportunity analysis should be of great benefit, since it not only provides a mechanism for identifying opportunity, but also helps in the process of monitoring competition and highlighting areas of potential risk before they are able to develop into too great a threat to the organisation. However, establishing such a unit is expensive and, in practice, it is often only the largest organisations that are able to bear the cost. Smaller firms have to rely instead upon the data inputs which are more generally available and hence which are not tailored to their specific needs. Nevertheless, even for smaller firms, business scanning in one form or another needs to be seen as an essential activity and one which should have a major input to the marketing decision-making process.

Developing an International Marketing Information System

In establishing an international marketing information system, the marketer is attempting to create a cost-effective communication channel between the environments in which the company is operating and the executives responsible for decision making. The essential component of such a system is therefore that the information provided is not only relevant and accurate, but also is continuous. In this way, it is possible to build up a far more meaningful profile of each market.

The breadth of information needed to do this is, quite obviously, considerable, although for the purposes of analysis here it can be categorised to form a hierarchy which starts with broad macro-economic, political and social data, and moves towards more specific data on market characteristics as follows:

Macro Data

(i) Economic data — growth rates, inflation rates, economic structures.
(ii) Political data — structures, stability.
(iii) Social data — family structures, sex roles, cultural norms and values.

(iv) Technological data — use of information technology, technological infrastructure.

Economic and Business Conditions Data

(i)   Monetary and foreign exchange regulations.
(ii) Tax policies.
(iii) Manpower skills and the structure of industrial relations.
(iv) Banking facilities.
(v)   National government regulations upon trade and industry.
(vi) Raw material supplies.

Specific Market Data

(i)   Market size and potential.
(ii) Competitor information including the structure of operations, product data, prices and predictions of intent.
(iii) Consumer behaviour characteristics.
(iv) The marketing services infrastructure in the form of advertising agencies, market research firms, media availability, and so on.
(v)   The structure of distribution channels.

The effectiveness of any information system is, of course, influenced to a very large extent by the quality of the information that is available or that can be generated. At an international level, these sorts of problems are often compounded by the way in which the availability and accuracy of market information varies enormously from one part of the world to another. In the majority of advanced Western industrialised nations, for example, there is often a wealth of data available either at low or zero cost for information systems managers to sift and analyse. In less developed nations, accurate data is either non-existent or hard to obtain. As a result, the international marketing information system may have to reconcile the problem of overload with regard to inputs from, say, the USA, and scarcity with regard to the LDCs. An additional complicating factor is that in certain parts of the world, and particularly the Eastern bloc, the information available may be distorted for political reasons. The implications for the information system are quite obviously considerable and it is therefore important that information inputs are assessed for their accuracy as well as their availability.

Information System Sources

Although the problems encountered in both primary and secondary data collection will be developed later in the chapter, it is at this stage worth exploring briefly some of the issues that are particularly pertinent to information sources for the system.

Keegan's investigations in the USA have pinpointed the importance of human sources of information both inside and outside the company.[3] It is essential, he argues, that international marketing executives develop a wide network of human information sources if the system is to develop effectively. It is not sufficient, he suggests, to rely solely upon published data, since far too often this lacks both the detail and the additional perspective that is really needed. Amongst the sources that he identifies as being of particular value are distributors, agents, commercial attachés, and the company's own salesforce. All too frequently, however, headquarters staff fail to recognise the true value of the information that is freely available from such sources, relying instead upon what is often uni-dimensional published data to which their competitors also have access.

This line of argument has, in turn, been developed by a number of other commentators and points to the need for sound interpersonal relationships between headquarters marketing staff and the staff of overseas companies and subsidiaries. If the links are marred by mistrust, or even in some cases headquarters arrogance, then the information system will suffer. In many situations strong affiliations develop between international staff of competing companies and these relationships can produce useful information; it is therefore essential that this source is monitored continuously and then fed into the system for evaluation.

Equally, firms need to make full use of the information that is generally provided by a variety of service organisations such as banks, advertising agencies, public-relations firms and marketing research agencies, all of which can provide general and specific information in areas such as foreign exchange rates, taxes, importing and exporting investment climates, and — very importantly — competitive activity.

Assessing Opportunities and Threats

Having established a marketing information system, a company is then faced with choice and priority decisions regarding market entry. As we observed earlier, three types of market opportunity present themselves to the international marketing executive:

(i) *Existing markets* in which customer needs are serviced by existing products;

(ii) *Latent markets* in which there are potential customers, but no one has yet offered a product to fill the latent need; and

(iii) *Incipient markets* that do not exist at present but conditions and trends can be identified that indicate the future emergence of needs in these markets.

Company executives therefore face a series of choice and resource allocation decisions in terms of each of these three types of market. The most appropriate way of doing this is by means of a detailed SWOT (strengths, weaknesses, opportunities and threats) analysis for all international product-markets, taking into account the data generated by the information system. Depending upon the results of the SWOT analysis, the company may then decide to switch resources away from existing markets towards latent markets. There are many examples that illustrate the existence of latent markets in which domestic manufacturers are unable or unwilling to react to the needs of potential customers and which therefore provide opportunities for international companies. During the 1970s, for example, many British caravanners and campers were attracted to the concept of caravanning but were deterred by the prospect of towing a full-size caravan. The folding caravan had long existed in other countries, but British manufacturers had traditionally operated on a very limited scale with little experience of product development. Recognising this, French manufacturers such as Esterel were able to enter the British market and, with comparative ease, attain a dominant position in the folding caravan market.

The major grouping of *incipient* markets is in the third world where many nations are beginning to develop patterns of consumption that are similar to those of the industrialised nations. Recognising this, a number of attempts have been made to forecast their future consumption and demand patterns. The best known of these are:

(i) *Demand Pattern Analysis.* Countries at different levels of economic development have different patterns of demand and consumption. Data at a macro-level are frequently available from UN sources and can be used to arrive at a broad estimate of the latent/incipient nature of demand in any given country.

(ii) *Multiple Factor Indices.* Here, the marketing researcher uses variables based on intuition or statistical analysis that are likely to correlate closely with potential demand for his company's product. Thus, the demand for electrical consumer durables may be related to factors such as household expenditure on durable goods generally and the number of homes with mains supply.

(iii) *Analogy Estimation.* This technique arouses mixed levels of enthusiasm, since experiences with it have been mixed. In addition, it is an expensive technique to implement and doubts have been expressed about the accuracy of its forecasts. However, those who have used it typically adopt one of two approaches:

(a) A cross-section approach where one relates the product-market size for one country to some appropriate gross economic indicator in order to establish a ratio. The ratio is then applied to the specific country under analysis to estimate the potential for the product-market in that country.

(b) A time-series approach based on the belief that product usage moves through a cycle. Thus, one assumes that the country under analysis will follow the same pattern of consumption as a more advanced economy, albeit with a pre-determined time lag.

(iv) *Regression Analysis.* This technique is typically used to complement an analogy approach. Regression analysis is particularly useful in enhancing the likely accuracy and eventual confidence that can be placed on cross-sectional studies.

An alternative approach for estimating demand in emerging countries is the macrosurvey technique that was developed by Carr.[4] The method is essentially anthropological in approach and can help companies to establish themselves early in emerging countries with obvious long-term marketing benefits. The technique is based on the notion that, as a community grows and develops, more specialised institutions come into being. Thus, one can construct a scale of successively more differentiated institutions onto which any particular country can be placed and its level of development — and hence its market potential — inferred. But despite the apparent simplicity of the technique, practical difficulties are often encountered, including the problems of developing a reliable and meaningful scale and, for the company, deciding upon the most appropriate stage for market entry.

Nevertheless, the macrosurvey approach is interesting and along with the other techniques outlined, offers scope for further development. However, even without further development, these techniques highlight the importance of comparative research and regular market screening if incipient demand is to be identified at an early stage.

The value of many of these techniques does however rest upon the assumption that all countries and their consumption patterns will develop along broadly common lines. Thus, if British, American, Japanese and German multinationals are to make effective use of many of these techniques, the assumption of common economic development patterns must stand. Increasingly, however, evidence is emerging to suggest that global commonality does not exist to this degree, and there are strong arguments for companies grouping markets for the purposes of this sort of comparative analysis.

Opportunities within the Pacific Rim

Over the past five years, many international planners engaged in market scanning have begun paying increasing attention to the opportunities and threats posed by the Pacific Rim. This region, which is made up of a large number of politically and economically diverse countries united by the access to the Pacific Ocean, has 1,800 million people, or 42 per cent of the world's population. In economic terms, the area is dominated by the United States and Japan (two of the three elements of the 'Triad' that we referred to in Chapter 1), although it also includes the ASEAN countries of Singapore, the Philippines, Indonesia, Thailand and Malaysia, and the NICs (Newly Industrialised Countries) such as South Korea, Hong Kong and Taiwan. Although many of these countries have very different cultural and economic backgrounds, their rapid growth in recent years has significant implications for European marketers. In broad terms, the implications can be seen in terms both of the opportunities offered by the sheer size of the region, and the threats posed by the growing production capacity and increasingly aggressive marketing strategies being employed. This theme has been pursued by Kiel and Howard who have suggested that:

> The developments in the Pacific Rim have had and will continue to have a major impact on the marketing strategies of many firms ... This impact will obviously be felt by those companies which have an opportunity to take an active part in Pacific Rim growth ... It will also be felt by those who will experience increased competition in their domestic and current international markets and who, unless they plan aggressively, will find themselves reacting defensively to Pacific Rim developments.
> For companies to whom Pacific Rim growth represents major market opportunities several decisions need to be made. These include prioritising markets for entry, determining entry strategies and the establishment of a marketing organisation in key countries ... However, for other corporations the effect will be felt in increasingly competitive markets and a reduction in market opportunities.[5]

Kiel and Howard also suggest that if firms are to succeed in this region a regiocentric strategy, of the sort that is reflected in the development of the world car concept by US and Japanese car manufacturers and which differs significantly from the traditional country by country development that many firms pursue, is essential.

The Costs of Opportunity Analysis

Quite clearly, techniques of market opportunity analysis are expensive to implement, particularly when there is a need for primary data to be collected. International marketing executives should therefore ensure that only the most potentially worthwhile research projects are pursued in detail. One way in which this can be done is by means of a series of screening criteria ranging from the highly formalised that are controlled by the headquarters marketing staff, to the rather more interactive judgemental form.

To help the screening process, companies often need to conduct a certain amount of exploratory research within potential markets. By doing this, it is generally possible to determine whether major obstacles such as barriers to entry exist, and hence whether further research is likely to be worthwhile. Although it is important to avoid confusing exploratory research with general information research, there are discernible links between the two. In this context, an investigation in 1977 found that European multinationals were likely to spend a much higher proportion of their research budgets on general research studies (e.g. general market studies, trade research studies, environmental scanning, and corporate image studies), than their American counterparts.[6] In addition to lending itself to a process of exploratory research, it is likely that such general studies are much more likely to highlight any threats to the company that may be developing in the environment.

One final area that is worth consideration at this stage is the problem of researching smaller markets. When multinationals allocate budgets for exploratory and major research, it is likely that this allocation process will lead to small budgets for smaller countries. This inevitably leads to the possibility of inadequate research being undertaken and inaccurate estimates being made of market potential. Because of this, international researchers should be especially creative when investigating smaller markets, using sources outside normal research methodology. It is particularly important, for example, to make use of the less formal sources such as overseas salesmen, distributors, advertising agencies, embassies and the trade assocations to which we referred earlier.

Sources of Data

As in domestic marketing research, there are in essence two sources of data: *secondary* data which has been collected by others, published and then made freely or commercially available, and *primary* data which the company itself collects for a specific purpose (see Table 3.1). However, perhaps the most frequently voiced criticism of international research concerns the quality of

Table 3.1: The Characteristics of Primary and Secondary Data

Primary Data	Secondary Data
Obtained from knowledgeable individuals.	Obtained from published sources or collected by other parties.
Sampling problems may be encountered.	Generally free or available at low cost.
Often costly to obtain.	Often available at short notice.
Results may be subjective or biased.	May be of only indirect value.
	May be out of date.
Often very specific to a problem.	Attention needs to be paid to the data's limitations.

the secondary information that is generally available. Nevertheless, when undertaking research projects in international markets, the old adage about the need for thorough desk research before committing the company to field research is, if anything, even more important, since international field research is generally far more expensive and time-consuming than in Britain.

The problems of obtaining meaningful secondary data on certain markets, particularly in the developing world, stem largely from the fact that the notion of accumulating economic and business data is still often very new and what data are available should be viewed with a healthy scepticism. The problems are also illustrated by the fact that countries such as Oman, Quatar and Laos had never undertaken a census before 1975. An additional and far-reaching problem regarding the accuracy of international data is that political considerations — often erring towards the optimistic — can lead foreign governments to produce distorted figures. It is widely recognised that even reputable organisations such as the United Nations and the Organisation for Economic Cooperation and Development (OECD), for example, have had their data distorted by the contributions of member states. Nevertheless, despite these problems, the major international organisations are generally excellent sources of data. OECD not only publishes *General Statistics* which give the major economic indicators for member countries, but also publishes a wide range of special studies which are of interest to companies involved in international marketing. Similarly, the European Community is a valuable source of data on member states. Equally, the World Bank provides a wide range of useful, and accurate, data. Almost certainly, however, the primary international source is the United Nations with publications such as *United Nations Statistical Yearbook*, together with a wide variety of market specific studies.

But even when the company is seeking data relating to an advanced industrialised nation, problems can arise as the result of differing classifications. Statistics on the level of ownership of television sets, for example, are classified under 'recreation and entertainment' in Germany, but under 'furniture, furnishings and household equipment' in the United States. It is these sorts of inconsistencies that often make comparative data analysis such a difficult and time-consuming task.

The Role of the British Overseas Trade Board and Other Agencies

Our discussion so far has concentrated largely upon sources of information produced by international organisations. For many companies, however, a far more useful and accessible source is the vast data banks produced by individual nations for the exporting/international business initiatives of their own companies. The USA is arguably the best example of a nation producing information to give its companies a competitive advantage in international markets, although all nations follow suit to a greater or lesser extent and British companies are now well supported in terms of governmental information provision. Whether they use it, however, is another matter. There is some evidence, for example, that many British firms involved in international markets never use primary or secondary information. David Wiseman, head of the Exports to Europe branch of the British Overseas Trade Board (BOTB) in 1981, said at that time:

> I think the real problem is that many British companies still do not regard selling to the rest of Western Europe as part of their normal activity. Of course, by this I do not mean just packing up the goods we sell here and sending them off; I mean getting to know the individual markets and producing goods to meet the needs.[7]

In an attempt to overcome this problem, the BOTB has expanded its research facilities considerably in recent years, a summary of which appears as Appendix 2 to this chapter.

The Comparability of International Data

At an earlier stage we referred briefly to the difficulties of obtaining truly comparable data, problems which have been elaborated upon by Mayer:

> In order to have truly comparable data from multinational markets, it is not sufficient to attempt to control sources of error. Since such error will never be completely eliminated, the data, having been collected, have to be adjusted for residual error sources.
>
> However before such adjustments can be done, much more knowledge is required. Such knowledge is generally obtained at a cost and usually requires some form of experimentation. And here is where one of the major problems arises in the multinational marketing field. First the funds for conducting such research may not be readily available as research budgets are generally controlled at the national level and, at that level, the concern about comparability across nations is not as strongly felt. More important, however, is the general nature of the problem — the subject does not lend itself to experimental design.[8]

Although, quite obviously, sample design is a perennial problem in market research, particularly in very different overseas markets, non-sampling errors do, in practice, prove to be the biggest single cause of a lack of comparability in the results. The major sources of non-sampling error include:

(a) *Differing Levels of Response.* Different national groups or cultures have proved to have distinct styles and levels of response to questionnaires. For example, a recent study indicated that in Malaysia, the Chinese are far more reticent than Indians and Malaysians when faced with an interviewer. Similarly, in the field of industrial marketing, European business executives have traditionally proved to be more reluctant to release company information than their American counterparts. In many countries, and particularly in those with a Moslem culture, problems arise in interviewing female members of family groups.

(b) *Language and Literacy Problems.* In certain regions of the world illiteracy problems are so great that any use of the written word in surveys would cause a major problem. Thus even in interviewer led questionnaires, prompt cards cannot be used. Language issues, and particularly accurate translations, are a major problem, however, even in cross-national studies involving advanced nations. Western Europe suffers from this problem, where individual nation-states such as Switzerland and Belgium have more than one official language. The meaning of individual words gets lost in translation and whole research projects can be ruined. Back translation is offered as a solution but this can be a tedious and costly business. Because of this, one account of a five-country piece of research in Europe for a pharmaceutical client advocated scope for interviewers to change and adapt the wording of questionnaires to cope with language and translation problems.[9]

(c) *Social Organisations.* This is a problem when cross-nation surveys come up against differing roles within families with regard to the purchase of goods. Green and Cunningham, for example, found great differences in husband/wife decision-making roles in the area of furniture, major appliances, life insurance, automobiles and vacations in a comparative study of middle-class families in the USA and Venezuela.[10] Although little work has been done in this area in Western Europe, anecdotal evidence suggests that significant differences exist between family decision-making roles in, say, the UK, West Germany and France.

(d) *Patterns of Consumption.* Quite often, differences in market data emerge as the result of historical and cultural patterns of consumption, and need to be identified before any conclusions are drawn from the data that have been collected. Majaro provides an amusing example to illustrate this.

> Research has shown that the per capita consumption of bananas in Germany is double that of the UK. On the face of it, it seems a puzzling bit of information which can easily lead to dangerous conclusions. However, on closer study, one discovers that whilst the consumption on a weight basis is double that of the UK, in terms of numbers of bananas

> per capita, the consumption is virtually identical. The reason is simple: the bananas imported from the Caribbean into the UK tend to be much smaller than those imported into Germany, hence the disparity.[11]

But in addition to non-sampling errors, problems also occur in terms of comparability due to sampling difficulties. Telephone interviewing may be limited by the existence or non-existence of telephones in the homes and offices of potential respondents. Similarly, the absence of street maps will affect both quota and random sampling techniques, and mail unreliability can affect postal questionnaires. Interviewer style can also have an impact. Interviewers of different nationalities employed in Western European research have, for example, proved in the past to have differing propensities to probe and this affects not only the response rate, but also the degree of detail of the answers provided.

Planning and Implementing an International Research Programme

It is clear that the tools and techniques used in international marketing research are broadly similar to those used in domestic research, but that the environment existing in many markets may limit the usage of those tools and techniques. Issues such as literacy, language, culture and technological infrastructure, for example, will frequently result in the need for the international researcher to be innovative, adaptive and creative if he is to overcome these problems.

Nevertheless, even against this background of possible improvisation, the research programme needs to follow a standardised format:

- problem definition
- statement of the research plan and objectives
- data collection
- data analysis and interpretation
- summary of the findings

We have already explored issues relating to data collection and analysis, but it is worth pausing to consider the need to define the problem accurately and establish appropriate research objectives. What is particularly important, if the research objectives are the province of headquarters staff, is to ensure that they make sense in terms of the country under investigation and are not oriented towards the country in which the headquarters is based.

One of the key elements in the planning and implementation of international research is the question of who should undertake the research programme. Companies researching in emerging countries will probably have faced the problem that structures such as consumer or trade panels do not exist; they then must decide whether to make use of a local or an international agency to carry out the project. The advantages of a local agency are for the most part that its staff will know the country and its people, will not encounter language problems with respondents, and will be readily available. On the other hand, there may be problems of a lack of experience and knowledge of the more sophisticated research techniques, and even issues such as the domestic attitudes to the work ethic. Companies also need to bear in mind the widely divergent costs of fieldwork in different countries, with costs varying a great deal even within Western Europe, with Sweden currently being the most expensive in terms of cost per interview.

One final point that is perhaps worth note is the differences that exist in the perceptions of the value of market research between European and North American managers. In a major study, Stephen Permut investigated the views of American and European executives towards the overall usefulness of marketing research and found that American respondents are much more convinced about its overall usefulness than are their European counterparts.[12] Thus, the will to undertake extensive international market research may differ significantly between executives in various parts of a multinational organisation.

Organising the International Research Function

The organisation of research activities within an international firm can create significant problems and lead to conflict between headquarters and regional marketing staff. In many ways, these sorts of conflict are simply a reflection of the problems that arise in any large organisation in which there is a large number of operational sites and a headquarters staff, where the relationship between the two has not been sufficiently well-defined.

The underlying issue of how best to organise international operations is discussed in detail in a later chapter, but quite obviously it is the firm's overall structure that will to a very large extent determine the nature of relationships and responsibilities within the marketing research function. Nevertheless, at this stage it is still possible to identify the sorts of issues that need to be recognised:

- Is marketing research to be organised on a centralised or a decentralised basis?
- If a *centralised approach* is adopted, what specific responsibilities does the operating unit have and what managerial arrangements exist between the unit and headquarters staff?
- Following on from this, what relationship is to exist between the local research staff, who are ultimately responsible to headquarters, and the local line management marketing group?
- If a *decentralised structure* is chosen, what arrangements exist for research findings to be transferred from one operating unit to another?
- Who has the overall responsibility for administering and overseeing the market research budget to ensure that resources are not wasted by a possible duplication of research effort?

Summary

Within this chapter, we have tried to illustrate the strategic importance of opportunity analysis and the contribution that the information system and market research can make to the decision-making process. International research is, in many cases, a complex, expensive and time-consuming task and evidence suggests that for these reasons, many international firms fail to research markets to the extent that is really necessary. The consequences of this are significant both in terms of missed opportunities and the failure to meet existing and developing market demand.

References

1. *Sunday Times.*
2. F. Aguilar, *Scanning the Business Environment* (New York, Macmillan, 1976).
3. W. Keegan, 'Multinational Scanning: A study in the Information Sources utilised by HQ Executives in Multinational Companies', *Administrative Science Quarterly*, September (1974).
4. R. Carr, 'Identifying Trade Areas for Consumer Goods in Foreign Markets', *Journal of Marketing*, October (1978).
5. G.C. Kiel and C.A. Howard, 'The Pacific Rim: Vision or Reality?', *European Journal of Marketing*, vol. 18, no. 4 (1984), pp. 21-2.
6. S. Permut, 'The European View of Marketing Research', *Columbia Journal of World Business*, Fall (1977).
7. A. Day, 'Why We Fail to Master Exports', *Marketing*, 21 October 1981.
8. C. Mayer, 'The Lessons of Multi-National Marketing Research', *Business Horizons*, December (1978).
9. C. Hamblin, 'What is involved in European Research for Pharmaceutical Clients', *European Research*, vol. 1, no. 6 (1973).
10. R. Green and I. Cunningham, 'Family Purchasing Roles in Two Countries', *Journal of International Business Studies*, Spring/Summer (1980).
11. S. Majaro, 'International Marketing: A Strategic Approach to World Markets' (George Allen and Unwin, 1978), p. 71.
12. Permut, 'The European View of Marketing Research'.

Appendix 3.1: British Exporters' Use of Market Research
(reprinted with the permission of Gordon Heald and Elizabeth Stodel of Gallup Poll)

In 1984, Gallup Poll conducted a survey on behalf of The Market Research Society and the Institute of Export to determine the extent to which British exporters make use of market research when developing their international strategy. The findings revealed that out of over 650 members of the Institute of Export (representing 18.5 per cent of all members and more than 40 per cent of companies belonging to the Institute) ONLY 4 per cent actually claimed to have bought market research. Instead almost half (43 per cent) relied on what they call 'market research carried out by their own firm' — and this is quite obviously open to a variety of interpretations.

The survey revealed that for the food and drink industries, 16 per cent use the services of a professional market research company. One reason for this is that the food and drink industry is consumer orientated and used to buying in within the UK market a

Table 3.2: Factors Influencing the Assessment of Main Opportunities for Exporting

Increased orders	71%
Increased enquiries	54%
Market research by own firm	43%
Export Intelligence Service	9%
Visits by export personnel	6%
Professional market research	4%
Syndicated multi-client studies	3%
Internal information	3%
External information	2%
Other	7%

large amount of consumer attitude and usage data and it expects the same information for its overseas markets. The chemical and pharmaceutical industry was the only other industry which spent anything (6 per cent) on market research. Otherwise the spending by the heavy goods industry, for example, machinery and transport, manufactured goods, forwarding and shipping, was about 2 to 3 per cent. Surprisingly, the spending by 'service' industries was only 2 per cent.

When it came to buying in professional research, it was only the very large companies with a turnover of £50 million or more who purchased any significant amount of market research, and about 10 per cent of these employed research companies. Companies with a turnover of less than £7.5 million purchased virtually no research at all.

The respondents were asked questions relating to where they saw the main 'areas' of opportunity. When they were asked about the basis of their answers to these questions most used an 'increase in orders' as their guide (71 per cent) and more than half (54 per cent) felt that an 'increase in enquiries' would be a sound gauge upon which to predict areas in the world where exporting potential exists. (Multi-coded answers.)

Another interesting point to emerge was the fact that British companies suffer from an extreme lack of foreign language skills for doing business in the various markets. One quarter of companies said that there was no one in their export departments who would be able to make sense of a foreign newspaper and only a bare majority (54 per cent) were fluent in French. German followed in second place (42 per cent), a third was Spanish (30 per cent) and fourth Italian (17 per cent). Other percentages were as follows:

Portuguese	9%
Dutch	8%
Arabic	7%
Russian	5%
Chinese	2%
Japanese	1%

In response to questions regarding the main areas of opportunity for British exports, the Middle East and North Africa rated as the main area (54 per cent). The EEC countries follow closely behind as the second most important area rated by 53 per cent of exporters, followed by North America (36 per cent) and other Western European countries (31 per cent).

Compared with five years previously, the perceived opportunities for British exporters in different countries had hardly changed, but 10 years ago when Britain was entering the Common Market and the dramatic increase in oil prices by Middle East countries was only just commencing, British exporters rated opportunities higher in EEC countries than the Middle East and North Africa. Over the last five to ten years, opportunities in North America have become more attractive to exporters than Western European countries outside the EEC, which is mainly the old EFTA group which Britain once belonged to.

Just as the Middle East/North Africa has become a fast growing area for British exports, so has South-East Asia which is now rated by nearly a third (31 per cent) of all exporters compared with only 14 per cent of exporters 10 years ago.

This is closely followed by South Africa (26 per cent) which is still seen as presenting increasing opportunities for British exporters compared to a decade ago. In contrast, Australia/New Zealand, whilst rated by nearly a quarter (24 per cent) of all exporters, are seen as presenting a stationary market with regard to export opportunities.

In contrast to the Middle East and North Africa, and South Africa, the other two major markets for British exports to Africa — West Africa and East Africa, have declined in relative importance over the last ten years. Currently only 18 per cent of exporters rate West Africa as a land of opportunity today compared with 28 per cent ten years ago, and only 11 per cent rate East Africa today compared with 16 per cent ten years ago. These two geographical areas present the largest perceived decline in opportunities for British exporters in the whole survey.

Another geographical area which has declined is South and Central America, which is only rated by 9 per cent of exporters today compared with 13 per cent five years ago. This is perhaps not surprising given the recurrent economic problems faced by these countries and the continual rescheduling of their debts.

A surprising result from the study is that whilst British exporters see increasing opportunities in Japan and Korea over the last decade, they are rated by only 15 per cent of exporters, only just exceeding the traditional British export markets of India, Pakistan, Bangladesh and Sri Lanka (14 per cent), and the Caribbean (13 per cent).

Eastern Europe, the Soviet Union and China are all seen as providing little or no opportunities to British exporters, and this view has not changed over the last decade.

Overall the study suggests that, whilst the Common Market has become an important market for British exports, it still has not replaced the old traditional markets mainly based on Commonwealth countries or territories where Britain has had strong political and economic historical ties.

Appendix 3.2: A Summary of the Services Offered by the British Overseas Trade Board

The British Overseas Trade Board has expanded its research facilities greatly in recent years. Amongst the information sources and services that it now offers are:

Information Sources

1. *Market Branches.* Tariff and non-tariff barriers, import and other regulations, general economic information and, in some cases, specific information on market sectors, are available for each overseas country through the BOTB's Market Branch which covers the country concerned.

2. *World Aid Section.* Details of projects to be funded by the

international lending agencies are available from World Aid Section. These are also published through the Export Intelligence Service.

3. Statistics and Market Intelligence Library (SMIL). A facility provided by the Government, SMIL is a reference library. The library has a great deal of published information on overseas markets: trade and other statistics; international trade directories and national trade and telephone directories from most countries in the world; development plans and supplementary sources like mail order catalogues; US Department of Commerce market reports; overseas business reports and market share reports.

4. Product Data Store. A central 'bank' of product and industry-based information about overseas markets which may be consulted by representatives of British exporters.

5. Publications
　　International Directory of Published Market Research. Published annually by the BOTB, this directory lists, on a classified basis, more than 8,000 market research studies prepared by over 350 of the world's leading research and consulting firms. The directory is an invaluable first check on whether or not a research report already exists.

　　International Directory of Market Research Organisations. A joint BOTB/Market Research Society publication, this directory is the most important source of reference for the services provided by over 1,300 market research organisations in some 60 countries.
　　British Business. Published weekly by the Department of Trade and Industry, this journal frequently carries reports on overseas markets.
　　Hints to Exporters. A series of booklets on over 100 overseas markets containing information on currency, exchange regulations, passport and entry formalities, methods of doing business, local holidays, economic factors, social customs, etc.

Services Obtaining and Providing Information

1. *Export Intelligence Service (EIS).* EIS is a computerised information service which daily distributes to its subscribers export

intelligence based on information received from commercial officers at nearly 200 British diplomatic and consular missions abroad. A profile of the subscriber's product and country requirements is matched to notices received on specific export opportunities, agency enquiries, market pointers, market reports for specific products, tenders, projects, etc.

2. *Market Prospects Service.*   This service obtains for an exporter, from Britain's overseas diplomatic and consular missions, an assessment of the prospects in an overseas market for his goods or services and advice about how he may best exploit them.

In addition to the BOTB, a variety of other organisations provide international market data, including the export departments of the major clearing banks, trade associations, Chambers of Commerce, export clubs which are organised locally under the aegis of the BOTB, and the commercial departments of the various embassies.

PART TWO

MARKET ENTRY DECISIONS AND APPROACHES TO INTERNATIONAL MARKETING PLANNING

4 MARKET ENTRY STRATEGIES

For many companies, the most fundamental and far-reaching decisions in international marketing revolve around the question of the market entry strategies that are to be used and the patterns of distribution that are subsequently to be developed. There are a number of factors that account for the significance of these decisions and it is to these that we turn our attention within this chapter.

Entering Foreign Markets

The question of how best to enter foreign markets is the first and in many ways the most fundamental to be faced by the marketer, since it is this choice that subsequently influences and shapes the whole of the international marketing programme. If, for example, the company opts for a distributor or licensee, its ability to influence pricing and promotion is likely to be limited. If, by way of contrast, it decides to opt for its own manufacturing subsidiaries, the degree of control that can be exerted will be far higher, although this in turn will be reflected both in the set-up and the direct operating costs.

In essence, therefore, the market entry decision involves a balancing of costs, control and risk. With this in mind, the marketer needs to consider carefully the various distribution alternatives that are open to him and what he wants to achieve. Once a choice has been made, he is likely to find that he has entered into a long-term commitment that can only be changed with difficulty and at a high cost. Recognising this, the three major options with which he is faced are indirect exporting, direct exporting, and foreign manufacturing. These are shown schematically in Figure 4.1. In deciding between these alternatives, several factors need to be taken into account, including:

(i) the company's objectives and expectations of the volume of business to be generated;

Figure 4.1: Methods of Market Entry

DOMESTIC
PRODUCTION

Indirect exporting
- via domestic purchasing
- export management companies
- piggyback operations

Direct exporting
- sales by foreign distributors
- sales agents
- overseas sales subsidiaries

and/or

FOREIGN
MANUFACTURING

- assembly operations
- contract manufacturing
- licensing
- joint ventures
- total ownership

(ii) the size of the company and its financial resources;

(iii) patterns of involvement in other foreign markets;

(iv) the managerial culture and levels of international marketing expertise within the company;

(v) the nature and degree of competition within the market;

(vi) the nature of the product and whether it has any distinct competitive advantages either in terms of its technology, patent protection or trademarks;

(vii)the market's political infrastructure and whether any tariff or non-tariff barriers exist or are likely to be introduced.

Although, quite obviously, this list is not exhaustive, it provides a basic framework within which the various market entry alternatives can be considered. Other more detailed and more pragmatic factors that need to be considered include the investment needs of each market; the manpower requirements; levels of political and financial risk; the administrative needs; the marginal marketing costs; and the degree of flexibility and control that is possible. Together, these can be used as the basis for a comparison of the degree of risk and the level of control of the alternative foreign market entry strategies as illustrated in Figure 4.2.

Figure 4.2: Control and Risk in Foreign Market Entry Strategies

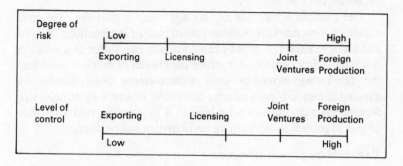

Indirect Exporting

For many companies, the simplest and lowest-cost distribution alternative when considering international marketing for the first time is that of indirect exporting, whereby the company's products are sold abroad by others. The obvious attraction of this is that little or no international expertise is required, since the strategy is little more than an extension to distributing the product domestically. It can, however, open up new markets at very little cost, although this approach does suffer from the firm's lack of control not only over the markets selected, but also over the marketing strategies used and the degree of commitment to each market. Nevertheless, indirect exporting is, for many companies, an attractive and low-cost introduction to international marketing. It exists in three distinct forms:

   (i)   overseas sales by means of a domestic buying department;
   (ii) export management companies; and
   (iii) piggyback operations.

Overseas Sales via Domestic Purchasing

In many organisations, the introduction to international marketing comes about almost by accident when a foreign buyer in the form of the buying department of an overseas manufacturing, wholesaling or retailing organisation makes the initial approach and then takes on the tasks of exporting, selling and distributing the product in one or more overseas markets. In these circumstances, the firm itself is not engaging in international marketing as such, but rather it is responding to an approach that is similar in manner to many domestic sales leads.

The obvious advantage of this approach is that the firm gains access to new markets without investment or international market knowledge, although equally the company can suffer as a result of not having any control over either the choice of markets or indeed the marketing strategies used within them. Nevertheless, for smaller companies particularly, this is the easiest way of achieving foreign sales and can in time lead to a more concerted and disciplined approach to developing an international business.

Export Management Companies

A second and rather more structured and deliberate approach to international distribution involves making use of specialist export management companies (EMCs) that act as the export department for a number of firms simultaneously. In essence, therefore, the EMC is similar to a manufacturer's agent and, for small and medium-sized firms in particular, offers a considerable number of advantages including:

(i) The manufacturer benefits immediately from the EMC's knowledge of foreign markets and can make use of previously developed contacts.

(ii) Payment to the EMC is generally based on performance and there is therefore a strong incentive for the EMC to increase sales.

(iii) The complementary products of a number of manufacturers are likely to have a greater impact than would the product line of just one firm.

(iv) The management costs of foreign sales are spread over a number of companies rather than being borne separately by each organisation involved.

(v) Transport costs for the individual firm are likely to be reduced as the EMC benefits from the savings to be made by the economies of large scale shipments.

Quite obviously, therefore, an EMC has considerable attractions, since not only does the firm gain from the instant market knowledge available, but it also enables costs to be kept at a far lower level than would be the case if the manufacturer was to attempt a more direct approach to exporting. The firm also benefits from being able to exert a degree of control over sales, since typically the EMC will negotiate on behalf of the firm and then get approval for orders and quotations.

But despite the obvious attractions of using an export management company, it needs to be borne in mind that this approach can also suffer from a number of shortcomings. The EMC will not necessarily, for example, have the degree or depth of coverage of all of the markets that the manufacturer is in and may specialise either by geographical region, product type or end user. The manufacturer is then faced with the choice of using more than one EMC, or cutting back his plans. Equally, because the EMC is paid on commission, there is a temptation for them to act for too many companies in unrelated product areas and, as a result, the manufacturer may not get the degree of attention that he had hoped for. Making use of an EMC can also lead to problems in the long term if foreign sales grow and it becomes more realistic for the firm to do its own exporting; when the company reaches this point, it will still be heavily dependent upon the EMC but have little detailed foreign market knowledge itself. Nevertheless, despite these disadvantages, many firms, particularly those in the early stages of exporting, find that export management companies are an extremely effective and low-cost means of international marketing and that their use has significant attractions.

Piggyback Operations

The third form of indirect exporting is piggybacking in which a manufacturer (the carrier) makes use of his own foreign distribution network to sell another company's products (the rider) alongside his own.

Although at first sight this might appear to be a somewhat strange arrangement, it can in practice offer a number of attractions for both parties; for the rider, the advantages are obvious, since it provides established export and distribution facilities. As such, it is similar in a number of ways to the export management company approach that we discussed in the previous section.

From the viewpoint of the carrier, piggybacking can be an easy and profitable way of broadening its product range which, in turn, leads not only to possibly greater economies of scale, but also provides the distributors with a wider and more attractive sales package. Piggybacking can also be an easy way for manufacturers of cyclical or seasonal products to keep their distribution channels operating throughout the year.

Insofar as problems with this system do arise, they tend to stem either from inadequately agreed payment and marketing terms, or from the technical nature of the product. With regard to payment, the carrier can either sell on a commission basis (in a similar manner to the way in which an EMC will operate), or he can buy the product from the manufacturer, thereby acting as an independent distributor. Branding and promotional policies need also to be agreed in advance and can range from the product being sold under the manufacturer's label, through to vendor branding in which the carrier or final distributor puts its own brand label upon the product.[1] But whatever approach is used, full agreement needs to be arrived at in advance if piggybacking is to work efficiently.

The second potential problem area in piggybacking concerns the product itself, particularly when it is of a technical nature. The carrier or distributor's sales and service force must be trained to handle the product and arrangements made for providing warranty and service back-up. Without this, the carrier–rider relationship is likely to encounter problems that may well undermine the whole of the exporting operation. Nevertheless, despite these potential problems, many companies make use of piggybacking. Colgate Palmolive, for example, acts as the carrier for numerous firms in international markets, including Wilkinson Sword (with razor blades) and Weetabix (with Alpen breakfast cereal).[2] Piggybacking was also at the heart of a joint venture established in 1983 between Colgate and the Kaa Corporation of Japan. Under the terms of the agreement, toileteries are now being manufactured in the United States, but being distributed worldwide by Colgate's distribution network.[3] Broadly similar piggybacking arrangements are used by Sony in the Japanese market in which it acts as the distributor for a variety of European and US companies.[4]

Direct Exporting

Our discussion so far has focused upon the low-cost and low-commitment approaches to international operations. Indeed, as we observed at an earlier stage, indirect exporting is in many ways similar to a domestic sales operation. An alternative to this is direct exporting in which all of the background work — such as building up contacts, conducting market research, and arranging the documentation and physical distribution, as well as establishing the pricing and branding policies — is done *in-house* by the firm's export department. The product is typically then sold overseas by other companies and sales agents, or through a sales subsidiary established for that specific purpose. On balance, therefore, direct exporting should lead to higher sales than are normally achieved by means of indirect approaches, although whether this is reflected in greater profits will depend upon the extent to which costs increase as a result of setting up an export department. The range of marketing activities involved in direct exporting is also considerably greater than those of indirect exporting and form the export marketing mix: the major components of this are illustrated in Figure 4.3.

For companies that have begun international operations by using indirect exporting techniques, the question of when best to switch to a more direct approach can be difficult to answer. In essence, the choice between indirect and direct exporting is similar to the choice between using sales agents and having a direct sales force in domestic markets. The advantages of the direct approach can be considerable and stem from the greater control that can be exerted, an improved system of information feedback, and the build-up of marketing expertise. Nevertheless, direct exporting is often a much more expensive alternative than indirect exporting, since all of the costs are borne by just one manufacturer, rather than being shared amongst a number of organisations. The decision must therefore be based upon a consideration of costs, benefits, company objectives, and short- and long-term market expectations.

Selecting Markets and Distributors

In the case of indirect exporting, the choice of markets is to a large extent outside the control of the manufacturer and is determined instead by the carrier in the piggyback relationship or by the breadth of coverage offered by an export management company. Quite obviously, other markets can be entered by using more than one carrier or EMC, although in these circumstances, care needs to be taken to ensure that territorial overlaps do not occur. In the case of direct exporting, however, the choice of markets is, in theory at least, a completely open one. In practice, however,

Figure 4.3: Elements of the Export Marketing Mix

- *The Product*
    Selecting the appropriate products for each export market.
    Developing suitable new products.
    Sourcing complementary products.
    Determining the most appropriate production sources.

- *Distribution*
    Developing and motivating the sales force.
    Establishing and motivating sales agents and middlemen.
    Determining inventory levels.
    Warehousing.
    Physical distribution both to and within the markets.

- *Promotion*
    Developing both local and umbrella advertising.
    Producing sales literature.
    Arranging trade shows.
    Developing appropriate packaging and labelling.

- *Pricing*
    Establishing a price and discount structure.
    Collecting information on competitors' prices.

- *Marketing Services*
    Commissioning market research.
    Providing technical assistance.
    Arranging quotations.
    Producing a sales catalogue.
    Training distributors' and agents' sales staff.
    Providing warranty and guarantee back-up.
    Arranging sales meetings and compiling sales reports.
    Generating competitive intelligence.

- *Finance*
    Budgeting.
    Arranging financial schemes for agents and buyers.
    Collecting invoices.
    Credit management.
    Auditing and control.

- *Technical Support*
    Ensuring products match local specifications.
    Product testing.
    Quality control.

> Providing spare parts.
> Training service staff.
>
> • *Others*
>   Providing data processing facilities, legal advice, insurance, tax advice,
>   translations, and specialist technical support.

companies do encounter constraints that limit choice. The nature of these constraints can vary enormously, but are typically economic (e.g. the market is too distant, too small or too poor); cultural (a significant and costly change in consumer's attitudes would be needed for the product to be commercially viable); competitive (few worthwhile market gaps are evident); or political (obstacles in the form of tariff barriers, trade restrictions and embargoes exist).

However, once the choice of markets has been made, the firm then needs to decide upon how it is to be represented within each market. In the case of markets that are sufficiently large and profitable, the obvious option is to establish a sales subsidiary which can then develop and control the marketing programme. For rather smaller markets where such an investment could not be supported or justified, the alternative approach is to select distributors or agents who are capable of providing the sales and back-up support that is needed. The criteria for choice in these circumstances are likely to be numerous, although quite obviously the factors that are of particular importance are financial stability, market knowledge and sales coverage of the territory. This information can be gained from a number of sources, including government agencies and banks, as well as from commercial organisations such as Dun and Bradstreet. Once the distributors have been selected, the focus of attention then shifts to control and support. Control of the distributor can be achieved in a variety of ways, including a strong initial contract which specifies in detail what is expected in terms of sales performance and the back-up support with which customers are to be provided. More pragmatically, however, the full co-operation of the distributor is more likely to be achieved if he sees it to be in his own interest. This can be done by providing marketing and advertising support, building effective lines of communication and, of course, by offering worthwhile profit margins.

Having appointed distributors and agreed upon the operating

terms, the company is then faced with the task of physical distribution. Although this is discussed in detail in a subsequent chapter, a number of points can usefully be made at this stage.

The most obvious difference between distributing nationally and internationally is the distance that is involved. This has implications for the time-scale involved in moving the product, the forms of transport that are to be used, cost levels, and, of course, for the documentation needed to move products across national boundaries. Indeed, it is in this final area that various studies have shown the greatest obstacles to international marketing to exist, with many managers of small and medium-sized companies in particular feeling that the complications that arise from international documentation are simply too burdensome and time-consuming to justify an exporting effort. But although international marketing does undoubtedly involve a considerable amount of paperwork, a variety of bodies exist to simplify the exporting process. International financing through the banks overcomes many of the problems encountered by companies in the early stages of exporting, whilst international freight forwarders take care both of the physical distribution and the associated documentation. Insurance of credit can be done both through commercial agencies, as well as by the government-financed Export Credits Guarantee Department.

Foreign Manufacturing Strategies

The discussion so far has concentrated upon the international marketing effort being based upon the supply of the product from home-based manufacturing plants. For many larger companies, however, international marketing involves manufacturing the product in one or more of the markets that is being supplied. Although the costs associated with this approach are considerably higher than for home-based operations, a number of factors help to explain why this option might be pursued. In the case of products that are particularly heavy or bulky, for example, high transportation costs may well mean that the delivered price to the foreign market is uncompetitive. Equally, tariff barriers or imposed quota levels may well make foreign-based manufacturing an attractive or necessary course of action. Indeed, it is for this reason that Nissan decided in 1984 to establish a manfacturing and assembly plant in north-east England.

Other attractions of foreign-based operations are that a far better system of market feedback can be developed, delivery and service levels are likely to be improved and, in certain parts of the world, production and distribution costs can be lowered substantially. In addition, customers within these markets may well view the company more favourably and the likelihood of gaining government contracts may be increased. One final advantage of foreign-based manufacturing is that because of the higher set-up costs involved and the consequent financial penalty of withdrawal, the development of an international marketing culture within the organisation is far more likely to emerge.

Various approaches to foreign manufacturing exist, including assembly operations, contract manufacturing, licensing agreements, joint ventures, and total ownership of foreign production facilities.

Assembly Operations

In the case of foreign assembly operations, the company manufactures all or most of the product's components in domestic plants and then transports them to foreign markets for final assembly. The attractions of this approach can be considerable, particularly when the product is relatively large, as in the case of cars and certain types of machinery, and where the transportation of the product in its final form would be high. In order to remain competitive the manufacturer therefore supplies the product CKD (completely knocked down) so that local labour can assemble the product for sale. It was this approach which was used by Chrysler in Iran for many years, since not only did it provide a more competitive basis for sales, but it also enabled the market to see the product as 'domestic' rather than foreign. A further reason for foreign assembly is that in some countries tariff barriers are lower on unassembled products than on the finished items. By imposing barriers of this nature, governments are able to increase employment levels at a relatively low cost.

'Assembly' is also used on a widespread scale in the pharmaceutical and soft drinks industries. Typically, the mixing and packaging is done locally with the key ingredients being shipped in and the bulky liquids being provided by the assembly operation. Thus Coca Cola sells its concentrate to the local agent who then adds water and bottles the product for sale.

Contract Manufacturing

An alternative to assembly operations is contract manufacturing in which the company's products are produced in one or more markets by another manufacturer operating under contract. Typically, such a contract would be limited to the manufacturing operation and sales would be handled by a sales subsidiary of the company. The attraction of operating in this way, assuming of course that a foreign manufacturer is capable of achieving and maintaining the quality and production levels needed, is that investment can be kept to a minimum and if the market subsequently fails to live up to expectations, withdrawal becomes a feasible and relatively low-cost strategy.

Other advantages of this approach are that the product can be advertised as being made locally, a factor which is often of considerable importance when trying to get government contracts; transportation and production costs may well be lower; and the company can concentrate its efforts upon developing the market without having to divert substantial sums of money into establishing production facilities of its own.

Insofar as there are disadvantages to this approach, they tend to stem from the difficulties in some parts of the world of finding a manufacturer who is capable of achieving and maintaining the production requirements that are needed. It is also often argued that long-term problems can arise if the foreign manufacturer decides at a later stage that he wants to terminate the relationship and make use of the expertise that he has acquired by marketing similar products himself. Whether in practice this is likely to be a problem is debatable, although the risk is minimised where strong branding policies have been pursued. Amongst the many companies which make use of contract manufacturing in one form or another in certain parts of the world is Procter and Gamble. In Italy, for example, the company concentrates its efforts upon marketing, whilst several local companies manufacture its products. A similar arrangement is used by Del Monte in politically volatile parts of Central America. Having begun by exporting to the region in the 1930s, the company decided in the 1960s to move towards local production. This was done initially by establishing contract production facilities with the Costa Rican canning firm, Del Campo, whilst Del Monte handled distribution. Because of the success of the venture, Del Monte subsequently offered a closer relationship and began providing production assistance and general marketing advice. The geographical coverage allowed for in the agreement was extended to cover all of the member countries of the Central American Common Market (CACM), and Del Campo took on the responsibility for marketing *within* Costa Rica. The success of this ultimately led Del Monte to begin negotiations for some two-thirds of Del Campo's equity.

Overall, therefore, contract manufacturing offers significant advantages, particularly in politically volatile parts of the world where, as we observed in Chapter 2, foreign investment is subject to periodic criticism and occasional seizure.

Licensing Agreements

A third approach to foreign manufacturing, and one which again minimises capital investment, is licensing through which a firm exploits its 'saleable know-how'. In a number of ways, licensing can be seen as an extension or development of contract manufacturing in that it generally covers a longer time period and involves the licensee in a wider sphere of activities. Typically, for example, the licensee would be given the exclusive rights to manufacture and market the product within an agreed area in return for a royalty based on sales volume. It is this responsibility for *marketing*, as well as for production, that is the distinguishing feature of a licensing agreement.

The attractions of licensing arrangements can be considerable, since not only does the company avoid the capital investment needed to establish production and distribution facilities, but it is also the fastest and least problematic way of entering a foreign market and gaining market knowledge. Indeed, in many communist countries, licensing is often the only way in which markets can be entered. From the viewpoint of the licensee, the attraction is that he avoids research and development costs and, in many cases, can capitalise upon the technological expertise of the licensor. Governments too tend to look favourably upon licensing, largely because of the implications for employment locally and the long-term benefits of technology transfer. For these reasons the large multinationals are often invited by governments to set up 'turnkey' operations. Under this arrangement, the investment capital is provided locally and management is eventually turned over to local personnel. Amongst the companies that have used this approach to penetrate the USSR market are Pepsi Cola and Fiat. Typically in these circumstances, the company will receive a continuing royalty on sales, as well as benefiting from being a preferred components supplier.

When problems with licensing do arise, the root cause tends to be the initial contract spelling out the responsibilities both of the licensor and the licensee; over time and as the market environment changes, the terms of the agreement may well become less appropriate and relevant. Other problems that companies have faced include the difficulties of dealing with a licensee who appears not to be putting sufficient effort into market development; the relatively low returns from the typical licensing agreement (3-5 per cent); and the entrepreneurial licensee who after a number of years decides to make use of the expertise he has gained by setting up a rival organisation.

On balance, however, many companies have found licensing to be an attractive method of entering foreign markets, particularly when strong international patents exist and steps are taken to minimise the likelihood of the problems referred to above arising.

One particular form of licensing that is currently growing rapidly and is worthy of note is international franchising. The companies that are most active in this area tend to be the American multinationals and by 1985 had established more than 26,500 franchises in other countries. The sectors in which the most rapid growth has been achieved are soft drinks (e.g. Coca-Cola and Pepsi Cola), fast foods (MacDonalds and Kentucky Fried Chicken), and car rentals (Avis and Hertz).

Joint Ventures

An extension to the idea of licensing which, when used properly, is capable of overcoming some of the problems associated with licence arrangements, is that of joint ventures. (The growth of joint venturing in the motor industry is discussed in the case study (Appendix 1) at the end of the chapter.) The important distinction between licensing and joint venturing is that in a joint venture, the firm takes an equity stake and has a management role in the foreign firm. Compared then with licensing, the two major attractions of a joint venture arrangement are, firstly, that the returns are generally higher and, secondly, that the company can exert a degree of control over the production and marketing operation. Other advantages include the expertise gained of international marketing and the levels of market feedback that are possible.

Insofar as problems do arise in joint ventures, they tend to stem from disagreements with the national partner about the goals of the operation, the level of earnings that is to be re-invested, and long-term product and market development. However, as an alternative to the *total* ownership of foreign production facilities, joint ventures have the attraction of requiring lower capital and management investment, are often politically more expedient, and, in countries which have an element of political instability, are possibly less likely to be taken over by the government. It is for these sorts of reasons that Japanese companies frequently opt for joint ventures, since they help to overcome possible trade barriers. Thus, Honda's joint ventures with British Leyland have provided a degree of access to the European markets that would otherwise be denied to them. Similarly, many Japanese firms have established joint ventures with American multinationals to avoid America's trade barriers. For their part, the Americans welcome the links because they provide an opportunity to tie-up American product innovation with Japanese low-cost manufacturing technology, as well as curbing an otherwise tough competitor.

But despite these sorts of advantages, many multinationals do have reservations about joint ventures and prefer instead to opt for licensing or total ownership. The major reasons for this are, firstly, that differences between managerial objectives, philosophy and culture are often too great to be easily reconciled; secondly, that integrating joint venture operations between countries is frequently difficult; and thirdly, that there is often a feeling that the market partner gets the best of the deal in that although he contributes market knowledge, he is getting in return the rather more substantial benefits of technological skill and access to more sophisticated managerial resources. It is largely because of these problems that multinationals tend to prefer total ownership of the foreign operation. With these comments in mind, it is perhaps worth turning to Appendix 2.1 since reference is made within this to Indian government attitudes to multinationals and the effect that these have had upon IBM (withdrawal from the market rather than accept joint ventures), Xerox (agreement to a joint venture with a 40 per cent equity after a decade of negotiation with its partner), and Gillette, which had to accept a far lower joint venture equity stake to ensure market entry.

Total Ownership of Foreign Production Facilities

The total ownership option is not only the most expensive of those that we have considered, it is also the approach that represents the greatest managerial commitment to international business. Once established, withdrawal is both costly and difficult.

However, before we go on to look at the various ways in which total ownership can operate, we need to clarify what is meant by the concept of 'total ownership'. Although in theory at least the firm needs 100 per cent ownership for total control, effective managerial control can in practice be achieved with a far smaller shareholding. The significant feature of total ownership is, therefore, the *degree* rather than the completeness of control.

The two strategies that can be used to establish foreign production facilities involve either acquisition by buying out an existing organisation, or establishing and developing a completely new company. Of the two approaches, the first is quite obviously the fastest and has the added advantage of providing a trained labour force, local knowledge, contacts with other companies as well as with the market, and an established distribution network. It was for these reasons that in the 1960s in particular, American organisations bought into European companies in large numbers.

The alternative approach which involves establishing completely new facilities, although more time-consuming, has its own advantages, particularly when the company feels there to be relatively few pressures. It enables the organisation to develop the new firm in the way that it wants, rather than having to change existing practices, and allows for a totally new image to be established.

But regardless of which of these two approaches to total ownership is pursued, costs are likely to be high. Nevertheless, for larger companies particularly, total ownership is often seen to be the only acceptable approach to international expansion, since the benefits in terms of freedom of action, higher profits and the absence of conflict with local partners are generally seen to outweigh the initial investment needed.

Market Entry and Marketing Strategy

The choice of a method of market entry has quite obvious and significant implications for marketing strategy. At one level, these can be seen in terms of the degree of freedom that the company has in choosing its target markets and in the ways in which it subsequently goes about the process of matching market demand.

At a rather deeper level, however, the choice of a method of entry has direct consequences for the firm's ability to develop an international image and reap the benefits of the economies of a large-scale and standardised production and marketing programme. The benefits of a standardised approach across all or most of the world's markets have long been recognised in a general way, although it is only in recent years that any more than a handful of companies such as Coca-Cola, Caterpillar, BIC and IBM have actually pursued it. However, with the apparent growth of an ever more standardised culture in the world's major markets, more and more companies have begun to modify their marketing strategies to reflect this. The arguments for and against standardised global marketing strategies are discussed in detail in Chapter 6 on product policy, although at this stage thought should be given to the way in which the choice of market entry either enhances or inhibits the marketer's freedom to operate in this way.

More fundamentally, however, it needs to be recognised that the choice of an entry strategy also affects the marketer's ability to target markets with any real degree of precision. If, for example, the company opts for one of the less direct approaches to entry, it is unlikely that it will be able to do anything more than suggest where opportunities exist and the areas to which priority should be given. The closer the firm moves towards *direct* international marketing, however, the greater the need and scope for precise targeting and market segmentation becomes.

The rationale for market segmentation is both straightforward and well-established; it simply gives recognition to the fact that users, be they in the industrial or consumer goods field, differ and that because of this it is rarely possible for a firm to satisfy the needs of every consumer simultaneously. As a consequence, there is a need to focus upon *groups* of consumers who exhibit similarities in their consumption habits, behavioural patterns, or in some other significant way. The degree of concentration that is at the heart of market segmentation has quite obvious advantages, although it does need to be recognised that, equally, it can in certain cases make the company vulnerable to a sudden change in patterns of demand. For this reason, some firms quite deliberately adopt the alternative policy of market aggregation whereby the market is treated as being largely undifferentiated. Any economic, social or cultural differences that do exist within the market are ignored and the marketing programme is standardised.

Although, quite obviously, the extent to which either of these two strategies is appropriate will vary from one market to another, the strategic importance of market segmentation should not be underestimated, since it is by means of segmentation that the marketer not only defines his market, but also determines the nature of his competition.

International Market Segmentation

Over the past twenty years, a variety of methods have been developed to help the marketer segment his markets. At this stage, it is not our intention to do more than make brief reference to these techniques, since the majority of marketing textbooks offer a reasonably full coverage of the material. Instead, we intend to focus upon the ways in which the concept can be used most effectively within the international marketing programme.

Bases for Market Segmentation

Despite the development in recent years of ever more sophisticated techniques, the best known and most commonly used methods of segmentation are still those that are based upon relatively straightforward criteria. They include:

(i) demographic variables such as age, sex, income, occupation, family life cycle, religion and social class;
(ii) cultural factors;
(iii) geographic differences; and
(iv) behavioural factors such as product usage rates, buying motives, and receptiveness to new ideas and products.

For the domestic marketer, information on most, if not all, of these headings can often be obtained relatively easily. In the case of demographic variables, for example, a considerable volume of information exists and can be incorporated into such socio-economic measures as the JICNAR (A, B, C1, C2, D and E) and ACORN (A Classification of Residential Neighbourhoods) frameworks. For the international marketer, however, this sort of information is often not available and even where it can be obtained, it only rarely lends itself to any real degree of comparative or cross-cultural analysis. One consequence of this is that the marketer is often faced with the need to develop his own measures of the market and assess the opportunities that exist.

Similar problems can be seen in the case of cultural differences between markets. Typically, the marketer defines his markets on the basis of geographical boundaries. In many cases, however, it may be rather more realistic to view the market as a series of cultural groupings. Majaro, for example, highlights the importance of this when talking about segmentation within Europe:

> In cultural terms the French part of Switzerland has probably more in common with France than with the German speaking part of Switzerland. In terms of market segmentation one is fully justified to cluster the French speaking part of Switzerland with France. This may be totally unworkable on political grounds, or in monetary/fiscal terms, but it is certainly logical on a cultural basis. Most international marketers accept political borders much too readily in their marketing planning; in fact there are many situations where such borders are quite meaningless in terms of marketing logic and potential synergy. The fact that a market is shown on a political map as a separate entity does not automatically make it into a separate marketing entity.[5]

Conceptually similar problems are encountered with most other methods of market segmentation and are, quite simply, reflections of the differences that exist between markets in terms of their culture and expectations. Nevertheless, it is only by recognising these differences and their significance that the marketer can decide upon the nature of his marketing strategy.

Market Segmentation and Marketing Strategy

In essence, the marketer operating either domestically or internationally has a choice of three strategies: undifferentiated marketing, differentiated marketing, and concentrated marketing. In the first of these, the firm uses a standardised marketing mix to sell a standardised product across a variety of markets and, quite deliberately, ignores any differences that exist between the various parts of the market. By way of contrast, differentiated marketing gives recognition to these differences, and both the product and the marketing mix are modified in an attempt to appeal more specifically to particular target groups. Concentrated marketing is, in turn, a more extreme manifestation of this policy and involves the firm in isolating a very limited number of segments upon which it subsequently concentrates its efforts.

In choosing between these three alternatives, the marketer needs to adopt techniques of cost-benefit analysis; in other words, what is the likely cost of marketing a series of differentiated products and what benefits in terms of greater sales revenue and profit are likely to emerge? It is this sort of analysis which is at the heart of one of the most fundamental and far-reaching decisions in international marketing: to what extent should the international marketing programme be differentiated? The decision has a number of quite obvious consequences not only for product policy and advertising, but also for the way in which the organisation of international operations develops. If, for example, the company opts for a standardised approach, the scope and need for decentralised management is reduced. If, by way of contrast, the firm decides to pursue a policy of concentrated or differentiated marketing, the likelihood of a centralised managerial structure being able to cope effectively drops significantly.

In order to decide upon the most suitable strategy, the marketer needs to begin by developing a broad picture of each of the potential markets and of the extent to which a standardised or a differentiated approach might succeed. From here, he can go on to identify any similarities between markets and hence the scope that exists for total or regional standardisation. In this way, he should then be able to begin developing the framework of a marketing strategy that reflects either a philosophy of concentration upon carefully selected market segments, or one of limited differentation in which there is a small number of marketing mixes, each of which has been tailored to a well defined cluster of market segments. A typical example of a concentrated policy involves segmenting world markets on the basis of such factors as geographical proximity and/or level of economic development and/or cultural similarities. By doing this, a number of major market clusters emerge such as the Scandinavian cluster (Norway, Sweden, Finland, Denmark), the Anglo-Saxon cluster (Great Britain, the United States, Canada, Australia, New Zealand, South Africa), the Iberian cluster (Spain, Portugal, Brazil), the 'traditional' European cluster (Germany, France, Belgium, the Netherlands, Switzerland), and so on. Within each of these clusters it should then be possible to pursue a degree of standardisation. In doing this, the marketer should ensure that he avoids the pitfalls of differentiated marketing in which the needs of an uneconomical number of market segments are being met.

A philosophy of concentration is therefore at the heart of world market segmentation and represents a quite deliberate attempt to focus upon those segments that offer the greatest profitability.

Summary

The choice of a method of market entry has fundamental and far-reaching consequences for the entire marketing programme. In choosing between the various alternatives, companies need to consider not only the cost of entry, but also the implications for future development, the levels of risk that are faced, the ability to control the nature of the marketing programme, and the ability to withdraw from the market if conditions subsequently change.

The relationship between market entry and marketing strategy is complex and reflected particularly in the scope that exists for segmentation and targeting. In selecting target markets care needs to be taken to ensure that sufficient similarities exist for a relatively standardised marketing programme to be pursued, since the consequences of a differentiated strategy are felt both in higher costs and in a reduction of central management control.

References

1. *Business Europe*, 4 October 1968, pp. 317-18.
2. 'Why Colgate sells Other People's Products', *Business Week*, 20 April 1974, p. 108.
3. 'Colgate Palmolive, Kao Join to Create Hair Products Line', *Asian Wall Street Journal*, Weekly, 24 January 1983, p. 22.
4. 'How Sony Piggybacks Foreign Products in Japan', *Business International*, 1 February 1974, p. 38.
5. Simon Majaro, *International Marketing: A Strategic Approach to World Marketing* (George Allen and Unwin, 1978), p. 45.

Appendix 4.1: The World Motor Industry: The Growth of Joint Ventures

---

The Pressures for Greater Co-operation

At roughly the same time that the 10 millionth car produced by Austin Rover rolled off the Longbridge production line in September 1985, the company signed a multi-million-pound co-operation deal to build Peugeot gearboxes. Although the agreement was seen by the two companies to be significant, it did in reality represent just one very small piece in the ever-more complex jigsaw of inter-company and international motor industry relationships that have emerged as companies have increasingly come to recognise that in order to survive, they need to co-operate.

Recognition of this fact has led to an intricate maze of links that now encircle the globe and range from simple component swaps to fully blown joint ventures, as illustrated in Figure 4.4. At the same time, however, motor industry analysts recognise that the shift towards greater co-operation has still not got into top gear, and that considerable scope exists for major deals to be made between the motor industry giants. The marketing implications of such deals are immense.

For the European companies, the major threat is likely to stem from increased links between Japanese and American manufacturers. In commenting upon this in 1985, Ray Horrocks, the chief executive of the BL Cars group, said that, 'Unholy alliances between the Japanese, with their manufacturing technology, and the Americans, with their huge domestic market, pose a real threat to Europe. We could be progressively squeezed and end up cutting each other to bits.'

To the average car salesman in British showrooms in 1985, it appeared that this had already begun.

In August of that year, Britons bought 373,000 new cars, the second highest monthly figure on record. Within the industry, however, few people were celebrating, since many of these sales had been achieved only by costly incentives and promotions. 'Moving the metal', as it is labelled in the industry, had become progressively more expensive in the early to mid-1980s, with the result that most European car manufacturers were losing money on each deal. The 1985 half-yearly figures for BL, for example, reported a loss of £44.8 million, whilst Talbot, part of the Peugeot

Figure 4.4: Patterns of Co-operation within the World Car Industry

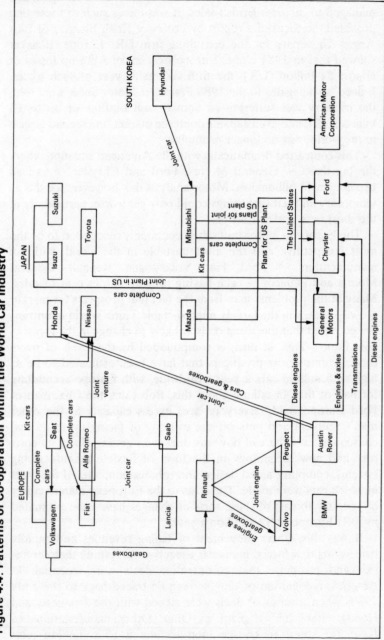

group, reported pre-tax losses of £13.1 million, even though it had managed to increase British sales. It was losses such as these that provided the focus of a report by Professor Krish Bhaskar of East Anglia University for the consulting firm DRI Europe. Bhaskar showed that in 1984 alone, Europe's car-makers ran up losses of almost £1 billion (UK), the fifth successive year of such losses. Indeed, as delegates to the 1985 Frankfurt Motor Show were told, the industry was suffering an annual cash outflow of up to £3 billion (UK), and even Japan's domestic market, the second largest in the world, was no longer profitable.

This contrasted dramatically with the American situation where the big three — General Motors, Ford and Chrysler — had all become profit billionaires. Motor analysts did, however, see this as temporary and felt that things could only get worse, particularly in the short term and in Europe.

The European motor industry is commonly recognised to be the most competitive and the most unstable in the world, with six manufacturers — Ford, Fiat, Volkswagen, Renault, General Motors and Peugeot — each having roughly 12 per cent of sales. Many of the problems stem from the fact that prospects for market growth, except in the largely unpredictable Third World countries, are poor and that this situation is unlikely to change in the foreseeable future. This, in turn, is compounded by the levels of over-capacity among car producers that have been estimated to be as high as 5 million cars a year worldwide, with Europe accounting for half of this. In talking about this, Bob Lutz, the Chairman of Ford Europe, said, 'Everyone sees excess capacity as the other man's problem and puts off the evil day of facing up to its real consequences.' The evil day was, however, getting closer as costs rose and new technology in the form of flexible manufacturing systems, computer aided design and robotisation, altered the ways in which cars were made. The costs to the European manufacturer of keeping abreast of these sorts of changes have been estimated by DRI Europe as $2.4 billion a year.

It was this pincer movement of falling revenues and rapidly rising costs that forced many car executives to rethink their strategies and recognise that co-operative deals were essential. In America, recognition of this fact can be traced back to the early 1980s when a series of deals were signed with the Japanese, and Honda established a plant in Ohio. Other manifestations of Japanese–American co-operation include a $500 million joint venture between Chrysler and Mitsubishi to produce 180,000 cars a year; the plan by Mazda, part owned by Ford, to build an American plant with annual capacity of 200,000 cars; and the deal by General Motors with Japan's Isuzi and Suzuki, in which it holds minority stakes, to take significant numbers of Japanese cars in a 'captive imports' operation whereby the imported vehicles are sold under the GM label. This 'vendor branding' deal followed Chrysler's vendor branding for Mitsubishi-made cars.

These deals, together with a variety of other projects through which Japanese manufacturers plan to have their own sole ventures, will mean that by 1990 Japanese companies could have the capacity to build more than 1 million cars on American soil. This projected 10 per cent market share has led many American critics to argue for a halt to be called; there does, however, appear to be little likelihood of the American government's responding.

The rationale for these developments is straightforward. For the Japanese, they have the advantage of ensuring a permanent place in the world's biggest market which traditionally has generated huge profits. For the American, there appears to be three main advantages:

(i)   *Cost.* According to a variety of reports, the Japanese can build small cars for $2,000 less than the most efficient American companies.

(ii) *Technology.* By collaborating with the Japanese, the Americans gain access to the most highly developed technology available for building 'sub-compact' cars.

(iii) *Expertise.* It provides the Americans with an opportunity to study at first hand the Japanese management techniques and production methods that have revolutionised car manufacturing.

Although many Americans are opposed to such high levels of Japanese access to the American market, the motor industry itself is confident that the links can only be beneficial and allow American manufacturers to close the cost and quality gaps that have traditionally existed between East and West.

European observers are, however, far more sceptical about collaborative deals. Although many admit to the need for partnerships, they point to the outcome of many such deals in the past. A study of the European motor industry in recent years, for example, indicates that previously intense competitors do not make good collaborators. This has been recognised by Ray Horrocks who, whilst having high hopes for the Honda–BL joint ventures, has admitted that it has often been difficult to find common ground when fighting for sales in the same market.

Sanjay Dabysing of DRI Europe has also highlighted these sorts of problems by pointing to the history of the Type Four Project between Fiat, Lancia, Saab and Alfa Romeo. The project's objective was to develop a car with the same mechanical components, but a different body shape for each market. After a good start, things began going drastically wrong when each wanted to start making parts in their own countries because of the job implications.

European scepticism has been further compounded by the relative lack of success in the past in finding partners outside the Continent. Several factors appear to have contributed to this, although the major obstacle has been that unlike the Japanese and the Americans, the Europeans have been negotiating from a position of weakness that has been aggravated by EEC regulations. It is against this background that many observers view the future of the majority of the European car manufacturing industry with concern, since it is in essence too highly fragmented to cope effectively with a major Japanese–American push in the 1990s.

Other observers view the situation somewhat differently and see major benefits emerging from possible collaborative deals between firms operating in Europe. In 1985, for example, Ford and Fiat reached a relatively advanced stage in negotiations that would have led to joint control of 25 per cent of the European market. The talks between the two firms eventually broke down, seemingly as the result of different views of how the two companies could best work together. Many motor industry analysts viewed the collapse of the talks with dismay, arguing that the strengths of the two companies are largely complementary (Ford with medium and large cars and Fiat with small cars) and that the potential pay-offs from such a deal could be so significant and far-reaching that they would overcome any incompatibilities between the two managerial cultures. They also pointed to the fact that without collaborative deals such as this, the future for most of the European car industry is gloomy.

5 INTERNATIONAL MARKETING PLANNING

Although marketing planning is an essential element of effective management and one which has received a considerable amount of attention in recent years, planning on an international scale is, for a majority of companies, still only a poorly developed activity. There are several reasons for this and it is to these, together with the ways in which international planning processes can be improved, that we turn our attention within this chapter.

The Nature and Purpose of Planning

The planning process has been defined as the way in which management attempts to reconcile the firm's objectives and resources with current and future opportunities. It is, therefore, a method of preparing for tomorrow and, as such, involves a series of decisions regarding *where* the company wants to go and *how* it intends getting there. This process of setting goals and formulating strategies is, in many ways, one of the most fundamental and far-reaching managerial tasks, since it is in this way that the nature and direction of the company's development is determined. In many companies, however, the benefits of planning are still only partially understood and, as a consequence, the planning processes only poorly developed. At an international level, the need for planning is, if anything, even greater than in domestic markets, since lead times and communication channels are often longer and the scope for misunderstanding rather greater. In addition, the opportunities open to the company, as well as the objectives pursued, are likely to differ significantly from one market to another. There is a quite obvious need, therefore, not only for a clear and unambiguous statement of objectives and priorities, but also of responsibilities and of the ways in which the objectives are to be pursued. It is this process of forward planning that is therefore at the heart of the international marketing effort. A great many commentators have observed, however, that planning practices for multinational markets are, if anything, far less well-developed than those for domestic markets. Several factors help to explain why this should be so, although arguably the most important single cause is the often confused relationship that exists between headquarters and subsidiary staff. Most typically, this takes the form of disagreements about who should be responsible for particular activities. Headquarters staff generally claim that because they have the advantage of a far broader perspective, they should be the ones to determine policy, with the subsidiary simply then having the task of implementation. Subsidiary staff often argue, however, that because they have a more detailed understanding of market conditions, they should play a far greater role in determining policy. The obvious and unfortunate casualty of this is the planning process and, subsequently, the organisation's performance.

There is an obvious need, therefore, for the relationship between headquarters and subsidiary staff to be clarified before the process of planning begins; the ways in which this can be done are discussed at a later stage. A starting point however is, quite simply, a far greater recognition throughout the organisation of the benefits of effective planning procedures and of the probable long-term consequences of unplanned development.

The benefits to the organisation of a well-developed planning process can be considerable and have been pointed to by a wide variety of commentators and include the ways in which:

(i)   it encourages a systematic process of thinking ahead;
(ii) the analytical process underlying planning forces the organisation to state its objectives and policies more precisely;
(iii) the organisation is more likely to anticipate environmental change and be ready to react effectively;
(iv) it leads to improved communication and co-ordination;
(v)   it allows for the development of performance standards which can then be used as a basis of control;
(vi) it broadens the base of participation in the managerial process; and
(vii) it minimises conflict and the scope for disagreement between different functional areas within the organisation when faced with a choice of strategies.

In practice, however, the extent to which these potential benefits are realised depends upon a number of factors, including the managerial philosophy and the evolutionary stage of planning that has been reached.

The Evolution of Business Planning

In many firms, planning procedures appear to develop through four quite distinct evolutionary stages, starting with the unplanned stage and culminating in strategic planning:

(i) The Unplanned Stage. In the early years of a business, there is a marked tendency for management to be preoccupied with searching for funds, markets and equipment, with little or no time or attention being paid to forward planning. The perspective tends to be almost exclusively short-term with the result that a managerial 'fire fighting' culture emerges in which problems are solved as they arise rather than being anticipated and avoiding action taken.

(ii) The Budgeting System Stage. Having got through the first stage, managers gradually come to recognise the need for a more formalised approach both for day-to-day operations and longer term development. In turn, this tends to lead to a system of budgeting in which estimates are made of sales for, say, the next twelve months and of the probable costs and cash flows. It needs to be recognised, however, that these budgets are essentially financial in nature and require substantially less thought and analysis than goes in to true business planning in which attention is also paid to such areas as marketing, research and development, production and personnel.

(iii) Annual Business Planning. Having developed a system of budgeting, the majority of companies eventually move on to a more formalised approach to planning which embraces a greater number of activities, including marketing and personnel. The time scale that typically is used for this is the same as for the budgeting system stage, and one of three distinct planning philosophies begins to emerge: top-down planning, bottom-up planning, or goals down/plans up planning. The first of these, *top-down planning*, is by far the most straightforward and takes its name from the ways in which senior management sets both the goals and the

plans for management at lower levels. Middle and junior management then simply has the task of implementation and, subsequently, of monitoring the results. *Bottom-up planning*, by way of contrast, takes a very different approach in that the various parts of the organisation prepare their own goals and plans, and then submit them to senior management for approval. Assuming that they are approved, they are then passed back for implementation.

The third approach is *goals down/plans up* planning and takes its name from the way in which senior management begins by assessing the firm's opportunities and needs, and then determines the corporate objectives that are to be pursued. The various parts of the organisation are then held responsible for developing plans that will help the firm achieve these goals.

(iv) The Strategic Planning Stage.   Having developed and made use of a system of annual planning, the process can then be taken an important step further by the addition of a system of *long-range planning* in which the annual plan represents just part of a far broader framework for the longer term development and direction of the organisation. In essence, therefore, the annual plan becomes quite simply a detailed version of the first year of, say, a five-year plan which maps out the way in which the organisation is expected to develop. The planning procedure can then be taken a step further still by reworking the long-range plan each year to take account of environmental changes and shifting market opportunities, a process which leads to what is referred to as a *rolling plan.*

One consequence of this is that planning tends to become far more strategic in nature with much greater and more specific attention being paid to long-term opportunities and threats. In the initial stages of planning, the plans that emerge tend to be relatively straightforward documents which focus upon tactics and operational issues, rather than upon the strategic development of the business. As the planning process develops further, this focus shifts and allows for other elements, including standardisation of the planning format to allow for comparisons across functions, as well as a greater use of financial analysis and contingency plans to be introduced.

In practice, however, many companies have experienced difficulties in moving through these stages, largely because of managerial resistance. The three most common reasons for this resistance are, firstly, that managers are often reluctant, particularly in a volatile environment, to commit themselves in advance to particular goals and strategies, arguing instead that more effective management will result from a fluid style that is unconstrained by written and specified plans; secondly, that managers frequently argue that the planning process is time-consuming and that this time can be spent far more profitably in managing the business; and, thirdly, that planning is often seen to be a process forced upon them by senior management rather than a mechanism by which managerial performance can be improved. In order to overcome these sorts of problems, there is a need to develop a 'planning culture' within the organisation in which the benefits of systematic planning are more widely recognised; a culture which is particularly important within multi product/multi market businesses in which co-ordination is essential. Within multinational corporations the most effective way of achieving this has proved to be by the development of a cadre of international strategic planning professionals who not only have a detailed understanding of the country or region whose plans they co-ordinate, but who also recognise how the problems of implementation vary from one market to another.

International Marketing Planning

Although the *process* of planning (see Figure 5.1) in domestic and international markets is in essence the same, international marketing planning is often complicated by potentially ambiguous relationships between headquarters and subsidiary staff, the greater uncertainties of geographically dispersed markets and, in some organisations, by ambivalent managerial attitudes to international markets. Together, these factors have led to much international marketing planning being operational and short term in nature, with relatively little attention being paid to strategic issues. If, however, international marketing planning is to be effective and the challenge of competition met, a far more formalised procedure is needed. This is most likely to be achieved by clarifying from the outset the nature of the relationship between corporate headquarters and the various operating subsidiaries. For a majority of companies, it is unlikely that a uniform relationship will emerge, or indeed be desirable, since markets differ considerably in terms of

Figure 5.1: The Strategic Planning Process

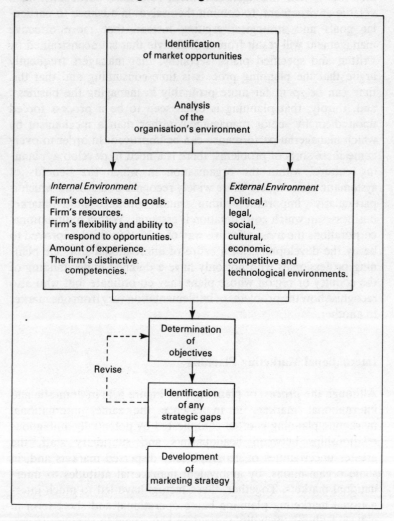

their size, importance and potential. Instead, what is rather more important is that the contribution that each is to make to the development and implementation of the corporate plan is understood from the beginning. Thus, in the case of a small market with limited potential and, in managerial terms, a relatively inexperienced staff, it may well be appropriate for all or most of the marketing planning to be done by corporate management using a top-down approach. However, even in those circumstances where a top-down philosophy is pursued, account still needs to be taken of the market's environmental realities; something that is most likely to be achieved by the development of a marketing information system that channels market data to the corporate planners. By way of contrast, in larger markets which offer a far greater potential and in which the levels of managerial skill are rather greater, a bottom-up or goals-down/plans-up approach is likely to be a far more effective means of planning.

But regardless of which approach to planning is used, corporate management has a responsibility for ensuring that staff are fully aware not only of the firm's overall mission, but also of the contribution that each subsidiary operation is expected to make. Without this sense of direction, any attempt at international planning is likely to suffer from an overly fragmented approach. By the same token, an additional corporate responsibility can be seen in terms of the need to develop a planning culture throughout the organisation, since in its absence the co-ordination of marketing policy becomes a far less realistic objective. In practice, however, the extent to which their responsibilities are recognised has been shown to depend to a large extent upon the international orientation of management and, in particular, whether it is ethnocentric, polycentric or geocentric. In commenting upon these philosophies, Jain has observed that:

> A company with a geocentric perspective tends to look at world markets as a whole, with no demarcation between domestic and international business. Its strategic focus will be global. But an ethnocentric orientation will view international business as secondary, a place to dispose of 'surplus' products left over after fulfilling domestic demand. The differences in these approaches have been illustrated by choices of branding policy.

- *Ethnocentric approach.* Branding policy in overseas companies stresses the parent country as a unifying feature, but not necessarily the origin of the parent country.
- *Polycentric approach.* Each local company brands products on an independent basis, consistent with local country criteria.
- *Geocentric approach.* A worldwide branding policy exists only for those brands that are acceptable worldwide.[1]

In turn, these three very different international perspectives have major and quite obvious implications for the *focus* of planning. But although international planning is typically done on a country by country or regional basis, an increasingly attractive alternative — once the initial product/market combinations have been decided upon — involves reorganising parts of the international business into strategic business units (SBUs). In essence, an SBU is a self-contained business that satisfies several criteria:

(i)   it is a single business or collection of related businesses;
(ii) it has a distinct mission;
(iii) it has its own competitors;
(iv) it has a responsible manager;
(v)   it consists of one or more programme units and functional units;
(vi) it can benefit from strategic planning;
(vii) it can be planned independently of other businesses.[2]

In focusing upon SBUs, it needs to be recognised, however, that they do not replace the existing organisational structure but rather that they are used as a means of determining strategy. This is illustrated by Jain who has said:

> An SBU may be established around products/markets in different divisions, in different countries. For example, a company may manufacture colour televisions in an electronic division in one country; while in another country radios and stereos are manufactured as a part of home entertainment division. For strategy development purposes TVs, radios, and stereo equipment may be pulled together in an SBU.
> Further strategic planning analysis henceforth is undertaken at the SBU level ... (and) each SBU conducts their opportunity analysis of the different product/markets under its control.[3]

It is in the light of these comments that the true complexities and difficulties of effective international planning can perhaps best be understood; the greater the number of markets in which the company operates, the more complex the planning process becomes. Recognition of this has led a number of multinational firms in recent years to make significant modifications to their planning procedures by reverting to an increasingly top-down process supported by a well-developed information system. The firms that have made this sort of change have justified it not simply in terms of the far broader market perspectives possessed by the corporate planners, but also by pointing to a long established argument that the starting point for planning has to be the strategic objectives. Thus:

> The aim of the firm is to satisfy a number of *stakeholders* with conflicting demands and expectations and the only people who are in the position of striking a balance among these demands are at the strategic level. They express the needs and expectations of the various groups of stakeholders in *corporate objectives* and these are the trigger point from which the firm's planning starts. In other words, according to this school of thought, the firm exists in order to meet certain expectations of various groups such as employees, shareholders, bankers, governments, etc., and the summation of the expectations is enunciated in corporate objectives — until these have been defined, no meaningful planning can be performed at the lower levels of management.[4]

It is against this sort of background that the conditions for successful international planning should be viewed. Thus, insofar as it is possible to identify the broad guidelines for success, they are:

(i) a widely accepted and well-developed planning culture;

(ii) a clear statement both of the short and the long-term corporate objectives; and a detailed understanding of the contribution that each part of the international operation is expected to make;

(iii) a well-developed and effective information system that provides the planners with information in the form that is needed;

(iv) a continuous monitoring process to review progress and ensure that changes are made to meet shifting patterns of opportunities and threats.

It is only once these sorts of guidelines have been accepted that it then really becomes possible to identify the specific planning responsibilities both of headquarters and subsidiary staff. In the case of short-term planning, for example, the process needs to reflect a series of inputs from both sides, beginning with a statement by corporate staff of the organisation's mission and objectives. In the light of this, the subsidiary can define its own goals and marketing objectives which are then submitted for approval. Most typically, this would be done by adhering to a standardised format to allow headquarters staff to establish a degree of homogeneity and comparative analysis between the various operating units. Once the objectives have been agreed, the planning process can then begin. The starting point for this is most typically a review of previous sales and their extrapolation into the future. The forecasts that emerge are then either revised upwards or downwards in the light of any environmental changes that are taking place nationally or globally and which seem likely to have an influence upon the firm. The responsibility for this environmental input can, again, be split between subsidiary and headquarters staff in the sense that the subsidiary is most likely to have an insight to local competitive, political and cultural moves, whilst headquarters staff are best placed for assessing the nature and significance of any changes on a larger scale. The modified sales forecast that emerges is then used to develop strategies and budgets which are submitted to headquarters or regional staff for approval. Once this has been given, the subsidiary has its operating plan for the next twelve months.

In the case of long-term and strategic planning, however, the nature of the interaction between the two sides is often very different. The reasons for this are discussed in some detail at a later stage, although in essence it is attributable to the far greater complexities and uncertainties of long-term planning, and to the belief in many firms that strategic planning is the prerogative of headquarters staff. Such an attitude can, however, create problems, since centralisation of strategic planning has a tendency to result in a greater standardisation of strategies across markets, and a much reduced recognition of market differences. These sorts of problems are, in turn, magnified in many companies by the way in which there is often a lack of relevant or adequate information on likely long-term market developments. Subsidiaries seldom have either the knowledge or the resources needed to scan the environment effectively and, in many parts of the world, published information on such things as national trends is often sketchy or outdated. An added complication for many multinational companies in the developing world is that the sheer pace of environmental change makes accurate long-term forecasting — and hence strategic planning — a virtually impossible task. These problems are often then compounded by the ways in which many organisations still fail to co-ordinate and disseminate the information that is available.

International strategic planning is also often hampered by the way in which many firms still adopt a predominantly short-term operational focus, with few managers being given the time, opportunity or resources needed to think strategically. This, in turn, has a knock-on effect to the subsidiary with emphasis being placed upon responding to the day-to-day demands of the parent corporation rather than allowing the subsidiary's managers to concentrate upon long-term market development.

It is against this sort of background, together with the changing international corporate environment, that Jain argues for a new approach to the management of international business planning, an approach which rests upon two major premises:

(i) Emphasis should be placed on the *fundamental* nature of each of the various businesses to be managed internationally. In this way, the level of risk and expected contribution of each overseas operation can be defined more readily.

(ii) The essential step in determining how best to manage international operations is the 'unbundling' of existing activities so that the functions to be carried out by headquarters and subsidiary staff become more evident.[5]

By doing this, he believes that a number of benefits will emerge: firstly, the organisation will gain a far clearer view of the nature and direction of each part of the business; secondly, management by strategy becomes much more attainable; and thirdly, the types of information needed to manage different businesses internationally become more apparent.

The Problems of Planning

In the light of our comments so far, it can be seen that many companies, but particularly those operating internationally, experience considerable difficulties in planning effectively. The nature of these difficulties varies enormously from one firm to another, but are, in essence, management-type problems or planning-type problems. Several factors contribute to this, including a lack of suitable information, poor communication, a lack of managerial skill, and an overly myopic approach to the nature and significance of environmental change. These are illustrated in Table 5.1. Although it is, quite obviously, unrealistic to underestimate the significance of these sorts of problems, management can do much to minimise and overcome their consequences if it understands their source. There is a strong argument, therefore, for a regular and detailed review of the entire planning process with a view to identifying any problems that are being encountered and modifying procedures so that they operate more effectively.

Table 5.1: A Framework of Planning Problems

Type of problem	Headquarters	Overseas subsidiary
Management	Unclear definition of planning responsibilities Unrealistic planning expectations Lack of awareness of foreign market conditions Inadequate guidelines	Managerial resistance to planning Managerial inadequacies Misinterpretation of data Opposition to headquarters guidelines Myopic perspective Misunderstanding of objectives
Planning procedures	Standardised bases for evaluation Inadequate data support Overformalised approach Poor report-back procedures	Inadequate market data Outdated information Underdeveloped information system Lack of planning skills Inaccurate data inputs

Source: William Brandt, James Hulbert and Raimar Richers, 'Pitfalls in Planning for Multinational Operations', *Long Range Planning*, December 1980, p. 26.

The Structure of the Marketing Plan

Although the structure and format of plans varies enormously from one organisation to another and reflects the planning needs and capabilities of management, there are several common elements of the marketing planning process, irrespective of the time scale covered or whether the plan is for a domestic or for an international market. They are:

(i)   a statement of stakeholder's expectations;
(ii)   an internal audit that highlights the firm's strengths, weakness and potential;
(iii)   an assessment of the external environment that focuses upon likely opportunities and threats;
(iv)   a statement of corporate objectives;
(v)   an exploration of the alternative strategies open to the firm;
(vi)   the selection of the appropriate strategy;
(vii)   the strategic plan which highlights the contribution each function is expected to make to achieving the goals.

Together, these areas can be aggregated to focus attention upon three distinct questions:

- Where are we now? (*situation analysis*)
- Where do we want to go? (*objectives*)
- How are we going to get there? (*strategy and tactics*)

Situation Analysis

As many companies have found to their cost, national markets can differ substantially. Before developing any strategy, the marketing manager therefore needs to be fully aware of the situation prevailing in each market and of the ways in which it is likely to develop. Situation analysis is the process whereby the organisation makes use of what is normally a standardised format to ensure that as precise a picture as possible emerges of each national environment, of how it is likely to change, and of the likely consequences for the firm. The advantages of using a standardised format across a variety of national markets are for the most part self-evident but, in particular, ensure, firstly, that specific issues are not ignored or overlooked and, secondly, that comparisons between markets are made easier. The first step in a situation analysis is market research which should focus upon such areas as direct and indirect competition, government policy, the legal environment, changes in the distributive infrastructure, cultural and social changes, and the buyer. Having collected this information, the analyst needs then to begin the far more difficult process of interpreting the results and, more importantly, assessing both the consequences and the significance of any changes that seem likely to take place.

Determining Objectives

Once a detailed situation analysis has been carried out, the short- and long-term objectives for each market need to be established. The procedures used for this often vary depending upon the size of the organisation, the significance of the market and the managerial culture that exist. It is therefore worth referring back to the earlier point in this chapter (pp. 127-8) at which reference was made to the various approaches to planning, ranging from top-down to goals down/plans up, since the choice of approach is often influenced by the managerial perception of the abilities of those in national markets and of their past performance. Nevertheless, regardless of which approach is adopted, it is important that each national plan is detailed so that those in the market know what is expected of them, the ways in which they have to operate, and how they will be assessed at the end of the period. The plan should therefore include targets for:

- sales (by volume and value);
- market share broken down by product category;
- profitability;
- the expansion of distribution outlets;
- levels of brand awareness;
- new product introductions.

In determining its objectives, the company does, however, need to conduct a full SWOT (Strengths, Weaknesses, Opportunities and Threats) analysis so that the objectives pursued reflect both the capabilities of the organisation and the realities of the market place, rather than an idealised statement of what it would *like* to achieve. An added advantage of this is that any strategic gaps that exist should also become evident and give scope for corrective action to be taken.

Strategy and Tactics

Once the objectives have been specified in detail, the company can then go on to develop the programme by which they will be achieved. This involves management in deciding upon the marketing profile that is to be adopted and, in broad terms, whether it will be based upon a strategy of price competition or non-price competition. Thus, the organisation may choose to put pressure on its competitors by emphasising price or, alternatively, it may emphasise product quality, place a high priority upon new product development, and allocate substantial funds to advertising and promotion.

Having decided upon the general approach to be used, the operating plan then specifies the tools and techniques that are to be used to implement the strategy. Included within this is the budget and the way in which it is to be allocated across the functional areas of marketing and how it is to be spread over the year. The operating plan also needs to allocate responsibilities both to people within the organisation, and to those outside but who work with the firm, such as market research companies and advertising agencies.

Although the structure of the marketing plan can, quite obviously, be broken down further, this formal three-stage process of analysing the environment, setting objectives, and determining strategy and tactics, is useful since not only does it provide a straightforward and consistent framework for short- and long-term planning, but it also provides a valid basis subsequently for assessing performance.

Short-term International Planning: the Specific Issues

Planning, in the short term, centres around three quite distinct tasks:

(i) developing an operational plan for each of the markets in which the company has a presence;
(ii) integrating the plans in such a way that they form a cohesive and logical international plan; and
(iii) ensuring that they provide a firm foundation for the strategic development of the organisation.

In broad terms, the amount of planning required for an individual market can be seen as a function of the organisation's level of business and degree of involvement in the market. Thus, in those markets where the firm has a relatively low level of involvement, there is often seen to be only a limited need for planning. The exception to this, of course, is when the firm has an objective of expanding its presence in that market.

A second factor which may well have an influence upon the amount of planning in any given market is the breadth of the product line offered which, for many companies, will vary significantly from one market to another. The third factor to influence the planning process is the overall nature of the organisation's involvement which, as we saw at an earlier stage, can range from exporting through to operating wholly owned subsidiaries. The implications of each of these for the planning process is likely to be significant, since the level of involvement and commitment on the part of those in the foreign markets may well be lower than that of headquarters staff. This, in turn, causes problems in terms of implementing plans, controlling and co-ordinating activities, and ensuring that an effective system of reporting back operates. These sorts of problems are most likely to occur when the firm is engaged either in exporting or licensing; with joint ventures and wholly owned subsidiaries, the firm has a far greater personal representation in the market. Even here, however, problems can arise when the objectives and strategies of local partners or national government conflict with those of the international firm.

Long-range International Planning: the Specific Issues

Long-range planning on an international level is a quite distinct activity from that of short-range planning and encompasses three major elements:

(i)   the analysis of the likely future international environment;
(ii) determining the appropriate marketing profile for each market sector;
(iii) establishing a long term strategy.

At the heart of this process is an assessment of the ways in which environmental changes are likely to affect the firm and the nature of any opportunities and threats that will develop. In this sense, therefore, there is a similarity between short-range and long-range planning. Apart from this, however, the differences between the two activities are marked and stem from the fact that long-range planning is for many companies still largely a matter of guesswork. This point is emphasised by a number of writers, including Schwendiman who investigated the planning practices of European and US based multinationals. He concluded that the majority of the techniques used are unsophisticated, undeveloped and unrefined, and that the art of long-range international business forecasting is still very much in its infancy.[5] Other differences between short-range and long-range planning that have been identified include the level of detail that is possible, the degree of uncertainty in the final result, and the personnel involved.

The Time Span of Long-range Planning.   The majority of short-range plans cover a twelve-month period. By way of contrast, long-range plans typically refer to a 5–10 year period and, as Terpstra points out, the planning process tends to be a continuing rather than a recurring activity which is often quite independent of the annual planning cycle.[6]

Environmental Assumptions.   A further distinction, and in many ways a far more important one than the time span involved, concerns the nature of any environmental assumptions that are made and which subsequently are built into the plan. Many of the constraints that in the short term are fixed become variable in the long run. An important objective in long-range planning therefore involves identifying and assessing the significance of possible changes in the environment so that the company can modify its profile in order to cope with them. Prominent amongst the factors that generally act as constraints within the short term but which are likely to change significantly in the long term are the nature of demand, the level of technological sophistication, socio-cultural issues, the number of countries in which the firm has a presence, the degree of involvement in each of these markets, the political and legal climates, consumer tastes and expectations, and the patterns of competition.

The implications of these sorts of changes are pointed to by Drucker who suggests that there is a need for senior management regularly to ask the questions, 'What business are we in?' and 'What business should we be in?' A third question that can then be added in the case of international marketing is 'And how do we intend to allocate effort between international and domestic markets?' The significance of these questions in the context of long-range planning needs to be seen therefore in terms of identifying long-term opportunities and threats and in deciding upon the organisation's future product and market profile. This process of identifying the long-term opportunities and threats can best be achieved by means of a systematic approach to environmental scanning which involves monitoring the economic, legal, governmental, political, social, demographic, technological, competitive and resource sub-environments.

Degree of Detail.   A further distinction between short-range and long-range planning is the degree of detail that is needed, or indeed that is possible. At an earlier stage in this chapter we commented that the short-range plan is, of necessity, specific since it provides a day-to-day framework within which individuals act and decisions are made. By way of contrast, the long-range plan is designed to alert management to possible opportunities and problems, and to provide a framework within which operational decisions are made.

Personnel.   A fourth major difference between short- and long-range planning concerns the personnel involved in the process. Effective short range plans are arguably best developed by those involved at an operational level. Long-range planning, however, is best done by staff who are not involved in day-to-day operations. Recognition of this has led many companies to set up separate strategic planning or forward planning groups who meet on a regular basis to monitor environmental changes, assess their significance and consider their long-term implications for the firm. The scope for error or misjudgement in such a process is, of course, quite considerable even when planning on a purely national basis. These difficulties are compounded significantly when the exercise is extended across a number of international markets where the level of economic and political stability may well be very different from that of the country in which the headquarters staff are based. It is for this reason that many firms in recent years have begun to make far greater use of outside expertise as a means of broadening the analytical perspective.

The Process of Long-range Planning

We commented at an earlier stage that the structure, if not the practice, of short-and long-range planning is broadly similar. This can be seen, for example, in the fact that, as in the short term, long-run planning involves the three-step process of situation analysis, establishing objectives, and then determining the strategy to be pursued.

Long-range Situation Analysis. Situation analysis at this level involves identifying every variable that is likely to have a significant influence upon the firm's performance and then forecasting how it is likely to change. The most prominent of these variables are:

(i) population levels both globally and in individual markets;
(ii) demographic and income levels;
(iii) developments in patterns of world trade;
(iv) the political climate;
(v) technological developments;
(vi) social and cultural factors; and
(vii) changes in the nature and patterns of competition.

But although it is a relatively straightforward exercise to list the areas to which attention should be paid, the process of forecasting how they are likely to change is infinitely more difficult. For this reason a variety of techniques have been developed to help in this process, although even their staunchest advocates acknowledge that the picture that emerges is at best partial.

The simplest of these techniques involves *extrapolating past trends* and rests on two assumptions: firstly, that any future changes will follow a straightforward and predictable pattern and, secondly, that major breakthroughs and significant developments are unlikely to occur. In making these assumptions, however, the planner is exposing a major and quite obvious weakness of the technique. Nevertheless, as a first step in the long-range planning process, many firms find that trend extrapolation is a useful process, since it provides an input which can subsequently be modified as other data become available. It is, of course, worth remembering also that extrapolating *certain* trends is likely to be a quite valid and reasonably accurate exercise. In saying this, we have in mind movements in population and patterns of world trade, both of which have followed broadly straightforward and predictable patterns over the past forty years.

An alternative to trend extrapolation involves *analysing the determinants of the major parameters* of the planning exercise. Thus in the case of population trends, Terpstra suggests that:

> rather than merely extrapolating major population growth rates, planners can look at the factors determining population changes. In a given country, they would look not only at birth rates and death rates but also at government population policies, family planning programs, and religious and cultural influences.[7]

The third major approach used by many multinationals involves looking outside the firm for specialist advice. This *outside expertise* can be found in a variety of research and academic institutions and has the major advantage of being unconstrained by the corporate philosophy and culture of the firm.

But although the need and significance of situation and environmental analysis would appear self-evident in the planning process, studies that have been conducted of the ways in which companies go about it suggest that it is an area of serious weakness and that few organisations go about it in a systematic way. Schwendiman, for example, comments that in the multinationals he studied, 'Headquarters capability and proficiency was poor in analysing political, economic and social factors around the world.'[8]

Determining Long-term Objectives.   Having arrived at a forecast of the ways in which the environment is likely to develop, the company needs then to set its long-term objectives both on a national and an international basis. In doing this, it needs to decide in some detail upon the overall international profile that it wishes to develop. One way of doing this is to polarise the alternatives by asking whether the organisation wishes to see an expansion or a contraction in its international presence. Once this has been established, the long-term objectives can then be developed and the implications for marketing objectives and strategy explored. In other words, the marketing planner must ensure that the strategies that he develops are consistent with the corporate plans that are being developed. It is only in this way that the two sets of strategies — the corporate and the marketing — will fully complement each other. In commenting upon this, Simon Majaro has said:

It is not difficult to perceive how corporate strategies can be paired with marketing strategies. A logical nexus exists between each corporate strategy and one or more marketing strategies. Thus, if at the corporate level the planners feel that the firm can only achieve its goals through *contraction*, it is more than likely that the marketing plan will incorporate a strong leaning towards *deleting products* which have ceased to show adequate returns. At the same time, if the word contraction has a geographical meaning in the sense that the planners feel that the firm must reduce its international commitments, the marketing strategy which needs to be studied carefully is *market concentration*. If efficiently implemented it may help to achieve the contracting strategy which in turn will help to achieve the corporate objectives.

In the case of marketing, these decisions therefore include market entry and exit, product development and deletion and, rather more broadly, the competitive posture that is to be adopted. Underlying all of this, however, is the fundamental issue of how the company wishes to allocate financial resources across markets. Thus, a useful basis for marketing decisions of the sort identified above is comparative analysis, whereby markets are ranked according to a variety of criteria. Typically, these would include political stability, patterns of growth, competitive profiles, income levels, and so on. In this way, a measure of long-term market attractiveness can be developed and incorporated into any decision concerning market priority and development. This information can then, in turn, be used as a basis for altering the company's operating profile in a market and shifting in one direction or another along the spectrum of exporting–licensing–joint ventures–wholly owned subsidiaries.

The Strategic Challenges for Multinational Corporations

As part of the strategic marketing planning process, there is a need to focus not only upon changing patterns of competitive and consumer behaviour, but also upon the very fundamental and far-reaching political and social changes that are taking place throughout the world. For many companies, their significance only becomes apparent at a relatively late stage and, as a consequence, the firm finds that its strategic responses are limited. In order to avoid this happening, long-range planning should include a regular review of what can loosely be referred to as the strategic challenges for MNCs. In commenting upon this, Brar suggests that the six major challenges for MNCs are:

(i) the more effective management of foreign assets in order to minimise the economic consequences of social and political upheaval;

(ii) expansion or growth policies which are becoming increasingly difficult in certain parts of the world as political conditions become more volatile;

(iii) decentralisation of production processes as more and more host countries begin to argue for domestic production facilities;

(iv) the ever greater automation of assembly lines and the consequent effect upon manufacturing costs;

(v) the pressures upon Western MNCs as the emerging nations with an abundance of cheap labour are becoming a more significant competitive force in world markets;

(vi) the globalisation of common tastes.[10]

Summary

Marketing planning is a fundamental part of the management process which for organisations with an international profile, takes on an added importance and complexity. The major problems encountered in planning effectively stem largely from inadequate market knowledge, poorly developed planning processes, and unrealistic expectations amongst either headquarters or subsidiary staff. Long-range planning is still a largely misunderstood activity from which many organisations shrink, with significant and far-reaching consequences. International marketing planning will, however, only be improved upon by far greater attention being paid to the development of more detailed and sophisticated data inputs and to a clear definition of the contribution that is to be made to the process by headquarters and subsidiary staff.

References

1. Subhash C. Jain, *International Marketing Management* (Kent Publishing Company, 1984), p. 661.
2. Philip Kotler, *Marketing Management: Analysis Planning and Control*, (5th edn), (Prentice Hall, 1984), p. 51.
3. Jain, *International Marketing Management*, pp. 670-1.
4. Simon Majaro, *International Marketing: a strategic approach to world markets* (George Allen and Unwin, 1978), p. 181.
5. Jain, *International Marketing Management*, pp. 668-9.
6. John S. Schwendiman, *Strategies and Long Range Planning for the Multinational Firm* (New York: Praeger, 1973), p. 134.
7. Vern Terpstra, *International Marketing* (The Dryden Press, 1978), p. 542.
8. Schwendiman, *Strategies and Long Range Planning*, p. 135.
9. Majaro, *International Marketing*, pp. 205-6.
10. Jagjit Brar, David Ramsey and Peter Wright, 'Six Challenges to Global Corporations', *The Collegiate Forum*, Spring (1982), p. 14.

Further Reading

For a discussion of the ways in which MNCs might go about developing a standardised planning process, refer to K. Shuptrine and B. Toyne 'International Marketing Planning: A Standardised Process', *International Marketing Strategy and Planning*, vol. 1, no. 1 (1981), pp. 16-28. For a detailed treatment of how best to develop the planning process, see Malcolm McDonald, *Marketing Plans — How to Prepare Them* (Heinemann, 1984). For a discussion of Japanese marketing and corporate philosophies, see W.J. Keegan, 'Strategic Market Planning — the Japanese approach', *International Marketing Review* (1983), pp. 5-15; W. Lazer, S. Murata and H. Kosaka, 'Japanese Marketing: towards a better understanding'. *Journal of Marketing*, vol. 49 (Spring 1985), pp. 69-81; and R.C. Christopher, *The Japanese Mind* (Pan Books, 1984).

Appendix 5.1: Japanese Marketing Strategies

Japan's international economic performance is remarkable. It achieved the fastest post-war rate of growth in the world averaging almost 8% between 1951 and 1984. During this period GNP per capita grew from below 25% of the British level to 25% above it. This growth was fuelled by the international competitiveness of Japanese companies. Exports grew from $6 billion in 1964 to around $170 billion in 1984. North America now takes 28% of these exports, Asia 23% and Western Europe 16%.[1]

Faced with such a highly competitive country, a number of Western commentators have attempted to identify the reasons for Japan's apparent ease of penetration of foreign markets. Amongst them is DeMente who has suggested that in North America in the 1960s, the Japanese recognised that established and entrenched American companies had begun to neglect consumers and that clear voids had been created with demands for quality, value, product features and after sales service not being met. Although in the early stages, Japanese firms were not necessarily able to fit the product gaps perfectly, they recognised the significance of the challenge and responded by emphasising product quality, increasing their marketing skills, and improving managerial talents. In doing this they were helped by their low prices stemming from cheap labour and large domestic markets. The learning curve, together with favourable reactions from American consumers, led to yet further reductions in costs so that Japanese companies, having selected target segments with a far greater precision than their competitors, were able to improve quality whilst at the same time maintaining a low price strategy.[2]

These themes have, in turn, been developed by Peter Doyle who conducted a comparative study of British and Japanese strategies within the British market. The work led him to conclude that there are four essential differences in the approaches adopted:

1. *Market share vs. short-term profits.* The marketing of Western companies is oriented to profitability, that of the Japanese to market share. Two factors have been used to rationalise this dichotomy: the characteristics of the Japanese financial system, and the need to provide long term employment security.

2. *Greater orientation to new environmental opportunities.* Japanese companies appear more adept at exploiting 'strategic windows' — opportunities created by new market segments, changes in technology or new distribution channels. Such an orientation is strongly encouraged from the centre by MITI and appears to be enthusiastically endorsed by many Japanese companies.

3. *Fast market adaptation rather than innovation.* Unlike some of the famous Western companies, Japanese firms have not been technological pioneers. This has been ascribed to a risk averse culture. ... Redesign, upgrading and rapid commercialisation of innovations made elsewhere appears the common priority.

4. *More aggressive marketing tactics.* The drive for market share leads to hypotheses about Japanese low prices, rapid product line extensions and high expenditures on advertising, promotion and dealer incentives.[3]

These factors are then, in turn, helped by the ways in which many Japanese companies are organised with a tendency for marketing decision-making to be decentralised so that local management is more easily able to tailor the marketing programme to local market conditions.

References

1. P. Doyle, J. Saunders, and V. Wong, *A Comparative Investigation of Japanese Marketing Strategies in the British Market* (Bradford Management Centre, 1985).

2. B. DeMente, *The Japanese Way of Doing Business* (Prentice Hall, 1981).

3. Doyle *et al.*, *A Comparative Investigation*, p. 3.

PART THREE

**DEVELOPING, IMPLEMENTING AND
CONTROLLING THE INTERNATIONAL
MARKETING MIX**

6 INTERNATIONAL PRODUCT POLICIES AND STRATEGIES

In international markets, as in domestic markets, the product is at the heart of the firm's marketing strategy, with the other elements of the marketing mix, such as advertising, price and distribution, playing a supporting role to ensure market awareness, acceptance and availability. It is, therefore, the international product policies and strategies that are central to the health and long-term development of the firm. Within this chapter we focus upon some of the key factors that impinge upon international product policy and influence its development within the firm. In doing this, it needs to be emphasised that the term 'product' is used generically and refers not only to a physical product, but also to services and franchises, as well as to the packaging, warranties, and after-sales service. In other words, therefore, the product is the total package that the buyer receives.

The Nature of International Product Policy

The starting point for determining the nature and shape of international product policy is the range of products that the company sells domestically. In the majority of cases, firms either sell exactly the same product overseas, or modify it only slightly. Relatively rarely do firms make substantial changes to their product range or develop completely new and different products for their international markets. The major reason for this is of course that, as we discussed earlier, the rationale for international marketing in many cases is that the firm is attempting to increase demand in the most cost-effective and least risky manner. It is, therefore, generally rather too costly to begin modifying the product in any significant way, since much of the firm's experience, knowledge, and competitive advantage stems from its domestic line. With this in mind, the two questions that the marketer then faces in developing an international product policy are, firstly: to what extent are the firm's existing products broadly suitable for international markets? and secondly: if changes in specification are to be made, what are they to be? Having arrived at an answer to these, the marketer can then move on to decide upon the product-related features, including packaging, labelling, trademarks, guarantees, and the brand names that are to be used. However, before we go on to examine these areas, it is worth emphasising that many companies move into foreign markets by selling their name and expertise in the form of the brand or the patent on the product or production processes, rather than becoming involved in selling the physical product itself. Brief reference was made to this in Chapter 4 and, as we observed, it can be seen most clearly in the rapid development of franchising over the past decade or so by companies involved in such diverse markets as fast foods, soft drinks, fashions, cosmetics, aerospace, white goods, glass and chemicals. Nevertheless, despite the rapid and continuing growth of franchising, international product policy for a majority of companies is still a decision that they make largely on their own.

Ideally, the international marketer would like to be able to sell a standardised product across most, if not all, of the markets in which he is operating. The benefits of this are quite clearly considerable and stem from the economies of scale that result not only in the area of production, but also in research and development, and marketing. It is from a far greater recognition of these sorts of benefits that much of the discussion in recent years about global brands and product standardisation has stemmed. The arguments regarding product adaption for individual markets are, however, equally well developed and centre around the different uses to which products are put in various markets, differences in consumer tastes, differing government regulations regarding product safety and specifications, and indeed a managerial culture within the firm which encourages individual operating units to make decisions that are tailored specifically to the needs of their markets. The question of standardisation or adaptation is, therefore, a fundamental aspect of international marketing strategy and one which manifests itself not only in the case of product decisions, but also in other areas such as advertising and promotion. The decision on whether to standardise and opt for global brands therefore has quite obvious and major implications not only for day-to-day marketing activity, but more fundamentally for the organisation as a whole and the managerial philosophy that is pursued. This can be illustrated by considering the way in which increasingly global strategies have given impetus to a policy of merger and takeover by international companies as a means of enhancing the possibilities of global brand and market domination. The food industry, for example, has proved to be one of the most fruitful areas for global product strategy and in recent years has been subject to prolific merger and takeover activity. Prominent examples of this include the takeover of Huntley & Palmer by Nabisco in 1982 and the successful bid by Nestlé for Carnation Foods in 1984.

International product policies have also been affected by a variety of other issues in recent years, including the question of the appropriateness of products in particular markets. The governments of emerging and Third World nations, for example, together with international agencies such as UNCTAD, are increasingly beginning to question the appropriateness for Third World markets of products originating in the more advanced nations and have posed a series of questions, including:

(i) Does the technology of the products support the goals of the country's development policy?

(ii) Is the finished product or service useful and acceptable to the intended user?

(iii) Does the production process make economic use of inputs? The Indian government, for example, has ruled that certain products should only be manufactured in labour-intensive cottage industries rather than in highly capital-intensive factories.

(iv) Do the production processes and finished products fit the culture and environment of particular countries? It is in this area that Third World nations have become conscious of the issues of 'Cocacolanisation' via the particular imported culture that accompanies certain products.

Without doubt, the importance of these sorts of issues will grow as Third World nations formulate firmer attitudes towards international companies and their products. Indeed, there is already evidence that some multinationals recognise this and are demonstrating a will to tailor their product mix to the needs of developing nations, not always it needs to be said with financial success.

One further issue that needs to be borne in mind when developing international product policy is the way in which products from particular countries are subject to stereotyping. Most typically this is in the form of national images for quality, price and reliability, particularly with regard to technological goods. The sorts of differences that exist have been highlighted by a variety of studies. Products imported into the United States by Western European nations, for example, are heavily stereotyped by American buyers.[1] Typically, for example, it is the case that West German products are viewed more favourably than Italian or French products in terms of quality. Similarly, the American market often perceives British products as being old fashioned. Japanese products, by way of contrast, benefit from a highly favourable image in the US market, although achieving this has been a slow and expensive process. Thus, although stereotyping is often ignored as an element in international business success, it needs to be seen as an important component in the whole image presented by the international corporation. (The implications of the country of origin and stereotyping are also discussed in Chapter 8).

It is in the light of these sorts of issues that decisions on international product policy need to be made.

International Product Policy: Objectives and Strategies

Product policy consists of two interrelated activities: management of the firm's existing product range, and the development of new or modified products. The underlying objective of international product policy should therefore be seen in terms of the development of the optimum mix of products that is to be offered internationally; the optimum mix being, of course, the one which contributes most directly to the firm's overall corporate objectives. Typically, these are expressed in terms of growth and profits, although it needs to be remembered that the extent to which these are pursued will depend upon two major constraints: firstly, the extent to which the firm is willing to pursue potentially risky but profitable strategies, and secondly, the extent to which the firm is truly committed to international operations. If, for example, international activity is designed principally as a means of exporting unsold domestic surpluses, then neither optimum growth nor optimum profits are realistic objectives. It is only for genuinely international and multinational corporations that such a declared objective is appropriate. However, even here, the terms 'growth' and 'profit' may need to be defined, since in terms of 'growth', the company may, for example, pursue a strategy of initial market concentration with only a gradual expansion of international operations. For companies not involved in world brand competition, this is an extremely common strategy with growth being achieved in a controlled and deliberate way. Similarly, the 'profit' objective needs to be clarified, since it may be that the company's pursuit of profit is essentially long term, with survival and growth being far more important in the short term. It is with these sorts of provisos in mind that the company can then begin to develop its product policy. Amongst the many other factors that ultimately influence the policy are:

(i)　the needs of the market;
(ii)　the company's financial and managerial resources;
(iii) the product itself, the stage reached on the life cycle, the universality of its appeal, and the level of support service needed;
(iv)　the nature of any legal constraints within particular markets.

Product Strategies

Internationally, companies tend to adopt a range of product strategies. Leroy, for example, found that product strategies differed within firms depending upon their circumstances. In a detailed study of fifty companies he observed a wide range of multinational product strategies which, it appeared, were determined by three sets of characteristics:

(i)　*Characteristics Specific to the Company's Environment.* Such as the stage of economic development of the country in which the product was originated, barriers to trade, and host country investment climates.

(ii)　*Characteristics Specific to the Company.* Including the international experience of the firm, the number of years abroad, and the company's management philosophy and operating policies.

(iii) *Product Characteristics.* Such as the complexity of production processes, economies of scale in production, and the ease with which the product can be sold.

In total, Leroy identified fifty-eight different product strategies, although their overly specific nature provides little real insight for the practising manager.[2] A rather broader and more useful analysis is instead provided by the five strategic alternatives proposed initially by Keegan.[3]

Strategy One: One Product, One Message, Worldwide

This strategy is perhaps best illustrated by the approach adopted by companies such as Pepsi Cola and Coca Cola. The cost savings of such an approach are enormous and, for this reason, the strategy clearly has great appeal. Globalists argue that it is this strategy that will dominate international markets in the future, although it needs to be remembered that there is a salutary list of companies who thought that their products were suited to this strategy when clearly they were not. Campbells' initial launch strategy for soups into the UK market is a classic example of this problem.

Strategy Two: Production Extension — Promotion Adaption

Here, the product remains unchanged, although the usage patterns of the product differ from one country to another. For this reason, the promotional message needs to be adapted in line with the differing usage. This is illustrated by the way in which greater leisure use is attached to motorcycles in the USA compared to the UK and how this, in turn, calls for very different advertising appeals.

Strategy Three: Product Adaption — Promotion Extension

This strategy has proved to be appropriate when a promotion campaign has been devised with proven international appeal but where, due to environmental conditions, the product needs to be adapted. Thus Esso were able to globalise the 'Tiger' while in fact adapting their petroleum sold worldwide.

Strategy Four: Dual Adaption

In many ways, this is the classic differentiated approach and has often been adopted second time around by American manufacturers in Europe who were unsuccessful when initially using Strategies One or Two.

Strategy Five: Product Invention

This is the approach that is often adopted by companies from advanced nations who are heavily involved in transactions with emerging nations.

From these five strategies, the choice adopted is likely to be determined by a combination of three factors:

1. the product, its functions and the needs it serves;
2. the characteristics of the market, together with patterns of consumer preference and the levels of purchasing ability;
3. the estimated cost of adaption both in terms of manufacturing and marketing costs.

Product Life Cycles in International Markets

Two types of life cycle are of particular importance in international marketing. The first of these was outlined in Chapter 1, and suggests that patterns of world trade can be explained in the following way:

(i) *The New Product Stage.* In which the product is manufactured in the developed home country and subsequently introduced into international markets in the form of exports.

(ii) *The Mature Product Stage.* In which the company begins production in other advanced economies in order to take advantage of foreign manufacturing facilities offering a more effective competitive posture, particularly in terms of price.

(iii) *The Standardised Product Stage.* Where due to ever-increasing price competition, the company moves manufacturing to an emerging nation to take advantage of low costs. Typically it is in this stage that many products are then exported back to the home country.

The second type of life cycle that exists and which, for our purposes, is more central to the discussion here is the rather better known product life cycle, which assumes that products in international markets have consecutive 'lives' in different countries; this is illustrated in Figure 6.1. This model does not concentrate upon

Figure 6.1: The Different Stages Reached on the Product Life Cycles within the Different Markets

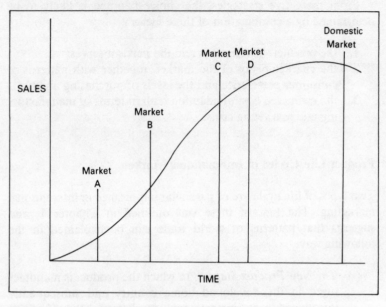

(Note the gap between the stages reached in Market A and the domestic market, and the consequences for the appropriateness of any given marketing strategy.)

the notion of phased changes in international manufacturing investment, but has as its primary focus a process of product saturation in one market followed by product growth in a less developed country. Thus, there could be consecutive life cycles for, say, a consumer durable moving progressively from North America to Western Europe, Australasia and finally to South America.

Quite clearly, the first of these two models will tend to involve a longer time span than the second. What they share, however, is that the validity of both has been reduced by the international communication revolution which has led to a general shrinkage in the time between product acceptance in different world markets. Thus, whereas the trade and investment product cycle model is often used to provide a rationale for US manufacturing investment in foreign countries in the post-1945 period, it is not really compatible with the operation of modern global corporations. This can be illustrated by considering the facility for environmental scanning and international marketing research that modern corporations possess and hence the scope for the specifically global nature of decisions that can be taken. In these circumstances, the sequential approach to marketing and manufacturing that is encapsulated in the original model is hardly likely to apply. However, as we established earlier in the book, not all companies operating internationally are global corporations, and it is therefore important not to ignore the model altogether.

The same argument applies when evaluating the notion of consecutive product/brand life cycles operating in world markets. Many consumer products developed by multinationals are subject to simultaneous global launches, thereby negating for these companies at least the second model. However, world trade is not confined to global fast-moving consumer goods brands backed by global advertising. The company that is simply exporting from an advanced economy is likely to be dependent upon the concept of phased life cycles if it is to achieve success. On balance, therefore, although the validity of the product life cycle has at various times been attacked by a variety of writers, it does have a role to play for certain types of company insofar as it is a model that provides a framework for thinking about product policy, new product development, product introduction and product elimination. Its application to international marketing is particularly significant for a number of reasons, including the ways in which the speed and shape of the life cycle will often differ from one market to another, and because overall the life cycle of the average product in world markets is shortening. The obvious implication of this is that pressures upon firms to introduce new products are correspondingly greater.

We can, therefore, draw a number of conclusions regarding the impact and importance of product life cycles in international marketing, particularly in the case of consumer products. They include:

1. Life cycles generally are shortening.
2. As a consequence, there is an increased need for a well-developed policy of new product development and differentiation in order to replace or extend the life cycle.
3. Global branding is becoming an increasingly important phenomenon with consequent implications for launch and development strategies.

4. To achieve market saturation in one country and then expect to move to another is likely to become increasingly difficult. This was illustrated by the way in which Cadbury took the lead in the Canadian chocolate market with Thick Bar, having introduced the brand before Rowntrees — the company which pioneered the chunky chocolate bar — was able to introduce Yorkie.[4]

But although these trends are evident in consumer non-durable markets, they do, however, need to be viewed with some caution when analysing present and likely future patterns of demand in world markets for capital goods as well as certain consumer durables. Even for genuinely global companies operating in these particular markets, world products are, on balance, likely to be less than appropriate. The needs of buyers of agricultural equipment, production machinery and plant, for example, are likely to be diverse world wide and it is in recognition of this that many companies are now pursuing a policy of increasing differentiation to satisfy specific needs rather than one of increased standardisation.

What lessons then can managers of international companies learn from these patterns? Quite clearly, the importance of product life cycles to companies is not based on a simple consumer/industrial dichotomy. Agricultural equipment sales appear still to be following a phased life-cycle pattern, yet in the truck market Ford is currently talking about the 'World Truck'. There is a need, therefore, for firms to undertake a careful analysis of the relationship between international life cycles of their products if an appropriate international product strategy is to emerge.

Standardised, Differentiated and Global Products

The most important and far-reaching product decision faced by the international marketer concerns the extent to which products are to be modified to fit the needs of specific market segments. Opinions on the need for differentiation vary greatly with many firms pursuing a policy of standardisation across a series of markets, whilst others adopt a policy of differentiation in which the product is altered for each of the markets in which the firm operates. The arguments in favour of each of these approaches are by now well-developed, although they have in turn been complicated by the emergence in recent years of a yet more extreme philosophy in which a global strategy entailing total standardisation, not only of the product but of the entire marketing mix, is pursued. The underlying rationale of this is that significant economies of scale can be achieved by total standardisation and companies typically move towards this position on a step-by-step basis as is illustrated in Figure 6.2. By referring to the figure, it can be seen that firms generally begin with a mix that differs for each market. They then gradually begin the process of standardisation by focusing upon specific elements of the mix and then broaden the process in such a way that increasing economies of scale come into play.

The Move towards Global Strategies

The debate concerning global strategies is tied inexorably to the arguments surrounding standardised or differentiated products, and stems from the fact that international business has now reached a point at which large numbers of truly global corporations exist. These corporations have moved significantly from the days when the overseas division was a poor relation and seen simply as a dumping ground for an excess of domestic produce. The modern international corporation takes instead a far broader perspective both in its strategy and planning, and in its analysis of opportunities for its products. One consequence of this has been the far greater recognition given to the strategic implications of the

Figure 6.2: The Standardised–Differentiated Strategic Continuum

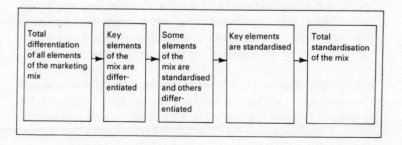

experience curve and to the ways in which its effective management can contribute to achieving lower production costs, and
hence greater opportunities for aggressive marketing in pursuit of
brand leadership. This greater awareness of the scope for international economies of scale has, in turn, focused the attention of
international marketing executives upon the possibilities of global
branding:

> When companies reach the stage where exporting begins to look
> attractive, the first thing they should decide is what would be
> the most appropriate marketing strategy. The choice can be
> summed up in three sets of initials — SWYG, SWAB and
> GLOB — which are defined as follows:
>
> * SWYG: Sell what you have got.
> * SWAB: Sell what people actually buy.
> * GLOB: short for global. Disregard national frontiers and
> respond to internationally emerging needs.[5]

The scope for global brands is, quite obviously, dependent upon
similarities in consumers' purchasing patterns and this had led to
the concept of the 'global village'. The notion of the global village
was first pursued in the 1970s and gives recognition to the fact that
purchasing patterns in world markets, at least amongst the
developed nations, are gradually coalescing to the point at which
geographically separate groups of consumers have broadly similar
aspirations and exhibit broadly similar patterns of demand. In
commenting upon this, Theodore Levitt has said:

> The globalisation of markets is at hand. With that, the multi-
> national world nears its end, and so does the multinational
> corporation. The global corporation operates as if the entire
> world (or major regions of it) were a single entity; it sells the
> same things in the same ways elsewhere. Corporations geared to
> this new reality can decimate competitors that still live in the
> disabling grip of old assumptions about how the world works.[6]

There is, therefore a clear distinction between a multinational
corporation and a global corporation: the *multinational* operates
in a number of countries and adjusts its products and practices in
each — at high relative cost. The *global* corporation, by way of

contrast, operates with a far higher degree of consistency and in this way should achieve far greater economies of scale not only in its production, but also in such areas as advertising. The obvious rationale for global strategies is a convergence of markets which in the case of the Western world at least, has been brought about by:

(i) greater demographic similarities as birth rates drop and an increasingly aged population emerges;

(ii) the decline of the nuclear family as divorce rates rise, the number of children per family decreases, and patriarchal influences decline;

(iii) the changing role of women as employment opportunities increase;

(iv) cultures becoming more similar as exposure to international media such as television increases.

The implications of demographic convergence along these lines is in turn compounded by the ever greater pressures upon manufacturing and marketing costs. The combined result, according to Levitt and others, is an inexorable move towards global brands supported by global strategies; this is illustrated schematically in Figure 6.3.

On the face of it, evidence in support of the increase in global branding appears impressive, although a number of critics have expressed reservations about the value of global strategies. There are also a number of practical problems. These were pointed to by *Marketing* in 1985:

> The global village idea may be attractive, but it's a snare, if only because it tidies away all sorts of problems which can actually

Figure 6.3: The Move towards World Brands

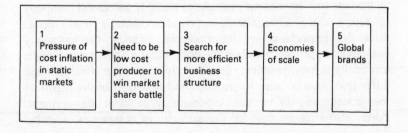

make or break a brand — regulations, quotas, preferences, climatic differences, language, religion, politics and — dare one suggest — racial characteristics. This can perhaps be appreciated by considering a company such as CPC. CPC, the US food company, owns brands like Knorr and Mazola, which are essentially international. It also owns others, like Frank Cooper and Brown and Polson, which are nothing if not national.

Soup, the thick, creamy sort readily made from a Knorr powder, is recognised almost universally, in Scandinavia, France, the Mediterranean countries, etc., and could be treated as an international brand with international support. But not so bouillon, the thin, stock based liquid which is understood and used differently in almost every market. Mazola, pure corn oil, has to be presented differently in northern and southern Europe.

Even within big national markets like the US, of course, the same radically different images and usages are sometimes encountered, particularly where large ethnic minorities form worthwhile markets of their own. But perhaps these distinctions are really missing the internationalists' point: on, say, a Japanese camera or VCR, the image is less important than the product features, and the aspiration to own one is the crucial common denominator. The precise positioning thus has less significance.

Even so, the state of development of individual markets is seldom identical. VCR use may be growing fast in many markets, but in the UK it already seems to have passed its peak. Unless the marketing strategy recognises the fact, the campaign is unlikely to be effective.[7]

Reservations about the need for global strategies have also been expressed by Michael Porter who has argued that companies do not necessarily need to compete globally in order to be successful and points to Nestlé as an example of a highly successful company operating with a differentiated approach. Although Nestlé recognises the importance of 'international' brands, the company pursues an approach based on the notion that marketing strategy is essentially a local problem, that the most effective strategies will differ from one country to another, and that the developments of the strategy should be the responsibility of local management. Porter also suggests that for the majority of companies, a global approach only makes sense if there are major strategic advantages in doing so, or major disadvantages in not doing so — if, for example, the firm's major competitor is adopting a global strategy.

A similar theme has been developed by David Thompson, the Vice-Chairman of the European Division of Rowntree Mackintosh. Whilst recognising the apparent attractions of a global strategy, Thompson suggests that in the majority of cases quite significant obstacles exist including tariff and non-tariff barriers, and legislative and cultural differences. The obvious implications of these differences are that the company is forced into pursuing a predominantly differentiated rather than a global strategic approach. To illustrate this, he points to the way in which the marketing of six of his company's products has to be tailored to the legislative needs of the French and German markets (see Table 6.1).

As Thompson points out:

> It can be seen that none of the products shown can be legally sold without considerable amendment. The problems of labelling and language can be relatively easily dealt with; problems arising from chocolate and other ingredients are less easy to overcome without important consequences on a brand's original strategy mix.

These problems are then, in turn, compounded by the ways in which different markets demand very different media strategies:

Table 6.1: Legality for Sale of Current UK Product and Packaging

	Kit Kat	Quality Street	Smarties	Rolo	Lion Bar	After Eight
France						
Labelling	no	no	no	no	no	no
Language	no	no	no	no	no	no
Chocolate	no	no	no	no	no	no
Ingredients	yes	yes	no	yes	yes	yes
W. Germany						
Labelling	no	no	no	no	no	no
Language	no	no	no	no	no	no
Chocolate	no	no	no	no	no	no
Ingredients	yes	no	no	yes	yes	yes

We are fortunate in this country to have considerable freedom and flexibility when determining media strategies for our brands. This is by no means the case elsewhere in the world. There are differences in supply, differences in cancellation procedures and again, even in Europe there is considerable variation in regulations. In Holland you are not permitted to use children in confectionery commercials and of course each film must display the toothbrush symbol. In France you can show children consuming your sweets but must not use their voices. In Italy you cannot use advertising which in any way at all pokes fun at public officials. Perhaps the further development of direct broadcasting by satellite will eventually remove these differences but I shall believe that when I see it.

Thompson also questions the most-frequently quoted rationale for global brands, that of the economies of scale:

The protagonists of globalization usually give pride of place to the economies that arise from greater scale, particularly on the manufacturing side of the business, as well as to experience curve benefits. Obviously these can be of tremendous significance, particularly if the products are highly price sensitive or margins are tight, and more so if a direct competitor is acting globally and is adopting a cost-leadership strategy. My own company is faced with just such a competitor who appears to act with considerable consistency across most markets and uses the resulting savings to fuel an aggressive value-for-money strategy.

There is in my view however a more important argument for globalization than scale economies, which appears to have been allocated insufficient emphasis. All branded packaged goods companies make their money by creating and then successfully commercially exploiting brands. Successful brands are not easy to create or to develop; success can take time; involves the investment of considerable resources, and on occasions a degree of serendipity. Brands which can survive successfully over a long period of time are scarce and are therefore very precious assets indeed.[8]

Broadly similar reservations about the feasibility of global branding have also been expressed by Greg Harris of the London Business School. Whilst recognising that there are companies such as Seagrams, IDV and Distillers which operate with a standardised product range across a variety of markets, he points to the way in which only rarely do they standardise the advertising. The reason for this, he suggests, is that markets differ to a far greater extent than the globalists will admit and that to pursue a truly global strategy is more often than not likely to fail. Harris does, however, recognise that some companies such as Coca-Cola, Pepsi Cola, McDonald's and Levi do pursue global strategies with a high degree of success but argues that these are very much the exception:

> The most interesting thing about these is how often you hear about them. Whatever you read and whenever you discuss the subject, it is always the same handful of brands that are cited ... However, I would be loath to draw any meaningful conclusions based on the evidence from such a small sample ... They should be regarded as one-offs and not pointers to the future.[9]

Doubts about the validity of global approaches have also been expressed by Alkarim Jivani of Marketing, although his reservations are based largely upon organisational constraints:

> Few companies have put a global approach into practice to any great degree.
>
> This is not to say that global marketers do not exist. Everyone can rattle off the names of a few international brands like Coke and Marlboro. But the telling point is that the names which leap instantly to the lips have been international for donkeys' years. The plethora of papers, books, workshops and conferences about globalisation have failed to produce a single new international brand which compares with the old-guard internationalists.
>
> The reason for this lack of progress is not that the multinationals remain unconvinced of the true value of globalisation. Far from it. There is widespread enthusiasm and interest, although, as with most new theories, the number of detractors is also sizeable. The real reason is that most companies' ideas about marketing multinationally are far ahead of the ability to put them into practice. The obstacles are largely self-made. Partly as a result of the rush to decentralise in the 70s, many large companies do not have the structure which would allow

them to take a marketing initiative straddling several countries at once.

The most spectacular example of a company coming unstuck as a result of trying to centralise too quickly is Cinzano. Faced with an ageing customer profile from Norway to Nicaragua, Cinzano decided to apply the global remedy by appealing to the world's youth, à la Coke. Under Swiss based general manager Luca di Montezemolo, all important marketing decisions were made centrally; this led to an expensive and, finally, futile exercise. It was also an organisational nightmare.

'Consolidating our research so that there was agreement wasn't easy,' says Alan Farrar, managing director of Cinzano (UK). 'Phone calls flew because everything had to be bounced off all the major markets for comment. The real cost was in planning, and I now believe that evolution, rather than revolution, is the key to international marketing.'[10]

A similar view emerged from a Campaign/Admap conference in 1985 on the future of successful branding, with delegates suggesting that 'globalisation is one of the great non-issues of our time' and that 'the idea of the world brand is synonymous with world bland'. This latter view was expressed by Michael Greenless, the joint managing director of the advertising agency Gold Greenless Trott. According to Greenless:

Much of the pressure for global brands stems from U.S. companies which believe that their society is a model for others. By way of contrast, the Japanese have a domestic market which is so individual that they are loath to make sweeping assumptions about international markets.[11]

Broadly similar lines of argument have been pursued by many other industrialists who, whilst recognising that global competition is growing, argue that its impact is not as straightforward as it seems. Globalisation is inexorably under way, but — contrary to conventional wisdom — this does not mean that most purchases by consumers around the world will soon be of identical, homogenised products. This is reflected in comments made by William Maeyer, head of Philips' small domestic appliances division, who has argued that 'Major producers of modern products must regard the world as their market and their battlegrounds and that in order to remain competitive, multinationals must become insiders in the "Triad" countries of U.S., Europe and Japan'. This does not mean, however, that companies should sell the same product throughout the Triad, but rather that they should emphasise commonalities to the greatest possible extent. In many cases, this is much more likely to occur with spare parts and components than with finished products.

Speaking at Worldesign '85, a congress of 2,000 of the world's leading industrial designers, Maeyer suggested that many companies have interpreted Theodore Levitt's global markets argument far too simplistically and that this is now being reflected in the policies both of multinationals and their advertising agencies. A far more realistic approach to globalisation is becoming increasingly evident in the car industry. Although future models are likely to be much less country-specific than previously, new technologies, such as flexible manufacturing, will permit more variations on common themes, and offer both economies of scale and specialised designs for specific market segments.

An additional qualification to this seemingly widespread misinterpretation of global homogenisation is shown by the way in which the development of sizeable markets of old people, one- and two-person households, and so on, provides far greater opportunities for world or regional rather than domestic demographic segmentation. Thus, it should be possible to develop new products that are tailored to specific new layers of customers around the world.

Recognition of this has led to an increasing number of companies pursuing a global strategy and this in turn is reflected in larger advertising budgets as companies attempt to attain world brand leadership. The trend has been particularly marked in Western Europe where per capita spending on advertising food, for example, is currently still only a quarter of the amount spent in the USA. In recognition of this and the potential benefits of leadership, Nestlé announced in 1984 that it intended to increase advertising spending by 20 per cent, even though the market was only growing at 5 per cent. By doing this, the company appeared to be hoping that the level of direct competition it faces would be reduced.[12]

The massive expenditure on advertising that can be afforded by global brand leaders appears likely to have a devastating affect on the number two and three brands. A Harvard Business School study has highlighted this by analysing a brand's net profitability relative to its ranking. The study found that the number one brand's net profit margin as a percentage of sales will average 17.9 per cent, whilst the number two will average 2.8 per cent, the number three will be −0.9 per cent, and the number four −5.9 per cent![13]

Standardised versus Differentiated Products

In the midst of debate regarding the future of global branding, it is important to remember that for the vast majority of companies operating in international markets, global branding is still not an issue of any real significance. Companies marketing many industrial, and indeed most consumer goods, are still faced with major decisions regarding their product strategy in terms of standardising or differentiating their product offering. However, before we present too severe a dichotomy between these issues and global branding, it is important to remember that global branding can also involve differentiated product offerings of the brand for major segments. This is illustrated in the case of Coca Cola which pursues a global branding strategy, but which at the same time recognises the significance of particular segments such as the slimming market, and with Diet coke has modified the product accordingly. For many companies, however, the major issue is the extent to which a product needs to be modified in order to ensure its acceptability. The obvious danger, of course, is of modifying the product too much and too frequently. Overall, therefore, the decision regarding which approach to adopt must be governed by cost-revenue analysis and the implications for profitability. Quite clearly companies should attempt to standardise, wherever possible, and this has always been the case. Serving identified segments by a differentiated product offering should only be undertaken when:

(i) the differences in need and taste that exist in identified segments are significant enough to justify the loss of standardisation; and

(ii) when sufficient demand exists within the segment for the company's adapted product offering to offset the increases in cost.

What is clear, however, is the reluctance on the part of many companies operating in international markets to differentiate their products. American companies, for example, have traditionally been slow to differentiate when operating internationally, seemingly on the grounds of the relative sizes of their home and international sales. A similar picture has emerged from a recent study by Kacker which pointed to the reluctance of many Indian companies to adapt their products for international markets.[14] In a sample of twenty engineering goods manufacturers in which exports accounted for between 4 per cent and 55 per cent of annual production, he found that many exporters quite deliberately aim for markets where only minimal adaption is required. In the majority of cases, it appeared that the reasons for this were:

(i) the existence of a readily available and sizeable home market; and
(ii) an inability on the part of these companies to afford the initial investment required for research and development and tooling.

When entering a new market, a company therefore has three choices:

(i)   to market exactly the same product as is being marketed domestically and/or in other international markets;
(ii) to modify the existing product to match the tastes and needs of the new market; or
(iii) to develop a completely new product.

This third option will be explored later in the chapter; at this stage we concentrate solely on the factors that encourage either standardisation or adaption.

The Arguments for Standardisation

A variety of factors need to be taken into account when deciding upon whether to adopt a strategy of standardisation. The potential benefits of standardisation include:

(i) economies of scale in production, stock control and servicing policies;
(ii) economies of scale in research and development;

(iii) marketing economies which result from standardising the format of sales literature and advertising material;

(iv) organisational and control benefits which result from the greater scope for centralisation.

These potential benefits are likely to be realised in a number of circumstances, but particularly when consumers are highly mobile and there is a need to standardise the product in order to maintain levels of brand loyalty. A strategy of standardisation is also likely to emerge if the firm does not perceive itself as a truly international organisation but rather as an exporter; in these circumstances, there is often a marked reluctance to modify the product because of the implications for costs.

The Arguments for Product Adaptation

By way of contrast, a strategy of adaptation is most likely to be encouraged by the following factors:

(i) Market circumstances which suggest a greater profit potential from adaption.

(ii) Where distinctly different use conditions exist, together with differences in service and maintenance expertise. An example of this is the differing needs for agricultural machinery, throughout the world, along with differing levels of workshop and maintenance skills.

(iii) Where consumer tastes differ distinctly.

(iv) Where legislation enforces adaption.

(v) Company growth patterns. An interesting corporate phenomena affecting standardisation or differentiation is the company's history of growth. Where the company has pursued an acquisition approach (possibly in disparate areas), then a differentiated product strategy will almost inevitably emerge. Where the company has developed internationally through internal momentum, then standardisation is likely to have been at least the preferred strategy.

The various arguments for and against standardisation are neatly illustrated by Majaro who says:

for Kodak to differentiate its range of 'Instamatic' cameras in different parts of the world would be a policy of indescribable wastage. At the same time it is difficult to see how a typewriter manufacturer can afford not to differentiate, in order to accommodate the special needs of language and script variations in different countries. It is unlikely that a typewriter that contains Germanic letters only would gain popularity in the French market.[15]

Overall, therefore, it can be seen that in deciding between standardisation and differentiation, companies need to take account of a number of factors, including their stage of international development, the characteristics of the product areas in which they are principally operating, the policies of their competitors, and the needs of their markets. The combined effect of these upon the major decision areas of the marketing mix and the strategic alternatives that follow is illustrated in Table 6.2.

The Use of Portfolio Analysis

Domestic product strategy has been well served in recent years by the introduction of portfolio approaches to product management. These approaches, which include the Boston Consulting Group's Growth — Share Matrix, the General Electric/McKinsey Screen, and the Arthur D. Little Business Profile Matrix, are designed primarily to clarify the current strategic position of a company and its competitors, and to help identify any future strategic options that may be emerging. Their main use in the past has been in domestic markets, since it is here that companies are most easily able to identify their competitors and their relative market positions. Once the analysis is extended to the firm's international

Table 6.2: Strategic Alternatives in World Markets

	Strategy 1	Strategy 2	Strategy 3	Strategy 4	Strategy 5
Product	Same	Same	Same	Same	Different
Price	Same	Same	Same	Different	Different
Promotion	Same	Same	Different	Different	Different
Distribution	Same	Different	Different	Different	Different
Type of strategy	Standardised				Differentiated

portfolio, the complexities and dimensions of the analysis increase considerably, since the competitive positions occupied by a product are likely to differ significantly from one market to another, as indeed will the nature and intensity of competition. Comparing the strength of a portfolio across a variety of markets is consequently fraught with difficulties as the analytical base is constantly changing. For these reasons, it has been suggested that attention needs to be paid to adapting the matrices to cope more effectively with international product strategy analysis. In terms of the BCG matrix, the analysis might feasibly be based on one product area with the circles in the matrices representing country sales instead of product sales. The analysis would then include:

(i)   the company's current international product/market port-
       folio;
(ii) the main competitors' portfolios; and
(iii) a projection of future portfolios.

The way in which this might possibly be done is illustrated in Figure 6.4 which shows the competing product/market portfolios of two firms. Company A is currently the market leader (see Figure 6.4a) with a portfolio which includes mature products (cash cows) in Great Britain and France, supported by a number of high growth products (Stars) in other parts of Europe (see Figure 6.5 for a discussion of BCG classifications). Elsewhere, its portfolio is relatively weak and the company has only a marginal presence in Japan. Company B, by way of contrast, is currently far smaller but has a sizeable presence in Japan and Singapore, both of which are rapidly growing markets. If company A then attempts to forecast the likely position in five years' time, the picture that emerges may be that of Figure 6.4b. At this stage, it can be seen that the decline in the demand for company A's products throughout Europe and the growth of company B in Japan and Singapore will have led to a reversal of the competitive positions. Faced with this, there is an obvious need for company A to make a number of strategic moves if it is to avoid its relative decline. Used in this way, the BCG framework therefore provides a basis for:

(i)   analysing the current international product portfolio;
(ii) assessing competitors' product/market strengths; and

Figure 6.4: Strategic Analysis and the Portfolio Approach

(a)

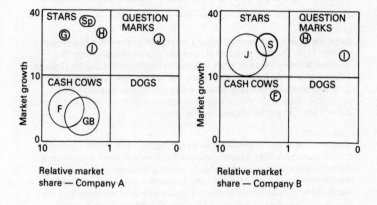

Relative market
share — Company A

Relative market
share — Company B

(b)

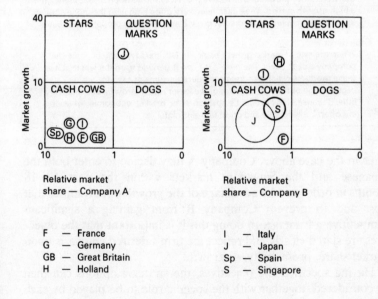

Relative market
share — Company A

Relative market
share — Company B

F	— France	I	— Italy
G	— Germany	J	— Japan
GB	— Great Britain	Sp	— Spain
H	— Holland	S	— Singapore

(iii) forecasting the likely development of future portfolios both for itself and its competitors.

Figure 6.5: The Boston Consulting Group's SBU Classifications

- Dogs
  Dogs are those businesses that have a weak market share in a low-growth market. Typically, they generate either a low profit or return a loss. The decision faced by the company is whether to hold on to the dog for strategic reasons (e.g. in the expectation that the market will grow, or because the product provides an obstacle albeit a minor one, to a competitor). Dog businesses frequently take up more management time than they justify and there is often a case for phasing out the product.

- Question Marks
  Question marks are businesses operating in high growth markets but with a low market share. They generally require considerable sums of cash since the firm needs to invest in plant, equipment and manpower to keep up with market developments. These cash requirements are, in turn, increased significantly if the company wants to improve its competitive position. The title of *question mark* comes about because management has to decide whether to continue investing or withdraw from the market.

- Stars
  Stars are those products which have moved to the position of leadership in a high growth market. Their cash needs are often high with the money being spent both on maintaining market growth and keeping competitors at bay.

- Cash Cows
  When the rate of market growth begins to fall, stars typically become the company's cash cows. The term *cash cow* is derived from the fact that it is these products which generate considerable sums of cash for the organisation but which, because of the lower rate of growth, use relatively little. Because of the product's position in the market, economies of scale are often considerable and profit margins high.

Thus in the case above, Company A may decide to enter both the Japanese and the Singapore markets within the next 12–18 months in order to take advantage of the growth opportunities that exist and to prevent Company B from gaining a significant competitive advantage. In doing this it is important that the objectives are stated clearly and reflect the firm's desired emphasis upon market share, profitability, or growth.

Having specified the objectives, the strategic options can then be considered, together with the specific role to be played by each of the elements of the marketing mix. If, for example, the firm pursues a share-gaining strategy, it may decide that this can be achieved most effectively by means of aggressive price competition. Pricing would, therefore, be the core strategy, whilst the other elements of the mix acted in a supporting role. The strategic perspective of each product/market combination is then used as the basis of the SBU strategic plans which subsequently are co-ordinated by corporate management to ensure that the organisation as a whole achieves as many synergistic benefits as possible. The way in which this is achieved is, in principle at least, relatively straightforward and involves plotting each SBU within the BCG matrix. Thus, SBUs which appear in the cash cow quadrant would be expected to generate cash and in normal circumstances would not receive further investment. SBUs in the question mark quadrant, however, may well offer considerable scope for develop-ment and conversion to the star category *if* funds are invested to support them. The principal advantages of this approach to portfolio analysis are therefore considerable and are manifested in terms of:

(i) the development of a global perspective upon the inter-national competitive structure;

(ii) a far more precise guide for the formulation of global marketing strategy; and

(iii) inputs for the formulation of marketing objectives for specific international markets.

Such international matrices would however be subject to the same limitations that exist for the use of portfolio approaches in domestic markets. Particularly important in terms of international marketing activity is the standard portfolio assumption that market share gains are easier to attain in the growth stage of the life cycle, an assumption that is rather dubious when related to the complex-ity of international markets.

International Products — Planning and Development

International product planning, which provides the focus of the three case studies at the end of the chapter, involves a similar series of activities to those of domestic marketing, including product introduction and elimination decisions, and new product develop-ment and launch strategies. However, the multidimensional nature of international marketing tends to make the decision-making and planning a far more complex process.

Designing an International Product Line

The international product line offered by multinational and international companies should, as we have observed, emerge from the objectives and strategic decision-making processes outlined in the last section. In practice, however, it is often a mixture of expediency and opportunism that determines its nature. Quite clearly though, one of the key aspects of any international company's product line is whether that line is specific to international markets or merely an extension (adapted or otherwise) of the domestic line. The nature of the product line will be mainly influenced by the company's international strategy which should, in turn, be based upon marketing information regarding the needs and tastes of consumers in the international markets in which the company is operating. As we have already observed, the international product line is typically shorter than that offered in domestic markets and provides an opportunity for companies to develop a range which, in BCG terms, is made up of 'Stars' rather than the 'Dogs' that are almost always a part of a long-established domestic product line.

As an alternative to the rather more conventional approaches to portfolio analysis, Wind and Douglas have developed an *analytical hierarchy process approach* designed to take specific account of objectives in a hierarchical fashion in which the ultimate decision criterion is the long-term welfare of the host country. The firm's worldwide portfolio of businesses is therefore developed in terms of:

- the goals that are to be pursued (in setting the goals, account is taken of optimistic versus status quo versus pessimistic scenarios);
- the objectives (profits, growth, and the demands placed upon resources);
- the importance attached to each country;
- the entry strategy to be pursued (export — licensing — joint venture);
- the target market segments;
- the product/technology combination appropriate for each segment;
- the alternative strategies for each product/market.[16]

New Products in International Markets

In Britain in recent years, it has become evident that an ever-increasing proportion of profits has been generated by new products. This trend, reinforced by evidence of shortening life cycles, has in turn led to a far greater managerial awareness of the importance of new product development and subsequently to an increasing proportion of company budgets being allocated to development activity. Similar patterns have also emerged in many international markets and there appears now to be a growing belief amongst many types of company that the key to international marketing success lies in the development of innovative new products. This, in turn, is reflected in a number of recent studies which have indicated that new products with a competitive edge can lead to greatly improved export performance. At the same time however, it needs to be recognised that overall it is still the characteristics of the company, along with its resources, that is ultimately likely to be a more important determinant of international success than the characteristics of just one or two innovative products. Nevertheless, amongst the work that points to the greater role of new products is an American study of machinery companies which showed that the percentage of sales accounted for by new products (i.e. those less than four years old) nearly doubled between 1960 and 1970. Subsequent work has shown that these trends have continued. Similarly, work by Davidson and Harrigan has also reinforced the evidence for this trend toward new products (see Table 6.3). Their survey of 44 companies and 733 commercially significant new products introduced internationally

Table 6.3: Number of First Foreign Introductions by Country Category (1945-76)

Country category	Number of first foreign introductions*	Percentage of total sample
English speaking	301	46.4
Other developed	241	37.1
Developing	107	16.5

*Of the 532 innovations introduced in a foreign market 63 were introduced in more than one market simultaneously, resulting in a total number of first foreign introductions in excess of the total number of innovations.

Source: W. Davidson and R. Harrigan, 'Key Decisions in International Marketing: Introducing New Products Abroad', *Columbia Journal of World Business*, Winter (1977).

since 1945 indicated that the rate of new product introductions across a wide variety of industrial sectors has increased by a substantial margin. Their work also highlighted two interesting elements of international new product development:

(i) That certain industries introduced new products more frequently into foreign markets than others. The textiles, paper and industrial chemicals companies, for example, introduced a high proportion of innovations abroad, whereas office machinery and instrumental innovations were much lower.

(ii) A 'roll-over' pattern of new product introduction could be discerned, supporting an hypothesis by Linden that companies tend to market their products to countries of similar culture and economic conditions before marketing products into less familiar territory. In the case of the American companies in their sample, for example, they found that the English-speaking markets of the UK, Canada and Australia accounted for nearly half of the initial introductions of new developments by the companies sampled, even though the relative importance of the UK and Canada had in fact declined over the years.[17]

Managing International New Product Development

There are several issues that need to be resolved by companies when managing new product development in international markets, including the global structure of development activity; whether to concentrate development at home or overseas; and how the whole process of development from idea generation to commercial launch is managed.

Types of R & D Investment

Small companies, with low-key international operations which amount to little more than ad hoc exporting, are rarely involved in genuine considerations of international new product development. Larger companies, however, need to consider what patterns R & D investments should take. Research has indicated that investment in R & D by multinational companies typically takes one of four forms:

(i) *Transfer Technology Units.* In which R & D units facilitate the transfer of technology from the parent company to foreign subsidiaries.

(ii) *Indigenous Technology Units.* Where R & D units are established specifically to develop new and improved products for foreign markets.

(iii) *Global Technology Units.* In which R & D units are established to facilitate simultaneous, or near simultaneous, applications of new products in the major world markets.

(iv) *Corporate Technology Units.* In which R & D units concentrate upon the generation of new technology of a long-term/exploratory nature specifically for the parent company.

In general, the R & D activities of international companies tend to follow an evolutionary path with R & D being concentrated initially in a transfer technology unit and moving gradually to a global technology unit. Whether R & D units then move on to become corporate technology units is more open to question, although the long-term trend appears to be a move away from the dominance of parent country R & D location, a development which, in turn, has implications for the question of where best to locate the R & D activities.

R & D Location: Home versus Abroad

In deciding where R & D activities should be located, the marketer should bear in mind that not only is there a long-term trend for R & D to move away from the home country, but also that with the development of the truly global corporation, the notion of a 'home country' becomes correspondingly less meaningful. In practice, however, many companies still concentrate a large proportion of R & D activity in their country of origin. It is therefore useful to consider the arguments for and against the centralisation of R & D activity in this way.

The major arguments for centralising R & D in the home country include:

(i) the economies of scale which result from centralisation, particularly in the light of the often high start-up costs of foreign R & D;

(ii) easier and faster communication and co-ordination with

fewer linguistic and cultural problems;
(iii) greater security for new ideas because of the closer control over personnel that is possible;
(iv) the greater synergy that can be gained from the interaction of R & D with marketing and production in the home country.

The arguments for decentralising R & D abroad include:

(i) Pressures from subsidiary companies for their own R & D resources. Although these pressures are not by themselves sufficient justification for a move, the likely increase in the motivation of subsidiary marketing staff may well justify its consideration.
(ii) Pressure from overseas governments to locate R & D in their countries with the resultant benefits that may evolve for the nation.
(iii) Possible public relations benefits.
(iv) A gain in human terms by utilising the talents of overseas personnel.
(v) Linked with (iv), financial savings may be made where development personnel in foreign markets can be paid on lower salary norms.
(vi) In the light of evidence from companies with international R & D facilities, such as IBM, Honeywell and Kodak, that truly international R & D can yield much greater creativity in terms of the production of ideas and yield faster and better results.
(vii) Local or regional R & D is likely to be much more sensitive to the needs and tastes of local or regional markets.

But although the general trend is towards greater decentralisation, R & D overall is still very much an activity that is centralised in the firm's country of origin. Nevertheless, evidence suggests that consumer goods companies in particular are increasingly coming to recognise the benefits of decentralisation, especially in their larger markets. This is particularly likely to be the case when the company has been involved in international activity for any length of time and international business represents a sizeable proportion of the firm's total turnover, a phenomenon which in part can be explained by the way in which acquisition is likely to have played an important role in the development of the organisation.

The Product Development Process

The process to be followed when developing products for international markets is broadly the same as that followed in domestic situations:

- Idea Generation
- Initial Screening
- Business Analysis
- Development
- Market Testing
- Commercialisation/Launch

Where the process does differ, however, is in the level of analysis, co-ordination and communication that becomes necessary when assessing the new product's suitability for a variety of markets. In doing this particular burdens are placed upon the managers of the information system since it is essential that the product is positioned accurately in each market from the outset. With this in mind, the international development process should incorporate the following key elements.

1. Idea Generation. Key elements:
  (i) Monitoring ideas worldwide so that duplication is avoided and synergy optimised.
  (ii) Using all sources effectively for new ideas, including employees, R & D departments, competitors, sales people, customers, distributors.
  (iii) Ensuring that all levels of the organisation contribute.

2. Initial Screening. Key elements:
  (i) Ensuring that the idea is screened at source initially but then is passed 'upwards' through the organisation if it shows any promise.
  (ii) Ensuring that sound *international* screening criteria which include both production and marketing factors are developed.
  (iii) Ensuring that product ideas are screened in terms of their applicability to all world regions so that opportunities are

not missed. Ideas that may, for example, be inappropriate for Western Europe might be appropriate for South America.

3. Business Analysis.   Key elements:
  (i) Establishing criteria for potential success/failure.
  (ii) Linking criteria with regions/markets.

4. Product Development.   Key elements:
  (i) Ensuring all relevant functions such as production, design, packaging become involved in the process.
  (ii) Selection of the most appropriate R & D centres for the development process with particular attention being paid to such factors as technological expertise and location near prime target markets.

5. Market Testing.   Key elements:
  (i)   Ensuring the test area is representative in terms of prime target markets.
  (ii) Ensuring that the test market has an adequate infrastructure in terms of test services such as advertising and market research agencies, and an appropriate distribution network.
  (iii) Maintaining a proactive stance in terms of potential competitor reactions both in the test market and globally.

6. The Launch.   Key elements: (assuming a satisfactory test)
  (i) Very importantly, determining whether the launch is to be sequential, with an initial concentration upon prime markets, or whether it is to be simultaneous.
  (ii) Making contingency plans for competitive activity.

Introduction and Elimination Activities

The increased pace of new product development activity has a number of consequences for product management both at the beginning and the end of the product life cycle. The question of when best to introduce a new product to any particular market can be determined by taking account of the firm's objectives, the company's existing range of products and degree of product overlap, the manufacturing capacity available, the likely receptiveness of the market to the new product, and the competitive structure. It is with regard to this final factor that the company needs to pay particular attention to the ability of competitors to copy the product and launch it in a separate market. In an attempt to prevent this, an increasing number of companies in recent years have either opted for strong patent protection, or have entered into licensing arrangements in specific countries to ensure that they have an involvement from the outset even though the financial returns are lower than if they were to undertake full market development themselves.

At the same time, however, product introductions also have implications for the existing product range in that the firm may well run the risk of overburdening the marketing system by having too many products. There is a constant need therefore for a regular review of the range and for elimination decisions to be made where a product is either in its decline stage or simply failing to generate sufficient profit. Yet again, however, the international perspective gives rise to complexity, since a product may be manufactured principally in one plant, and be a 'Cash Cow' in Market A and a 'Dog' in Market B. Careful analysis is therefore needed before the product elimination decision is taken. Insofar as it is possible to identify broad guidelines, they need perhaps to be seen in terms of profit and opportunity cost, tempered with a degree of marketing expediency.

Summary

International product policy involves a degree of complexity that is only rarely encountered in domestic markets. In developing the policy, the marketer needs to take account of a wide variety of factors, including the nature and length of the product life cycle, the strength of the international product portfolio, the pros and cons of standardisation and adaption, and the move towards global branding. New product development, with its associated activities of introduction and elimination, is a major element of product policy and care needs to be taken to ensure that the product mix is modified in such a way that the firm's competitive profile allows as few opportunities as possible to competitors.

References

1. P. White, 'Attitudes of U.S. Purchasing Managers towards Industrial Products, Manufactured in Western European Nations', *Journal of International Business Studies*, Spring/Summer (1979).

2. G. Leroy, 'Multinational Product Strategy: A Typology for Analysis of Worldwide Product Innovation and Diffusion' (Praeger, 1976).

3. W. Keegan, 'Multinational Product Planning: Strategic Alternatives', *Journal of Marketing*, January (1969).

4. *Financial Times*, 25 October 1984.

5. M. Van Mesdag, 'The Frontiers of Choice', *Marketing*, 10 October 1985, p. 39.

6. T. Levitt, 'The Globalisation of Markets', *Harvard Business Review*, May-June (1983), pp. 92-102.

7. *Marketing*, 25 October 1985.

8. D. Thompson, 'When is a Global Strategy Advantageous?', *Admap*, September (1985), p. 425.

9. G. Harris, 'International Product Standardisation — Progression or Regression', *Admap*, September (1985), pp. 420-2.

10. A. Jivani, *Marketing*, 4 July 1985, p. 19.

11. Campaign/Admap Conference on 'Successful Long Term Branding', (Madrid, October 1985).

12. *Financial Times*, 11 October 1984.

13. Ibid.

14. M.P. Kacker, 'Export-oriented Product Adaption — Its Patterns and Problems', *Management Internatonal Review*, vol. 6, no. 1 (1975).

15. S. Majaro, 'International Marketing: A Strategic Approach to World Markets' (George Allen & Unwin, 1978), p. 86.

16. Y. Wind and S. Douglas, 'International Portfolio Analysis and Strategy: The Challenge of the '80s', *Journal of International Business Studies*, Fall (1981), pp. 69-82.

17. W. Davidson and R. Harrigan, 'Key Decisions in International Marketing: Introducing New Products Abroad', *Columbia Journal of World Business*, Winter (1977).

Further Reading

For a discussion of country of origin stereotyping, see Curtis Reierson, 'Attitude Changes towards Foreign Products', *Journal of Marketing Research*, vol. IV, November (1967) and Akira Nagashima, 'A comparison of Japanese and U.S. Attitudes towards Foreign Products', *Journal of Marketing*, vol. 34, January (1970).

For a detailed discussion of how to make use of the Boston Consulting Group's Product Portfolio in International Marketing, refer to Jean-Claude Larreche, 'The International Product Portfolio', in Subhash C. Jain (ed.) *Research Frontiers in Marketing*, Educators' Conference Proceedings (Chicago, American Marketing Association, 1978).

For a further discussion of the arguments surrounding global issues, see S. Winram, 'The Opportunity for World Brands', *International Journal of Advertising*, vol. 3 (1984), pp. 17-26.

Appendix 6.1: The Launch of a New Ford Transit

Launched in 1965, the Ford Transit is firmly established both as Western Europe's most popular medium-size van and as Britain's best-selling commercial vehicle. Its emergence as one of the most successful products to be launched in Europe in the post-war period is due largely to the way in which Ford pioneered the concept of a range of vans, buses and chassis models with variations in wheelbase, payload, engine, transmission and door types, all sharing a pool of common components. (The flexibility that this gives is reflected in Ford's estimate that it could build the Transit for 30 years without repeating one single specification.) It was the first vehicle Ford developed, not just for the UK or West Germany but for all the European markets, and has led to a situation in which the van contributes 65–70 per cent of Ford's total commercial vehicle units but, in a normal year, 80 per cent of the company's commercial vehicle profits. Its importance to the company is also shown by the fact that it is Ford's most profitable individual model, cars included.

Since the product's initial launch, the European commercial vehicle market has, however, become infinitely more competitive with a steady stream of new products having emerged both from European and Japanese manufacturers (see Table 6.4). In the case of the Japanese, for example, their European penetration increased between 1980 and 1984 from 11.8 per cent to 21.6 per cent. This was achieved primarily with a range of vans that were slightly smaller than the Transit and which, because of their very low prices, began to open up new market sectors, but also by the Japanese having developed manufacturing capacity in Europe itself (Nissan, for example, manufactures its Vanette at its Motor Iberica subsidiary in Spain). The problems caused by this were, in turn, compounded by significantly higher levels of new product development activity on the part of European manufacturers. At the end of the 1970s, for example, Fiat and the Peugeot group launched jointly produced medium vans (sold as the Peugeot J5,

Table 6.4: The Medium Commercial Vehicle Market: European market shares

	1971	1975	1980	1984	1985
Total units	444,000	411,000	665,000	641,200	521,500
	%	%	%	%	%
Japanese	0.3	3.0	11.8	21.6	22.1
Volkswagen	29.9	21.7	20.2	14.9	14.8
Ford	16.0	20.0	18.5	13.4	12.3
Fiat	8.8	6.7	6.4	9.2	9.5
Diamler-Benz	8.1	9.4	8.8	8.6	9.2
Peugeot-Citroen-Talbot	N/A	14.4	11.1	9.8	9.1
Renault	5.3	5.0	3.2	8.6	8.7
British Leyland	6.5	5.9	4.3	4.5	4.4
General Motors	6.5	6.0	6.8	3.6	3.5

Fiat Ducato, Citroen C25 and Talbot Express) from a new factory in Southern Italy, whilst in the early 1980s Renault introduced the Trafic/Master range of vans.

The combined effect of these moves led Ford to take two major steps. Firstly, it began the long and extremely costly process of developing a replacement for the Transit (Ford's total investment is estimated to be in the region of $500 million, $150 million of which was spent on developing a new 2.5 litre diesel engine) and secondly, it added a van produced by its Japanese associate Mazda to its range in West Germany. The market into which the new Transit was launched showed considerable evidence, however, of becoming ever more competitive. Although the market share enjoyed by Ford in Britain had only once dropped below 30 per cent, the company had not been so fortunate in the rest of Europe where it had lost ground to its Continental rivals. In 1980, for example, Ford had sold 122,000 built-up Transits throughout Europe, but by 1985 this had dropped to around 85,000 units.

Although the new Transit had quite deliberately been designed to be an evolutionary rather than a revolutionary new product (about one-third of the components had been used in the earlier model), the improvements made to load space, volume, access, driver environment, ride and manoeuvrability were calculated to restore annual sales to their 1980 level. Unlike its predecessor, however, the new Transit was not designed to be distributed widely outside Europe. With production of the model being split equally between Genk in Belgium and Southampton, with 40 knocked-down kits a day being sent for assembly at Ford's factory in Portugal, a number of observers in 1986 felt that Ford's sales forecasts were optimistic. Their comments were based on the knowledge that Volkswagen, Renault and Fiat/Peugeot were all involved in further product development and that in each case sales of 100,000 units a year were necessary if the investment levels involved were to be justified. An additional threat to the company was posed by agreements reached by Daimler-Benz and General Motors to begin assembling vans based on Japanese designs. In the case of Daimler Benz, arrangements had been made to produce a Mitsubishi van in its Spanish subsidiary, whilst General Motors' Bedford plant had begun making vans based on Suzuki and Isuzu design. It was in the light of these sorts of developments that a number of critics asked whether Ford had perhaps left the development of the new model a little bit too late.

Appendix 6.2: Black and Decker and the DIY Market

Black and Decker, the US multinational, dominates the European DIY market with a performance that is viewed by many commentators as being little short of extraordinary. The company has operations in every European country, which buy, sell and, in many cases, manufacture for each other. It is as Black & Decker's UK marketing director has observed, 'a fully integrated European manufacturing policy ... That means that certain plants are assigned the role of supplying Europe with specific products. For instance, the UK makes all low cost jig saws, and Germany makes all circular saws.'[1] The result of this is that 60 years after the British subsidiary was founded, the European arm of the company has a sales turnover of $478 million, and brand shares are higher than anywhere else in the world. In the United Kingdom, for example, B & D's share of the indoor power tool market stands at around 88 per cent, whilst elsewhere in Europe competition from other firms appears at best to have had only limited success.

The European division can be broken down into manufacturing and marketing-only subsidiaries. Thus, the company manufactures in Germany, France, the UK, Italy and Spain, with marketing divisions elsewhere that are free to buy from whichever plant is most appropriate. A well-developed communication network then helps to ensure that the manufacturing operations do not compete with each other and waste resources. This policy of strict manufacturing co-ordination is also reflected in the firm's advertising which adopts a common style, even though patterns of media usage differ substantially from one country to another.

In the 1980s the firm decided to build upon its success and its reputation by diversifying into gardening equipment and subsequently into housewares. The rationale for this diversification was in part that the firm was pursuing a strategy of growth, but was also a recognition that the general European economic recession which had initially benefited the DIY market had, in 1984, also begun to affect DIY firms. The effect was that the power tool market had seemingly moved into the mature stage of the product life cycle.

With an enormously successful record of innovation, the firm began in the early 1980s to place even greater emphasis upon a strategy of new product development and launched a variety of new products such as a hot-air paint stripper and the Dustbuster portable vacuum cleaner. Although neither product was conceptually new, they reflected a philosophy of finding motorised alternatives to manually arduous tasks and demonstrated a clear understanding of consumers' wants. The move into the European housewares market illustrated a similar philosophy and was prompted by the firm's acquisition in 1984 of General Electric in the USA. However, any thoughts that the company had about simply transferring GE's range to Europe were quickly dispelled as the significance of differences in styling and electrical specification became apparent. Faced with this, the firm began developing a totally European range of products which were launched in 1985.

As with the firm's DIY and gardening products, manufacturing of housewares was divided up within Europe, depending upon each country's strengths. The cordless products, for example, including the Dustbuster are made in France, the UK concentrates on garment and personal care products, whilst Germany has responsibility for developing motorised products such as knives, can openers and food processors. In this way, the firm once again made full use of its resources and ensured that the European marketing effort was fully co-ordinated.

Reference

1. 'B & D Homes in on Housewares', *Marketing*, 10 October 1985, p. 20.

Appendix 6.3: Ford's American Import Strategy

At the beginning of the 1980s, Ford set itself the target of becoming the leading exporter of luxury cars from Europe to the United States. Their first year of operation proved, however, to be a disappointment with only 13,000 cars being sold in 1985 rather than the target of 20,000. Nevertheless, the company was confident that by 1990 its objectives would be achieved.

The decision to begin selling in North America an annual 100,000 cars was designed not only to boost market share and profitability, but also to provide extra work for Ford's factories in Belgium, Germany, Brazil and France, and to strengthen the group's up-market Lincoln–Mercury division in North America. The model imported to the United States is the Merkur, a range based on cars designed by Ford of Europe: the Sierra and the Scorpio-Granada. In the States, Ford's advertising strategy places heavy emphasis upon the car's West German origins, and gives recognition to the fact that American buyers perceive German cars to be high quality, high performance and safe vehicles.

Although the Sierra was designed primarily for the European market, it was acknowledged from the outset that it had also to appeal to American buyers. Because of this it was the first Ford model to incorporate features that would enable American regulatory requirements to be met. The Merkur that was launched into the North American market at the beginning of 1985 was assembled in Germany by Karmann, an independent company, making use of parts supplied by Ford's Sierra factory in Belgium, its transmission plant in Bordeaux, and its engine factory in Brazil, as well as those parts that are produced by Karmann itself.

The market sector for which the product was destined — luxury cars from Europe — has for the past decade proved to be recession-proof with sales having risen steadily from 0.7 per cent to 2 per cent of the total market between 1977 and 1980, a period which coincided with the worst post-war slump in the market. This part of the market accounts for some 40,000 units annually with Volvo, Audi, Mercedes, BMW and Saab being the biggest competitors with sales in the region of 100,000, 85,000, 84,000, 80,000 and 38,000 respectively.

Recognising that the choice of distribution network would be crucial to the success of the venture, Ford considered a variety of approaches, including:

- (i)   a totally new dealer network;
- (ii) adding the new range to all existing Lincoln–Mercury dealers;
- (iii) offering the product to selected dealerships.

The first of these was rejected on the ground that the projected sales volume would not have justified the necessary dealer investment (estimated at $2 million per dealer). Similarly, it was felt to be inappropriate to offer the product to all 842 independent Lincoln–Mercury dealerships. Instead, it was decided to limit the product to those dealerships which had consistently demonstrated high levels of customer service and which were prepared to invest in the new facilities needed to support the sales push. An additional unanticipated benefit of this was, that it had the effect of indicating to other dealers that their standards needed to improve.

The market research which had preceded the product's launch had been used to develop a detailed profile of potential buyers. It suggested that the typical customer would be 33 years old with an annual income of $42,000; 68 per cent would be males and 60 per cent graduates. It suggested also that they would opt for fairly spartan interiors. In the event, although age, education and sex profiles proved to be accurate, buyers' annual incomes averaged $64,000 and exhibited a massive preference for cars with high specifications, a factor which led to supply and demand imbalances. The research also failed to indicate that the product would prove to have a significant appeal for buyers who had previously opted for Japanese and American sports cars.

Within the company there was therefore a general feeling of satisfaction, even though the initial sales target had not been achieved. It was felt that the product had established itself as well as having provided a substantial underpinning for the broader strategy designed to position the Lincoln–Mercury range further away from the mainstream Ford division and to increase the firm's overall market penetration.

In recent years international pricing decisions have, for a majority of firms, become more critical and more complex. A variety of factors have contributed to this, including increasing fluctuations in exchange rates, accelerating inflation in certain parts of the world, more intense international competition, and the rapid growth of alternatives to traditional methods of pricing in the form of leasing, barter and countertrade. The overall effect of these changes has been significant with many firms now recognising that the key to international success is less likely to be by means of direct price competition, but rather it is through far greater attention being paid to areas of non-price competition, such as higher product quality, faster delivery schedules, a more aggressive sales approach, a more detailed understanding of the market, and a more effective after-sales service. Nevertheless, despite these changing attitudes, price is, of course, still a marketing factor of considerable importance, since it not only affects revenue and profitability, but is also a major determinant of the way in which the product itself is perceived within the marketplace. It is to these sorts of issues that we turn our attention within this chapter.

The Strategic Role of Price

The first and in many ways the most fundamental issue in international pricing concerns the relative roles that are to be played by head office and subsidiary staff. In some firms, for example, the majority if not all pricing decisions are made centrally, whilst in others the responsibility is delegated almost entirely to staff operating locally. The implications of these two approaches are both significant and far-reaching in the sense that a firm's ability to develop a truly effective and integrated international pricing strategy is either enhanced or inhibited. In practice, however, the role that is assigned to price within the marketing mix appears, in part at least, to be influenced by the firm's corporate culture and the markets in which it is operating:

Traditionally, U.S. companies have relied more on nonpricing competition than on pricing. For example, U.S. companies generally avoid price competition in the Common Market and more often go after competitive leverage through advertising, selling, and product differentiation. This sort of behaviour can be attributed to the fact that U.S. manufacturing costs are usually high, which makes it difficult to compete pricewise. Further, the quality of U.S. goods is considered high, which permits targeting the product for a segment in which price does not matter.

In the last few years, however, price competition has been stressed more than before. Sales promotion, pre-sale and post-sale service, advertising and product differentiation, and product quality are no longer depended upon exclusively. This change has been necessitated partly by the importance of focusing on mass markets overseas, particularly in Western Europe. A small decrease in price can be an effective way of increasing penetration in many foreign markets, especially wherever there is considerable price consciousness and where products are not highly differentiated. For example, the Italian appliance industry in the 1960s made significant inroads in the Western European markets through price competition. By 1965 Italian-made refrigerators accounted for 32 percent of the total French market, and for 40 percent to 50 percent of the Benelux market (Belgium, the Netherlands, and Luxembourg). Furthermore, costs in many countries, Germany for example, have been rising faster than in the United States. Thus price competition is feasible in some cases.[1]

The strategic role of pricing is, however, often far broader than indicated above and numerous examples exist where pricing has reflected a very long-term strategic objective. The Japanese, in particular, approach a new market for a specific product on the basis that the purpose of the initial few years of sale is to establish the product, its trade name, and its associated distribution, dealer and repair networks, and to provide the basis of a reasonable expectation of the realisation of substantial market share in the medium to long term. This market share approach which has featured in many markets from motor cycles, through consumer electronic equipment to zip fasteners, and forms the basis for what the economist might label long-term oligopoly profits. This approach, which appears to be unique to Japanese international companies, reflects their willingness to take a very long-term perspective to profit. This may be linked in part, at least, to the willingness of Japanese banks to see themselves more like shareholders than outside providers of finance and their willingness to see returns on any loans based on a twenty-year view, rather than the five-to-ten-year view which is more common in Europe in general and the UK in particular.

This, in turn, leads on to the question of whether international firms should aim for a broadly uniform price structure or pursue a policy of price differentiation and who should be responsible for determining pricing policies. The obvious argument in favour of uniform prices is simplicity, although as many commentators have observed, it is a policy that because of the very different economic legal and competitive features of each market, is only rarely realistic. Nevertheless, it is a policy that is pursued by some firms with a considerable degree of success. Aircraft manufacturers, for example, typically adopt a uniform pricing policy with the same price being charged in each market regardless of whether the customer is an airline based in the United States, Europe, the Far East, or the Third World.

Insofar as it is possible to identify the market conditions that allow firms to adopt this sort of approach, they are that the firm's competitive position does not vary significantly from one market to another, and that it enjoys a monopolistic or differentiated oligopolistic position. Equally, standardised pricing policies may be feasible if an innovatory product follows a broadly similar pattern of diffusion worldwide. At the same time, however, uniform prices can lead in certain markets to allegations of dumping when the price being charged is lower than that of domestic firms. For the vast majority of companies, however, these sorts of conditions rarely if ever prevail and a differentiated policy, reflecting each market's different competitive structures, legal environment, channel structures, market opportunities, diffusion processes, perceptions of the product, and stage reached on the product life cycle, becomes essential.

The strategic significance of these sorts of differences has been reflected in the findings of a variety of studies of multinationals; *Business International,* for example, in a study of European markets, pointed to the ways in which a country's wholesale and retail distribution structure has major implications for eventual market prices. Amongst the examples cited were television and audio equipment which had the lowest prices in the German market, and convenience foodstuffs which were least expensive in the Benelux countries and most expensive in Italy. In each case, it appeared that the most important single influence upon price was the level of efficiency within the distribution network.[2] A very similar picture emerged from a study of the performance of 59 items imported into the Japanese market:

By the time a £3 bottle of whisky makes it through Japan's complicated import and distribution system to their consumer it costs more than 10 times as much. Most of the mark-up goes into the importer's pocket, although wholesalers, retailers and the government all also take hefty cuts ...

As an example, a bottle of Scotch whisky that costs about 900 yen (about £3) to import will eventually retail for 10,000 to 11,000 yen (£34-38).

The cost is boosted by liquor tax and import tariffs — about 1,900 yen; miscellaneous transaction charges — up to 900 yen; importer's margin — up to 4,500 yen; wholesaler's margin — up to 800 yen; and retailer's margin — about 2,000 yen.

The markups for whisky in the distribution stages account for 65–73 per cent, with the importer's margin 35–40 per cent, compared with 23 per cent for domestic products.[3]

The importance of adapting prices to local market conditions was also reflected in the findings of a study of multinational practice carried out by Boddewyn, with more than two-thirds of consumer-nondurable firms and almost 50 per cent of industrial goods manufacturers adapting prices to local market conditions. The principal reasons cited for doing this were that manufacturing costs, taxes and competitors' prices often differ greatly from one country to another, and modifying prices in line with these different conditions is therefore essential.[4]

Amongst the other arguments in favour of a policy of price differentiation is that the firm's objectives and opportunities often vary considerably depending upon a country's stage of economic development, the competitive infrastructure, and the point reached on the product life cycle. In one market, therefore, it may be necessary to pursue a policy of rapid market penetration with low prices helping to create barriers to entry, whilst in others a far more leisurely price skimming approach may be feasible. Equally, pricing flexibility can be influenced by consumers' perceptions of the product's country of origin. In discussing this, Turnbull has suggested that:

> All companies, whether operating in home markets or striving to establish and maintain a foothold in overseas markets, must seek to project an appropriate image for competence and trustworthiness. In short, reputation is an essential element of long term marketing success ... if British companies have a general reputation for trustworthiness, then a buyer will be influenced by this when considering and forming an opinion about a particular British supplier company.[5]

Pricing Responsibilities

If a firm is to develop a logical and co-ordinated international pricing strategy, it is essential that the responsibilities for price setting are clearly allocated and understood. The three principal ways in which these responsibilities can be allocated are (i) by centralising all pricing decisions so that they are made by headquarters staff; (ii) by decentralising them so that subsidiary staff can more easily tailor prices to local market conditions; and (iii) by developing a procedure in which decisions are made jointly by head office and subsidiary staff. In practice, relatively few firms pursue a policy of total centralisation, largely because of the sorts of differences in market conditions that we referred to earlier and of the difficulties of coming to terms with them from a distance. Instead, a majority of firms either allocate the responsibilities to local management, or develop a broad framework within which subsidiary staff are free to operate. Typically, this framework would consist of a series of guidelines concerning expected margins and whether a penetration or skimming policy should be pursued.

The Determinants of Price

Although the major determinants of price in domestic and international markets are broadly similar (see Figure 7.1), international pricing often proves to be a far more complicated and risky activity because of the difficulties of having to come to terms with a generally higher level of environmental uncertainty. Thus, while it may

Figure 7.1: Influences upon the Pricing Strategy

- The firm's corporate and marketing objectives
- The firm's product range
- The existence or scope for unique selling propositions
- The degree of product differentiation
- Costs
- Resources
- The firm's market position
- Previous strategies
- The nature of the market
- The nature and structure of competition
- Opportunities for market growth
- Demand elasticities
- Consumers' perceptions and expectations
- The need for credit
- Government influences upon price
- Inflation rates
- Currency fluctuations

seem reasonable to suggest initially that the principles which lie behind pricing in international business exactly parallel those in domestic pricing, the practice involves a number of elements which are unique to international business. Firstly, the system of floating exchange rates which emerged following the first oil crisis in 1973 and the consequent differentially accelerating inflation rates of different countries raises particular issues about the attitude of businesses to the opportunities and threats created by potentially large movements in exchange rates. For example, a rising dollar against European currencies generally will increase the domestic currency value of dollar earnings without any change in business performance in the USA; while a fall would have the reverse effect. Thus a key question arises therefore, as to the timing of remittances to the main company. This issue can be pertinent in terms of an internal company's approach to transfer pricing. A second problem that is specific to international business and which arises in particular as a result of trade with Eastern Bloc nations is their lack of so called 'hard' currencies with which to pay for their purchases. An option which often arises is a barter deal in which the exporter accepts, for example, a shipload of Baltic timber in exchange for his machine tools. The whole issue of barter and counter-trade is a detailed one and is explored at a later point in the chapter. However, we must be clear at this stage that a price is involved in countertrade transactions. It is not one that is expressed in sterling or dollars, but rather it is in our example in timber. As such, it involves judgements about relative valuations and ultimately has a claim on organisational resources.

Because of these sorts of problems, the marketer needs to develop a 'price profile' of each of the markets in which he is operating (see Figure 7.2), together with a broad framework which is then used to provide both head office and local management with a series of pricing guidelines within which pricing decisions are subsequently made. The five essential parameters of this framework are the firm's corporate objectives; the nature and structure of competition; the stage reached on the product life cycle and the expectations regarding the recouping of investment within the market; any legal constraints that exist; and the company's approach to international organisation.

Corporate Objectives. By starting with a statement of the firm's overall objectives and of what it is trying to achieve within each market, it is possible to identify the broad dimensions of the pricing strategy and the role that prices are expected to play. In commenting upon this, Majaro suggests that:

> A firm may achieve a volume of profit by catering for a small number of consumers with a high quality product and at a high price. A competitor may opt for a different approach: he may wish to attain a substantial penetration of the market with a lower quality product at a lower price and yet achieve virtually the same amount of profit. The net result of these two extremes may be the same in terms of profit but totally different in terms of turnover, production load, productivity and so on. The underlying considerations in each situation will be different, and it is essential for a person responsible for determining the price of a product to understand these considerations and the goals of the firm that result therefrom. It is the role of the strategic level of the firm to communicate such a fundamental 'input' to the marketing personnel wherever they may be located.[6]

The Nature and Structure of Competition. Having identified the firm's overall objectives, the focus of attention switches to the nature of competition and to the ways in which the competitive environment is likely to influence the implementation of a pricing strategy. If, for example, the market is dominated by a large and

Figure 7.2: The Market's Price Profile Analysis

COMPETITION
- Who are our direct *and* indirect competitors?
- What pricing strategies does each pursue?
- Is price competition an important element of their marketing mix?
- How are they likely to behave when faced with price competition?
- What financial resources do they have available to cope with a price war?
- Are competitors' prices related to particular market segments?

LEGAL
- Are there any constraints upon pricing and re-pricing decisions?
- Are there legal constraints upon margins within the distribution network?
- Is there freedom to engage in price promotions?
- Do prices have to be printed on the product and/or package?
- Does retail price maintenance exist?

CUSTOMERS
- How do consumers perceive these types of products?
- Is there a tradition of haggling?
- How important is the product's country of origin?
- How is our country perceived?
- Do any social or cultural factors exist that might influence the prices that consumers are willing to pay?

DISTRIBUTION
- What are the implications of the patterns of distribution for costs and subsequent prices?
- What margins typically exist throughout the channel?
- How are price promotions and special offers likely to be received?

OTHER
- Are there any trade associations which need to be consulted before setting prices?
- Is there a consumer group (e.g. Consumers Association) which publishes comparative analyses of products and which might influence consumers' perceptions of prices?
- Will our price strategy be affected by the behaviour of others in the market in the past?
- How is the market as a whole likely to respond to price changes?
- How are changes within the country moving and what are the implications for pricing?

aggressive competitor, the firm is likely to be forced into the position of having to follow the market leader with little or no real control over the price charged. This, in turn, may have consequences for prices in other markets either because a policy of price standardisation is being pursued or because it is seen to be necessary to increase prices elsewhere to compensate for these pressures. By way of contrast, the firm may find itself in a market in which it has a degree of technological leadership or in which its manufacturing or marketing expertise provides it with a significant competitive advantage that can then be reflected in the pricing policies pursued.

The Product Life Cycle. The role of the product life cycle in international marketing strategy was discussed at an earlier stage in the text and at this point, therefore, we need to do little more than to remind the reader that as the firm's products move through their life cycle, so the role of each element of the marketing mix changes. At the international level, of course, the stage reached may vary greatly from one market to another and in determining the pricing policy consideration should therefore be given to three main factors: firstly, the probable length of the product's life cycle; secondly, the scope that exists for a competitor to introduce a new product or new technology — possibly from another market — thereby artificially shortening the length of the life cycle; and, thirdly, the firm's profit expectations.

Legal Considerations. In many markets the multinationals' pricing policies are a potentially controversial issue with some governments — particularly those in the Third World — viewing their strategies as unduly manipulative and against the consumer interest. Because of this, a number of countries, including those in the developed world, have at various times experimented with price legislation in one form or another. The nature and significance of this legislation varies enormously, but most frequently takes the form of anti-monopoly rules in an attempt to protect small companies, domestic manufacturers, and consumers from abuses by large firms. A second area of concern for governments which has also led to the emergence of legislation is that of price dumping whereby an international firm uses its revenues from one market to subsidise abnormally low prices in another. The consequences of dumping have often proved to be disastrous for indige-

nous manufacturers and at one time or another have affected the
steel industry, textile manufacturers, electronics companies, and
agricultural machinery manufacturers throughout the world.

At a rather broader level, the influence of the government
regulations upon prices has been discussed by Henley:

> Perhaps the most obvious difference can be found in the realm
> of legal and philosophical approaches toward competition.
> Europe, Japan, and the U.S., for example, have far different
> approaches toward competition policy. In the U.S., antitrust has
> a long history. Structure and conduct are the principal bases
> upon which public policy toward competitive activity is formu-
> lated. In Europe, antitrust has a history of less than 15 years.
> Performance is far more important than structure and conduct
> which would be unheard of in the U.S., provided that perform-
> ance in terms of public benefits (price, products, service, stable
> employment, etc.) is acceptable. The Japanese, if the literature
> is to be believed, coordinate industry, financial institutions,
> unions, and governments in a manner impossible to duplicate in
> the other advanced countries. In the developing countries, anti-
> trust is virtually unknown and competition may even be seen as
> wasteful of fixed plant and equipment.[7]

The International Organisation.   A further influence upon pricing policies is the structure of the organisation itself and the degree
of centralisation or decentralisation that exists. Reference was
made to this at an earlier point in the chapter and its significance
discussed in terms of the scope that exists for either a standardised
or a differentiated pricing policy.

The Nature of Pricing Objectives

Having developed the framework within which pricing decisions
are to be made, the marketer needs then to decide upon the
specific marketing and pricing objectives that he intends to pursue.
The nature of these objectives and their implications for the
eventual price charged can vary greatly, although the most
commonly pursued objectives are:

(i)   *Return on Investment.*   Prices are set partly to satisfy the needs of consumers, but more importantly to achieve a predetermined level of return on the capital or investment involved.

(ii) *Market Stabilisation.*   Having identified the leader in each market, the firm determines its prices in such a way that the likelihood of the leader retaliating is minimised. In this way, the status quo is maintained and market stability ensured.

(iii) *Maintain and Improve Market Position.*   Recognising that price is often an effective way of improving market share, the firm uses price partly as a means of defending its current position, and partly as a basis for gradually increasing its share in those parts of the market where gains are most likely to be made and least likely to result in competitive action.

(iv) *Meet or Follow Competition.*   Having entered a market in which competitors are firmly entrenched, the firm quite simply takes its lead in pricing from others until it has built up experience and established a firm reputation on which it can subsequently build.

(v) *Pricing to Reflect Product Differentiation.*   For a firm with a broad product range, differences between the products can often be made most apparent by means of price variations related to each market segment. The differences in price are not necessarily linked to the costs of product, but are instead designed to create different perceptions of their products' value, and indirectly to increase profits.

(vi) *Market Skimming.*   With a skimming objective the marketer enters the market with a high price and only gradually lowers it as he seeks a greater number of market segments. In this way, profits are likely to be relatively high and, by minimising the degree of commitment at any one time, the levels of risk are minimised. However, for this to be a realistic objective, certain conditions must exist, the most important of which is that the firm has a degree of security in the form of new technology or a new product which prevents others from undercutting the price and upsetting the strategy.

(vii) *Market Penetration.* As an alternative to the gradual entry of market skimming, the firm may adopt a far more aggressive approach in which prices are set at a deliberately low level to ensure a high level of sales and to keep competitors at a distance. The use of this approach in Third World markets has been discussed by Leff[8] who argued that the high elasticity of demand for consumer products together with the highly skewed income distributions of developing nations offers considerable scope both for developing mass markets at a high profit and enhancing the rate of economic development.

(viii) *Early Cash Recovery.* Faced with problems of liquidity, the firm may opt for a policy designed to generate a high cash flow and lead to an early recovery of cash. This can be achieved in a variety of ways, including a rigorous credit control policy, and by a series of special offers and discounts to increase immediate sales and achieve prompt payment.

(ix) *Preventing New Entry.* Because of the potentially powerful role that price can play, a low price may have the effect of preventing others from entering the market as they recognise the low returns available and the dangers of becoming involved in a price war. In this way, the firm may be able to minimise the amount of competition, whilst recognising that his returns may be relatively unattractive.[9]

Methods of Pricing

In essence, there are three major approaches to setting prices both in domestic and in international markets: cost oriented, market oriented, and competition oriented. It is not our intention to discuss the pros and cons of each of these methods here since they are adequately covered in most standard marketing textbooks. Instead it is of rather more value to relate the objectives that are discussed above to each approach to pricing. Thus:

Cost Oriented

  (i) return on investment;
  (ii) early cash recovery.

Market Oriented

  (i)   market stabilisation;
  (ii) market skimming;
  (iii) market penetration.

Competition Oriented

  (i)   maintaining and improving market position;
  (ii) meeting and following competition;
  (iii) pricing to reflect product differentiation;
  (iv) preventing new entry.

Issues in Export Pricing

Throughout this book we have emphasised that many firms selling overseas do so as exporters rather than as international marketers. For an exporter, the problems of pricing differ considerably from those faced by international and multinational corporations and before going on to examine approaches to international pricing, we therefore need to consider the problems that are peculiar to the exporter.

Financial Elements of Exporting

A number of issues arise in relation to the financial arrangements associated with exporting. For example, a manufacturer who is considering exporting must ascertain how a foreign market price in, say, Deutschmarks can be converted into an ex-factory price in, say, Sterling. Since an exporter normally sells to an importer and loses control of the process thereafter, the real issue for the exporter is the price he is to receive from the importer and the currency in which the agreement is to be struck. Over the past decade, the period of floating exchange rates, offset only by the relative exchange rate stability of currencies within the European Monetary System, has meant that some exchange rate risk does exist and either has to be borne by the importer, the exporter, or shared. Many agreements are expressed in terms of one of the national currencies that perform a reserve role, such as the US dollar, but equally they may be in either the exporter's or the importer's currency. For the exporter it is important to ensure that the currency specified is one which does not have undue downside risk as measured in his domestic currency. If, for example, we have a UK exporter who requires an ex-factory price of £10 to cover his costs and has agreed to sell to a West German importer at 35DM at an exchange rate of 3.5DM, he will be in serious danger of losing money if the exchange rate moves to 4DM (which is only £8.75), unless the contract can be renegotiated. If on the other hand the exchange rate moves to 3DM he will receive £11.65 and his profits will rise. In negotiating the contract, therefore, he will prefer it to be specified in DM if he believes Sterling will fall, and in Sterling if he believes it will rise. The importer on the other hand is likely to have exactly opposite preferences.

Careful consideration also needs to be given to the point within the delivery chain at which prices are specified. The price may, for example, be quoted:

(a) ex factory;
(b) FOB (free on board);
(c) CIF (cost, insurance, freight);
(d) FAS (free-alongside-ship);
(e) delivered duty paid.

In each case, the level of costs incurred by the exporter will differ and there is an obvious need therefore for prices to reflect this.

Elements of the Export Pricing Strategy

In developing an export pricing strategy, some assessment has to be made of whether the firm which exports has a long-term commitment to such activity, or whether it is merely a short-term expedient to dispose of surplus production. If it is the latter, there are few issues of general significance and so the discussion here will focus on export pricing strategies where a longer view has been taken. This approach may also be taken to imply that the objectives that the firm has in mind in formulating its prices (domestic and export) are essentially long term. They may be profit-orientated or they may relate to some other objectives or group objectives, although even here it is likely that there will always be a profit constraint as part of the prerequisite of long-term survival.

Once a firm is committed to exporting, a number of questions then arise which are not normally present in domestic sales:

(i) What tariffs will have to be paid?
(ii) How much will transport costs be?
(iii) Will special packaging be required?
(iv) How much will extra insurance cost?
(v) What foreign tax liability will be generated?

All of these concerns then feed into the more general question of the relationship that is to exist between the domestic and export price structures and whether:

(a) costs incurred in export sales are greater than for domestic sales;
(b) prices should be related to costs of all production, or to average or marginal costs in particular;
(c) exports are a mainstream or marginal element of the firm's activity.

In relation to the first of these, it is apparent that there are several types of cost which are specific to export sales. These include the costs of translating and processing orders; credit and collection costs which are often higher overseas; and the costs of operating the export sales department. Logically, all of these should be reflected in export prices, together with the directly attributable variable costs and an appropriate proportion of general overhead expenses. In practice, however, even though the costs associated with export sales are greater than those for domestic sales, it does not necessarily follow that export prices should carry all of these costs differences. Indeed, conventional economic theory suggests that any firm which has a degree of monopoly power (i.e. is not a perfect competitor) should charge different prices in different markets to reflect differing elasticities of demand. Although, in practice, the difficulties of pricing by equating marginal costs and marginal revenues in each market apply equally to international markets, the principle of prices in markets reflecting specific market conditions is well established.

With regard to the third issue raised, this clearly goes back to the question of the firm's degree of commitment to export markets and, in turn, to the issue of dumping which was raised at an earlier stage. Although dumping has been defined in a number of different ways, the critical feature is the sale of goods in an export market at prices which are below those which are sustainable over the long term. While the consumer benefits in the short term, these actions are likely to drive other suppliers out of business and by reducing the long-term supply of the product, force the long-term price upwards. Clearly, if the 'dumper' could continue to supply over the long term at these low prices it would be in the interest of the consumer for domestic producers to switch their resources to other activities. On occasions, the practice of dumping develops political overtones. Exports from the communist countries of Eastern Europe, for example, are very often priced at very low levels and certainly below the costs of production in an equivalent Western country. The issue is whether this is truly dumping, since the communist nations have very different political structures and production relations with the result that their costs are often not directly comparable with those of the West. They also tend to pursue production rather than profit targets. In addition, they often have a need for 'hard' Western currencies to pay for grain imports so that their major concern in pricing exports is to generate adequate hard currencies to pay for these imports. Quite obviously, this is an area of particular sensitivity and difficulty, but has been addressed within the USA which views sales from Eastern Europe at prices below the costs of production in a capitalist country at a similar stage of economic development in an unfavourable light.

Market Based Export Pricing

In the foregoing analysis the main focus of attention was on the way in which different cost structures affected export prices. It is also clear that some assessment of market condition and therefore the revenue potential of overseas markets need to be undertaken. However, there are certain dimensions which are specific to exporting. If we assume that an analysis of a particular overseas market has been completed, then the firm is likely to have reached some assessment of the price, or more realistically the price range, at which it could sell the kind of volumes it has in mind. The issue which then arises for an exporter is to deduct from this market price all the costs incurred in getting the product from the factory gate to the market place. Approaching the problem in this way allows the firm to compare the unit revenue generated by each market in relation to its ex-factory unit production cost, and hence to identify the most attractive markets in which to sell. This process is absolutely vital since it is typically the case that the difference between the ex-factory price and the market price is substantial. The reasons for this become clear if we work back from the market price. From this must be deducted the following:

(a) retail margin on selling price
(could be as much as 50 per cent or even more in some specialised products);
(b) wholesaler's mark up
(perhaps of the order of 10 per cent of his buying price);
(c) importer's mark up
(perhaps 5 per cent of his buying price);
(d) duty and taxes payable on landing
(together these two could be as much as 20 per cent);
(e) Insurance and freight costs to transport the product to the market.

Clearly the sum total of these deductions will vary widely according to the product, the country, the distribution network, tax and duty rates, and so on. Nevertheless, approaching the problem in this way allows the exporter to identify the most desirable opportunities both at home and abroad and also to identify which areas to concentrate on in attempting to reduce the costs incurred in getting the product from the factory to the market place. This might suggest alternative distribution channels, different packaging or may suggest that some other market entry strategy than exporting is appropriate.

The Role of Credit

The area of export credit is one in which governments typically play an important role and is illustrated in Appendix 7.1. While credit is typically available from banks and other institutions, the problem the firm faces is that it must balance its preference for cash payments in advance with the likelihood of gaining greater market share if the terms provided are more generous. Bearing in mind the fact that many countries can be viewed as being economically, financially or politically unstable, it is not surprising that governments in the main industrial countries have sought ways of helping to provide credit finance for exports and to guarantee payment to firms in the event of default by the customer. In the UK, this role is played by the Export Credits Guarantee Department (ECGD).

The strategic importance of a well-developed export credit strategy has been the subject of a considerable amount of research in recent years with writers such as Michell,[10] Pass,[11] and Udell,[12] suggesting that relatively few marketing executives perceive credit provision as a significant influence on their firm's success. Others, however, including Neale and Shipley have argued that:

> Although few purchasers rate sellers' credit packages among the two or three most important *patronage* determinants, many buyers do regard the credit terms offered as an important selection criterion.
>
> Viewed in this light, it would appear that sellers can only ignore credit conditions at the risk of losing sales and profit opportunities. It has been pointed out by (various) writers that the ultimate determinants in source selection need not be the most highly rated factors such as product, delivery and price. Rather, when rival sellers offer an equally attractive mix of these attributes, other criteria like breadth of product range, efficiency of sales quotation procedures and credit offerings may become decisive. In particular, these factors are likely to become the most significant influences on marginal patronage decisions in some oligopolistic markets.
>
> These arguments suggest that many firms may be able to achieve a position of competitive advantage through the development of an effective credit strategy. Accordingly, manufacturers might be expected to offer credit packages differentiated from those of competitors by, say, duration of payment period or by interest charges.[13]

Neale and Shipley's comments are based on the findings of a major international study of credit strategies and led them to conclude that, 'If suitably insured, sellers could have much to gain and little or nothing to lose from providing credit.'[14]

Transfer Pricing

The problem of transfer pricing is one which is not unique to international business. It arises whenever a business is divided into separate operating units which have their own management structure and organisational objectives, and products are transferred from one unit to another. The transfer price is the price at which this trade or transfer takes place and creates problems because it is not determined in the market place through the interaction of willing buyers and willing sellers in the way in which conventional prices are. If a transfer price is set at too low a level, the 'seller' will suffer from a depressed profit performance while the 'buyer' will achieve substantially better profits. Conversely, if the transfer price is set at too high a level, the 'seller' gains but only at the expense of the 'buyer'. While it might appear at first sight that the aggregate profit for the business as a whole is no different regardless of the transfer price and that it does not therefore matter what transfer price is chosen, that is rarely the case in practice. The reason for this is that if the business has been separated into divisions or groups, each with its own objectives and managerial responsibilities, arbitrary transfer pricing is likely to have the effect of preventing one unit achieving realistic objectives while making it far easier for the other. The net effect of this is likely to be that the effectiveness of the organisation as a whole will be undermined. Thus in some general way, the transfer price has to reflect the individual needs and aspirations of each of the units involved. There may, however, be specific circumstances in international business where the international pattern of taxation leads to a particular pattern of profit distribution and this may be most easily realised by setting transfer prices at levels which encourage profits in low tax-rate countries, and restricting them in high tax-rate countries. Clearly, the authorities in the high tax country will be especially concerned to ensure that tax revenue loss does not result from such action.

The transfer pricing issue therefore usually arises in the context of the transfer of products from the producing division to the international division and subsequently to a range of overseas subsidiaries which may be either marketing agencies, or engaged in assembly and production work. In these circumstances it is quite obviously important to find a transfer price which encourages both units to maximise their contribution to *overall* organisational objectives. The transfer price which produces this outcome is, not surprisingly, likely to be one which neither party is entirely happy with. This can be illustrated by considering the various ways in which firms go about the transfer pricing process. One rather extreme method that is employed involves the producing division being judged on general efficiency and cost criteria. with the transfer price including no profit element. However, because the producing division is receiving a price which is well below what it could achieve in the open market, and in some cases what it is in fact receiving from open market sales, this solution can lead to problems with delivery reliability, since there is no real incentive for an improved performance.

As an alternative, the firm can make use of *arms length transfer pricing* in which the producing division charges the same price (or price structure) to all its customers whether they are internal, such as the international division, or external. There are, however, instances in which no external market exists and it is not clear what the arm's length transfer price would be. Even here, however, it is possible, in principle at least, to construct an artificial arm's length price. Although popular in practice, problems can arise with this approach largely because of the way in which the international division may find that it is uncompetitive on such a basis and cannot sell even though the organisation as a whole has determined that international sales growth is strategically important. Secondly, and perhaps more critically, there is no rational reason why domestic external market prices should necessarily determine what the overseas price should be given different market demand conditions. Indeed, as we have already observed, economic theory tells us that a discriminating monopolist should charge prices which reflect the elasticity of each market's demand.

Because of these sorts of problems, a compromise often emerges in which the transfer price is based on full unit cost plus some negotiated mark-up. At least one advantage of this approach is that, in principle at least, it is possible to envisage that this mark-up is determined not by bureaucratic procedures, but by reference to the market demand conditions faced by the various internal buyers whether domestic or international.

The comments made so far are applicable in a general sense both to domestic and international transfer pricing. Where the international division or the producing division directly sells to an overseas subsidiary, other issues do, however, arise. Not only are there tax issues of the sort referred to earlier, but also problems that arise from the action of customs officials. While overseas tax authorities will be concerned to ensure that transfer prices are not set at too high a level and thus limit the overall tax liability in that country, the customs officials will be concerned to identify transfer prices which are set unduly low in order to prevent customs duty avoidance. Thus the tax authorities and customs office both watch transfer prices closely, albeit from opposite perspectives. At the same time, domestic tax authorities also look for unduly low transfer prices because of the implications for lost tax revenues at home. Despite all this, the firm should not look solely at tax rates in determining its response to the fiscal environment, but should also take account of levels of financial economic and political stability, since these not only influence exchange rates, and hence the value of profits accruing in low tax nations, but also the legal framework within which accumulated profits may be remitted to the parent company.

In the light of these comments, it can be seen that transfer pricing decisions are influenced by a wide variety of factors including:

(i)   tax liabilities in the host country;
(ii) tax liabilities in the country of origin;
(iii) exchange controls;
(iv) profit repatriation restrictions;
(v)   quota restrictions;
(vi) credit constraints;
(vii) the level of involvement within the market.

The relative importance of these factors has been examined by Kim and Miller who found that the most important single variable for multinationals operating in the industrialised world is the tax liability. In the developing world, however, restrictions on profit repatriation and constraints upon exchange control proved to be far more important,[15] and have in turn led Jain to identify a series of transfer pricing guidelines:

- All domestic and foreign units are profit centres, and transfers must be set at levels that yield a reasonable profit to both the selling and buying units.
- Profit is divided according to functions performed in

producing and marketing goods to unrelated buyers.

- Gross margins (the spread between production and distribution costs and the sale to an unrelated buyer) are divided more or less evenly between domestic producing and foreign marketing units.
- Overall impact on consolidated profit is the paramount consideration and profit is taken where it is best for the total corporation.[16]

Clearly, therefore, the establishment of appropriate transfer prices is a complex and difficult area for managerial judgement. While cost-based transfer prices and arm's length prices may be appropriate in certain circumstances it is likely to be generally the case that some form of cost plus pricing will be the best compromise since it gives all parties some share of the profits available. To refine this approach further and to attempt to reflect in some detailed way the political, economic, financial, fiscal and legal dimension would tend to lead to an overly cumbersome and bureaucratic system, which would not allow effective responses to changing market conditions.

Foreign Market Pricing

Both export pricing and transfer pricing are concerned essentially with the task of delivering products to foreign markets at a price level that satisfies or contributes to corporate goals. As such, they can be seen as techniques of *international* pricing. Foreign market pricing is by way of contast more akin to *domestic* pricing in that it is concerned directly with the specific prices that are to be charged *within* each market. Typically, therefore, multinationals operate by developing an overall pricing strategy based on export or transfer pricing principles which is then used by local management as the framework within which national market prices are set. Foreign market pricing is, therefore, for the reasons that we discussed at an earlier stage in this chapter, generally the responsibility of local rather than head office management. Nevertheless, foreign market prices are still of importance to head office staff and, for two reasons, need to be monitored carefully: firstly, the prices charged in a domestic market are often related directly or indirectly to supply and demand factors outside the market's boundaries; and, secondly, co-ordinating the behaviour of domestic markets and the policies pursued is an integral part of the international marketing task. Without this co-ordination, the firm runs the risk of each market operating too independently with the result that medium or long term conflicts begin to arise.

This was illustrated quite dramatically within the European car industry in the early 1980s when the pricing policies pursued in a number of markets began to move too far apart and British buyers began to recognise the size of the possible savings that could be made by buying a new car in Belgium, Germany or Southern Ireland and then taking it straight back to Britain. Faced with a rapid escalation in the number of car buyers who were willing to do this, both the British government and the major car manufacturers began to look for obstacles that would prevent or at least hinder the trade. Amongst the methods used by the manufacturers was a restriction upon the number of right-hand-drive cars that Continental European dealerships could sell and a consequent lengthening of the delivery schedules. Attempts were also made to place restrictions upon the trade by limiting the 'type approval' which is needed before the car could be brought legally into Britain on a permanent basis. In the face of unfavourable publicity, customer dissatisfaction, and — perhaps most importantly of all — the intervention of the European Commission which pointed to the ways in which competition law and the principle of the free movement of goods was being infringed, manufacturers were obliged to lift their restrictions, and guidelines designed to ensure greater parity between the prices charged in each market were developed.

The approaches used to set foreign market prices are, in essence, the same as those used in domestic markets, although it should of course be remembered that foreign market pricing is often only necessary when the firm operates within a market with its own marketing subsidiary. Where it operates through a series of distributors or other intermediaries, the responsibility for anything other than transfer or export pricing rests with the intermediary rather than with the parent company. However, for those companies that do become involved in foreign market pricing, the basic principles of domestic pricing apply, although in many cases a variety of additional factors need to be taken into account in arriving at the final price. Prominent amongst these is the question of which *costs* are to be taken into account. For a firm operating in just one market, the identification and allocation both of direct and variable costs is relatively straightforward. However, as we observed at an earlier stage, allocating costs in a fair and acceptable manner once the company operates in a variety of markets often becomes a more difficult exercise, largely because of the problems of determining which specific costs are relevant. These problems are, in turn, compounded when subsidiaries are part of an international network within which different stages of the manufacturing process are carried out. Insofar as it is possible to identify broad and generally acceptable guidelines for coming to terms with this they are, firstly, that the manufacturing and distribution costs should provide a base price below which the company should go only in exceptional circumstances; and secondly, that the market price should incorporate all of those costs which can be attributed directly to the product.

A second factor which is peculiar to foreign market pricing is the structure of *tariffs* throughout the world:

> Because tariffs can be an important part of delivered cost, the subsidiary will tend to prefer a source from a country having favourable tariff relations with its own. Thus a subsidiary in the E.C. will usually choose another E.C. subsidiary because no tariff barriers exist. For the same reason, U.S. firms have often supplied Australia or India from Canadian or British subsidiaries rather than from the United States. Because these countries were in the British Commonwealth, they had lower tariffs for each other than for non-member countries like the United States.[17]

Equally, the foreign market price can be influenced by differential rates of *inflation.* Although virtually all countries experience some degree of inflation over time, pricing in countries which have a history of significant levels of inflation (10 per cent or above) becomes a far more complex problem since not only do many costs increase at a faster rate than prices, but the governments of these countries often tend to introduce price legislation to limit price increases, whilst at the same time imposing restrictions on foreign exchange. In this way, foreign companies find it more difficult to repatriate their profits and, for them at least, the market ultimately becomes far less attractive.

Foreign market prices are also affected by the *nature of demand*

and the *structure of competition*. With regard to patterns of demand, the key issue is the extent to which the product satisfies local tastes and whether the product has an advantage over those already on the market. Where this is the case and a unique selling proposition exists or can be developed, the degree of price freedom increases significantly. This, in turn, is helped or hindered by the structure of competition and whether competitors are pursuing a price or non-price strategy. For a foreign company, a price war locally often proves to be counter-productive and, in general terms at least, American and European multinationals try to avoid significant levels of price competition by emphasising the non-price elements of the marketing mix.

The final major determinant of foreign market prices is the *government* of the country and its attitude towards business generally and the multinationals in particular. At its broadest level, government influence upon price can be seen in terms of the nature and structure of its competition policy, together with the influence of any additional regional competition policies that exist (e.g. British companies are affected not just by British law but operate also within a series of constraints imposed by EC competition policy). The legislative techniques used to control prices vary greatly, but at one time or another have included *resale price maintenance* (now largely abolished in Japan and Western Europe, although still in use in some countries in Latin America, Africa, and Asia); *economy wide controls* such as Brazil's Interministerial Council on Prices, and in Britain, the Prices Commission of the early 1970s; and *selective controls* which are used within a particular market sector either to control prices for the public good or to correct an apparent price abuse. This third approach has been used in the majority of countries at certain stages, including in Britain agreements between the National Health Service and the pharmaceutical companies, and in Germany between the government and the major oil companies.

The Influence of Fluctuating Exchange Rates

The significance and strategic importance of price as an element of the international marketing mix has long been a source of debate with many commentators arguing that the relative cheapness of the Yen, Franc or Mark has greatly contributed to the growth and strength of the Japanese, French and German economies. Others, however, argue that in many markets, particularly in the developed world, price is a far less important element of the mix than is often claimed and that international marketing success is ultimately determined by a more detailed understanding of market needs, higher product quality, faster delivery schedules, and a more aggressive sales approach. In support of this, analysts point to the ways in which in the long term at least, fluctuating exchange rates appear to have little real impact upon the willingness of a firm to enter a particular market, but rather they have the opposite effect by increasing the level of uncertainty. At a more specific level, fluctuating exchange rates create significant difficulties for the international marketer, since they have the effect of altering a market's profitability quite dramatically in a very short period. Faced with this, he then has to decide whether to alter his prices to reflect the different relative value of the currencies involved, or to adopt a far longer perspective in which losses today may possibly be counterbalanced by greater profits tomorrow as the currencies fluctuate yet again. In making such a decision, consideration also has to be given to the probable reaction of distributors, since frequent changes in price not only lead to a degree of disillusion and disenchantment, but also to confusion within the market place. Because of this, it is essential that a pricing policy reflects a long-term perspective in which currency fluctuations are, as far as possible, absorbed.

The possible size and violence of currency movements — with obvious implications for marketing — were illustrated in a quite dramatic fashion by the way in which the pound and dollar moved against each other in the early 1980s. From a peak of $2.40 in late 1980, the pound slumped in February 1985 to $1.03. Over that period, the profitability of shipping goods from the US to Britain collapsed, while many UK exporters enjoyed a profits bonanza. Within a matter of months, however, the pound had recovered to $1.30, altering the equation yet again. During this time though, British companies found access to the American market far easier than ever before with the result that, in 1983 alone, non-oil exports to the USA increased by £1.3 billion (UK), or 30 per cent, to £5.7 billion (UK) (see Figure 7.3). Fluctuations such as these do not, however, benefit all industries and companies equally. Typically, consumer goods are best placed to take advantage of currency movements, followed by such areas as office equipment,

Figure 7.3: Patterns of US–UK Trade (1981–4)

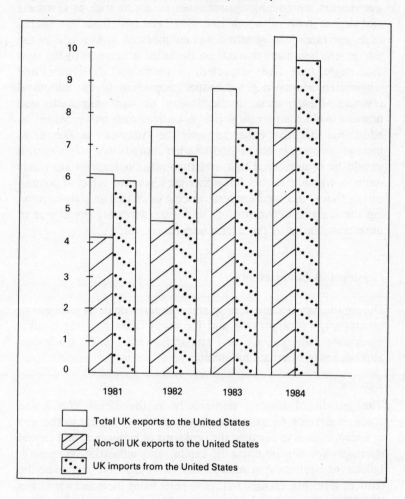

Total UK exports to the United States

Non-oil UK exports to the United States

UK imports from the United States

contract furniture, carpets, and finally capital equipment manufacturers. (A case study on the effects of fluctuating exchange rates appears at the end of the chapter, see Appendix 7.4.)

The effects of currency fluctuations such as this are not always, however, as beneficial or self-evident as might appear at first sight. The relative decline of the pound in this case was due largely to the overall international strength of the dollar, a situation which of course also benefited most other Western currencies. As a result,

British firms found themselves in what was still a highly competitive market, competing against other countries such as Germany and Japan, both of which had also benefited from the altered exchange rates. The situation was complicated further still by the way in which in many markets profits failed to increase by the level that might have been expected, as importers, distributors and wholesalers absorbed a substantial proportion of the additional revenue. Nevertheless, a fluctuation of this magnitude was however welcomed by most British businessmen and provided an additional incentive either to enter the American market or to increase existing levels of sales. Rather more broadly, however, it should be remembered that exchange-rate fluctuations are rarely quite as dramatic as this, but rather they have the effect of complicating short- and medium-term pricing decisions and, by narrowing the margins between profit and loss, increasing the degree of uncertainty faced by the international marketer.

Leasing and Countertrade

During the past decade, leasing and countertrade deals have grown enormously in importance and for many firms now represent a significant alternative to straightforward and traditional approaches to international pricing.

Leasing

The growth of leasing, particularly in the Third World and amongst developing nations is attributable very largely to the way in which it helps to alleviate the problems of high prices and capital shortages for the purchase of capital and industrial equipment. Leases for equipment normally run from one to five years with the costs of servicing, repairs and spare parts being included within the rental fee. The essential advantages of leasing are, therefore, that not only does the lessee get expensive equipment at a low cost, but also receives a level of maintenance which often would otherwise not be available. Leasing can also be an attractive proposition for a company when governments offer *investment grants* for new plant and machinery, supported by a series of *tax* incentives. The lessor in these circumstances can often taken advantage of the tax provisions in a way that a lessee cannot and a portion of the savings can then be passed on.

Countertrade

The term countertrade is used to refer to a variety of forms of exchange (see Figure 7.3), the four most common of which are:

(i) *Barter* where no cash is involved, and there is simply a direct exchange of goods. (This is illustrated in the Hawker Siddeley — Indonesian Railways and Saudi Arabia — B. Ae. case studies at the end of the chapter, see Appendices 7.2 and 7.3.)

(ii) *Compensation deals* where both cash and goods are involved in the transaction.

(iii) *Counterpurchase* where two contracts are negotiated. In the first the seller agrees to sell the product at an established price to a buyer and to receive his payment in cash. In the second and simultaneous contract he agrees to buy goods from the buyer for an equivalent or proportionate cash payment. This is often part of aerospace deals and can involve national governments in supporting the arrangement.

(iv) *Product buy-back agreements* where the transaction involves production/manufacturing equipment. The seller accepts a proportion of the output of the equipment in payment or receives full cash payment initially with an agreement to purchase some of the output later.

The ways in which these forms of exchange operate are illustrated in Figure 7.4.

A variety of criticisms have been made of countertrade deals largely because they have been used by some countries to offload goods of inferior quality onto world markets. However, it is clear that emerging nations are determined to use countertrade practices not only to stimulate exports, but also to earn foreign currency and save on foreign exchange for imports. Because of this, American companies and bankers who were initially very wary about participation, have adopted a very different approach with banks such as Bank of America, Citicorp and Chase Manhattan now not only having specialist personnel, but also a series of trading companies to handle bartered goods. This trend has, in turn, been encouraged by the major British clearing banks, all of which have specialist departments, and by the formation in London in 1984 of Batis International Business Services which offers computer-based barter services to its clients. It is services such as these together

Figure 7.4: Common Types of Countertrade

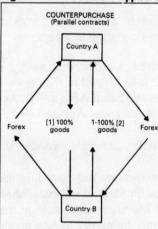

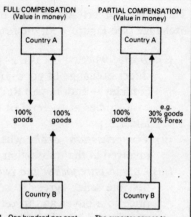

COUNTERPURCHASE
(Parallel contracts)

FULL COMPENSATION
(Value in money)

PARTIAL COMPENSATION
(Value in money)

1. Contracts [1] and [2] are negotiated and signed simultaneously but fulfilled and settled in foreign exchange separately.
2. Contract [2] could contain penalties for non-fulfillment.
3. Contract [2] can often be assigned to a third party e.g. trader, subject to the agreement of Country B.
4. Costs incurred in disposing of the counter-trade goods have to be built into the price in Contract [1]
5. The contracts are not usually cross-referenced, so Contract [1] could be eligible for ECGD support, where available.

1. One hundred per cent two-way transfer of goods, by means of a single contract.
2. The goods are valued in monetary units.
3. Settlement is achieved by setting off the sale proceeds of the compensation goods against the amount due from the importer in Country B.
4. The compensation obligation may be transferred to a third party, against payment to that party of a subsidy, called a disagio.

The exporter agrees to accept cash in partial settlement for the goods supplied and enters into a compensation agreement for the balance. This agreement follows the procedure for full compensaion contracts.

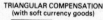

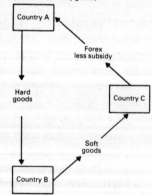

TRIANGULAR COMPENSATION
(with soft currency goods)

The procedure follows that for triangular compensation for hard currency goods, but as the goods are less easily saleable, Country C will accept them only where a subsidy is paid by Country A. Allowance for this subsidy will have been made by Country A in pricing their hard goods exports to Country B.

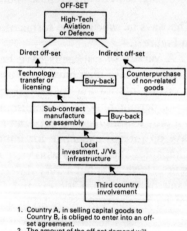

1. Country A, in selling capital goods to Country B, is obliged to enter into an off-set agreement.
2. The amount of the off-set demand will often be expressed as a percentage of the main contract.
3. Direct off-set usually involves the technology of the seller and is most often connected to the products to be supplied.
4. Indirect off-set involves goods unrelated to those of the seller.

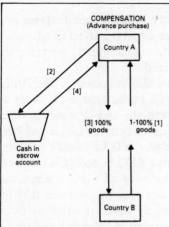

COMPENSATION
(Advance purchase)

1. The exporting country will take delivery of, and sell, the countertrade goods first.
2. The proceeds are placed in an escrow account with an institution sanctioned by Country B.
3. The exporter then delivers his goods to Country B.
4. Against agreed documentation the exporter is able to reclaim the funds held in escrow.

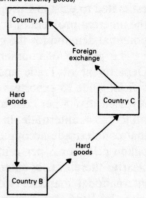

TRIANGULAR COMPENSATION
(with hard currency goods)

1. Triangular compensation involves the movement of goods between three countries.
2. This arrangement is appropriate when the hard goods offered in compensation by Country B are readily saleable, but not necessarily in Country A.
3. The goods are sold in Country C who then settle in foreign exchange with Country A.

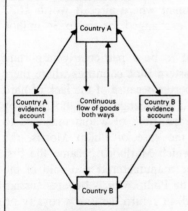

EVIDENCE ACCOUNTS

1. Resulting from an agreement whereby a company in Country A undertakes to buy and sell products from and to Country B; over a given period.
2. Such sales and purchases are recorded on evidence accounts maintained by Country B with a bank in that country and with a bank in Country A.

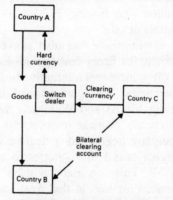

SWITCH

1. Country A exports to Country B, where no hard currency is available.
2. Country B has a clearing arrangement with Country C, which is out of balance in B's favour.
3. A portion of the clearing balance is bought by a Switch dealer who pays A in hard currency (less a discount).
4. The Switch dealer will sell the clearing 'currency' to another country trading with C, or will use it to acquire goods from C.

with 250–300 countertrade advisory organisations that are now estimated to exist in Europe, that have had the effect of alleviating the inherent problem of countertrade of determining the value and potential demand for the goods offered.

The growth of countertrade was also reflected in the British Department of Trade and Industry's publication in 1984 of an official guide to exporters on countertrade, and by a survey which revealed that 5 per cent of £3 billion of British exports had been subject to countertrade. In the same year, a GATT study estimated that countertrade accounted for some £133 billion (UK) to £167 billion (UK) or 8 per cent of the value of all world trade. Quite clearly, therefore, countertrade is likely to be an issue that the international marketer will increasingly have to come to terms with. In 1984, for example, Volkswagen do Brasil negotiated a triangular countertrade agreement with Iraq which involved the sale of passenger cars in return for petroleum to sell to Petrobras, Brazil's state oil company. The deal also necessitated gaining the permission of the Jordanian government to install an oil storage terminal at Aqaba. At the same time, Boeing Commercial Aircraft Company, in partnership with Rolls-Royce, agreed a deal with the Saudi-Arabian government where aircraft worth £833 million (ten Boeing 747s) were exchanged for up to 34 million barrels of oil.

Countertrade has also proved to be a particularly important activity for firms dealing with Eastern Bloc countries where there is often little real alternative to barter because of the lack of hard currencies. The significance of this was recognised in the 1970s by Philip Morris and Wilkinson Sword, both of whom managed to enter the Russian market. In the case of Philip Morris, the company negotiated a deal in which Marlboro became the first foreign brand of cigarettes to be manufactured and sold in the USSR. This was made possible by Philip Morris buying Russian tobacco for sale in the West and, in return, getting a royalty on each 'Russian' pack of Marlboro cigarettes. Similarly, Wilkinson Sword established a Russian manufacturing plant for razor blades and, as part payment, took back an agreed proportion of the output.

Summary

International pricing is for many firms a difficult and complex exercise requiring decisions not only on the pricing strategy, but also on precisely what costs are to be allocated to each product. Although the determinants of price both in domestic and international markets are broadly similar, the added problems of fluctuating exchange rates and greater levels of environmental uncertainty conspire to increase the significance of the decision and of the consequences of a poorly formulated approach. A variety of pricing techniques exist, although in many cases the starting point is pricing for export. Over time, the development of the organisation internationally alters the nature of the pricing problem and leads ultimately to companies engaging either in transfer pricing, countertrade or leasing.

References

1. S. Jain, *International Marketing Management* (Kent Publishing Company, 1984) p. 382.
2. 'Why Common Market Does Not Mean Common Prices', *Business International,* 2 February 1973, p. 47.
3. 'Why Scotch is £34 in Japan', *The Guardian,* October 1985, p. 13.
4. J.J. Boddewyn, 'American Marketing in the European Common Market, 1963-1973', *Multinational Product Management* (Harvard, Marketing Sciences Institute (1976), pp. VII-1 to VII-25.
5. P.W. Turnbull, 'The Image and Reputation of British Suppliers in Western Europe', *European Journal of Marketing,* vol. 19, no. 6 (1985), p. 39.
6. S. Majaro, *International Marketing: A Strategic Approach to World Markets* (George Allen & Unwin, 1978), pp. 111-12.
7. D.S. Henley, 'Evaluating International Product Line Performance: a conceptual approach', in *Multinational Product Management* (Marketing Sciences Institute, 1976) pp. II-10, II-11.
8. N.H. Leff, 'Multinational Corporate Pricing Strategy in the Developing Countries', *Journal of International Business Studies,* Autumn (1975), p. 55.
9. Majaro, *International Marketing,* pp. 116-19.
10. P. Michell, 'Infrastructures and International Marketing Effectiveness', *Columbia Journal of World Business,* Spring (1979), pp. 91-101.
11. C. Pass, 'Pricing Policies and Market Strategy: An Empirical Note', *European Journal of Marketing,* vol. 5, no. 1 (1971), pp. 94-8.
12. J.C. Udell, 'How Important is Pricing in Competitive Strategy?', *Journal of Marketing,* vol. 28, no. 1, January (1964), pp. 44-8.
13. C.W. Neale, and D. Shipley, 'An International Comparative Study of Credit Strategy', *European Journal of Marketing,* vol. 19, no. 6 (1985), p. 24.
14. Ibid., p. 25.
15. S.H. Kim and S.W. Miller, 'Constituents of the International Transfer Pricing Decision,' *Columbia Journal of World Business,* Spring (1979), p. 71.

16. S.C. Jain, *International Marketing Management* (Kent Publishing Company, 1984), p. 403.

17. V. Terpstra, *International Marketing* (The Dryden Press, 1978), p. 504.

Further Reading

For a discussion of the growth of barter see J.G. Kaikati, 'The Reincarnation of Barter Trade as a Marketing Tool', *Journal of Marketing* April (1975), pp. 17-24. For a review of the implications of fluctuating US/UK exchange rates in the 1980s, see 'Making Sense of the Dollar', *Marketing*, 4 April 1985, pp. 26-34.

Appendix 7.1: The Use of Soft-credit to Win International Contracts

Complaints by British industrialists about the low levels of government help for trade have long been a feature of business-government relationships. In the 1980s, however, after a series of trade failures in world markets, discontent amongst large British contractors and their supporters in Parliament became increasingly vociferous over what they alleged was the ambivalent government policy towards aid for capital goods exports. In this, they were supported by the findings of a review of 29 contracts worldwide for railway locomotives conducted by the Hawker-Siddeley Group, a summary of which appears in Table 7.1. In the light of their findings, Hawker-Siddeley claimed that British exporters were being 'gazumped' by foreign governments in the international bidding for large contracts, and that the British government was failing to match the generosity and 'flexibility' of France, West Germany, Japan, Canada and — to a lesser extent the USA — in offering soft loans and tied aid in support of their own exporters' tenders.

One result of this, Hawker-Siddeley claimed, was that its subsidiary, Brush Electrical Machines, 'definitely' lost five orders for lack of matching help from Whitehall. In a further eleven cases, the company did not even receive an invitation to tender because other governments had already secured the contract with a soft-credit package.

The Government rejected these criticisms, however, arguing that it was committed to helping exporters win orders for large

Table 7.1: How Some Recent Railway Contracts Were Won

Customer	Requirement	Approx. value	Evaluation Commercial	Evaluation Financial	Award	Major reason	Hawker-Siddeley/ Brush involvement
Egyptian Railways	104 Mainline Co-Co locos (3 separate orders)	£60m	Negotiated contract (no international tender)	Soft, long-term credit	Thyssen-Henschel (W. Germany)	Attractive finance	Not invited to participate
East Africa Kenya, Uganda and Tanzania Railways	74 General purpose locos (4 separate orders)	£30m	3 negotiated contracts and 1 international tender	Soft, long-term credit	Thyssen-Henschel (W. Germany)	Attractive finance	Not invited to participate
East Africa Railways	36 Mainline locos	£18m	International tender	Long-term interest-free credit	Bombardier (Canada)	Attractive finance	Quoted and shortlisted
Iraq Railways	72 Mainline locos	£48m	International tender	Cash terms	MTE (France)	Political pressure and armament deal	On shortlist of 3
Busan Metro, S. Korea	Turnkey project for Metro		International tender		Hitachi (Japan)	Political pressure ensured business placed in Japan	Brush/H.S. were close to receiving order
Turkish Railways	50 General purpose locos	£20m	International tender	Long-term soft credit	Krauss Maffei (W. Germany)	Attractive finance and political pressure	Brush price and technical offer no. 1 but finance not equal to German

Source: Hawker-Siddeley.

projects by means of ministerial visits abroad, the aid-and-trade programme, and by means of marketing, pre-contractual assistance, and project finance. Hawker-Siddeley retaliated by saying that the evidence suggested that the French, West German and Canadian governments had pursued a specific policy to support their railway industries.

The company also pointed to their worldwide reputation for technical excellence and world-competitive prices, citing an order in 1984 for 22 locomotives for New Zealand won against intense competition where no aid or special financing was called for. It went on to identify Canada, France and West Germany as principal suppliers of tied aid to win orders in Asia and Africa. UK bilateral aid, by way of contrast, is rarely tied to the purchase of specific goods, except in the case of India. Hawker-Siddeley also highlighted the policy of many other governments which offered pre-emptive aid, whereas the UK would match but not initiate such deals. This policy, the company claimed, had cost its British subsidiary 'a number of orders'. This was illustrated by the way in which the West Germans had pre-empted the UK for a Turkish order for 50 locomotives worth £50 million, and by the failure to match a French bid for a Jamaican order for six.

An additional complaint made was that the UK has a policy of offering aid, together with separate finance, only at internationally agreed concessionary interest rates. Foreign competitors, however, tend to offer a mixed credit package in which aid is used as a means of cutting interest rates and extending the terms of the loan even further. To illustrate this, the company pointed to a West German mixed-credit package for Turkey repayable over 30 years with a ten-year period of grace, compared with a UK offer of fixed aid and credit at 11.35 per cent payable over ten years. Hawker-Siddeley concluded its analysis by stating unequivocally that the way in which the government implements its bilateral and aid-and-trade programme 'effectively precludes British companies from a number of markets'.

Appendix 7.2: Hawker-Siddeley and Indonesian State Railways

In 1984 Hawker-Siddeley Canada was awarded a contract by

Indonesian State Railways to supply $20 million of railway carriages. However, before the contract could be approved, Hawker was obliged to enter into a counter-purchase agreement equivalent to the full value of the contract for the purchase of Indonesian paper, rubber, cocoa, textiles and plywood. In turn, this involved a series of separate negotiations between Hawker and Indonesian Railways, Hawker and MG Services (the firm which Hawker contracted to take on the obligation to buy and dispose of the countertrade goods), Indonesian Railways and the Department of Trade, MG Services and the Department of Trade, and finally MG Services and the firms which were the ultimate recipients or outlets for the goods (see Figure 7.5).

Figure 7.5: Hawker-Siddeley — Indonesian Railways Counter-Purchase Deal

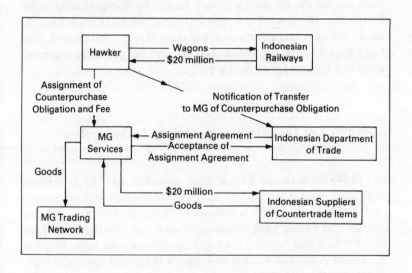

Appendix 7.3: Saudi Arabia and British Aerospace

A barter deal was also at the heart of a $3 billion contract in the mid-1980s to equip the Saudi Arabian airforce with 48 Tornado fighter aircraft and 30 Hawk jet Trainers, together with a complete range of weapons, radar, spares and a pilot training programme, all of which were to be supplied by British Aerospace. The Saudi Arabian contract followed hard on the heels of the sale of eight Tornados to Oman, although whereas the Omani deal was handled directly by British Aerospace, the Saudi negotiations took place at government level and, because of the politically sensitive nature of the deal which was strongly opposed by Israel on the grounds that it undermined stability in the Middle East, political factors played an important role. Indeed, it was the possible political repercussions and the strong pro-Israeli lobby in the US Congress that had led to the Reagan administration being unwilling to guarantee the supply of F15 E fighter aircraft, and to a relatively straightforward fight for the contract between British Aerospace and the French with their Mirage 2000.

A substantial part of the $3 billion barter deal involved Saudi oil and led to a degree of political controversy since Britain had little use for the oil, which is very similar to that produced in the North Sea. Because of this, the intention was to begin selling the oil on the international market, although this in itself proved difficult because of the quantities involved and the generally depressed nature of the market at the time.

Appendix 7.4: The Effects of Fluctuating Exchange Rates

In 1984 Jaguar's profits almost doubled to £91.5 million, compared with £50 million in 1983. Although the company's performance was partly a reflection of the healthy and growing demand for Jaguar cars, the main reason was the strength of the dollar which had boosted their US operations. The importance of the North American market to Jaguar's long-term success is highlighted by the fact that while 55 per cent of the company's total output is destined for the United States, it accounts for between 65 per cent and 70 per cent of total revenue. In addition, whilst the average price of a Jaguar car in the United Kingdom is around £20,000 (1986 prices), it is about $35,000 in the United States. The net effect of this is that fluctuations in the dollar/sterling exchange rate can have a dramatic effect not only upon the company's profitability, but also upon its marketing strategy. A strong dollar provides the firm with a far greater degree of pricing flexibility and this, in turn, influences every other element of the marketing mix.

As in many other industries, however, the influence of exchange rate *fluctuations* has to be viewed as an essentially short-term determinant of marketing behaviour. Stringent US safety legislation means that a decision to export a vehicle to the USA must be taken at the planning stage. This, together with the lengthy period involved in launching a model and developing a market, militates against UK vehicle manufacturers adopting a short-term perspective by taking advantage of a strong dollar and then withdrawing temporarily when the dollar weakens and profitability subsequently drops. Quite obviously, however, a *consistently* strong pound does exert a far more significant influence upon strategy. In the 1970s, for example, despite strong American demand for MG and Triumph sports cars, British Leyland withdrew from the market when the pound was worth $2.40 and the company was losing £900 on every car sold.

On balance, therefore, exchange-rate fluctuations are often viewed by the international marketer as just one other factor within the international business environment with which they have to come to terms. Relatively few markets are willing to accept frequent price changes and as a consequence the marketer, particularly in the Japanese and North American markets, is often obliged to opt for price stability by absorbing exchange-rate fluctuations as far as possible.

INTERNATIONAL PROMOTIONAL DECISIONS

Having decided upon the nature of the international product range and the pricing and distribution policies that are to be pursued, the marketer needs then to consider how he is to communicate most effectively with the target market. In the majority of markets, a variety of promotional tools are available to the marketing planner, including advertising, personal selling, point of purchase displays, direct mail, publicity, and special promotions ranging from money-off offers to commercial sponsorship. In practice, of course, not all promotional tools are equally available or, indeed, equally effective in all cultures and societies, and the international marketer is often faced with the task of adapting the promotional mix to each of the markets in which he is operating. In doing this, he needs to give consideration to a wide variety of factors, including the nature of the market, the company's objectives, its marketing philosophy, the degree of competition, the type of product, the stage reached on the product life cycle and the degree of centralisation or decentralisation in the company's organisation. Within this chapter, we consider each of these factors and show how they influence the communication process and need to be reflected in the promotional strategy that is developed. However, in doing this it needs to be remembered that, more than any other marketing activity, advertising lends itself to misinterpretation. Whilst this is, quite obviously, a potential problem area in domestic marketing, it is a veritable nightmare in international marketing where the company is often trying to appeal to buyers across a variety of markets, each of which has its own cultural norms and language. The scope for error that exists because of this has been pointed to by Ricks *et al.*, who have identified numerous examples of international communication failure,[1] some of which appear in Table 8.1. These sorts of problems were also experienced in Johnnie Walker Scotch in Japan when they ran an international advertisement in which the whisky was left in a decanter bottle. The advertisement was received unfavourably because the Japanese decant only poor whiskies. In order to avoid, or at least minimise, the likelihood of these sorts of ambiguities and misinterpretations occurring, it is essential that the source (i.e. the company) knows and understands how the recipient behaves, what it is that motivates him, and how he is likely to interpret and respond to a given message. It is this awareness and understanding of the differences that exist between the cultural, political, legal and economic environments of the various target markets that is likely to contribute to success in international advertising. Unfortunately, however, many international marketers still fail to recognise fully the need for such a detailed understanding and the result is the sort of communication failure illustrated by Ricks.

Table 8.1: International Communication Failure

Message intended	Message received
'Body by Fischer' (General Motors slogan)	'Corpse by Fischer' (Flemish)
'Schweppes' Tonic Water'	'Schweppes' bathroom water' (Italian)
'Put a tiger in your tank' (Esso slogan)	'Put a weakling in your tank' (Animals are inferior to man in Thailand)
'Come alive with Pepsi'	'Come alive out of the grave' (German)
Cue toothpaste	Pornographic word in French
'Cleans the really dirty parts of the wash'	'Cleans your private parts' (French Canada)

Advertising in International Markets

Although advertising is the major means of communication for many companies, and particularly those marketing consumer goods, attitudes towards advertising are often unfavourable. In the United States, for example, some consumer groups view advertising as being manipulative, whilst classical economists consider it to be a largely unproductive activity which simply adds to the ultimate cost of the product. In many other countries, including those in the developing world, views of advertising are even more negative and have, in turn, led to a variety of constraints upon the advertising practices of the multinationals. One consequence of this has been that the World Health Organisation (WHO) of the United Nations has published a series of directives aimed at the pharmaceutical companies on the grounds that it is felt that advertising has led to over-consumption.[2] The WHO has also examined the advertising practices of the manufacturers of baby-formula products following the unfavourable publicity that Nestlé received in the less-developed nations in the 1970s.[3] Elsewhere, advertising has been viewed as a means of economic penetration by the larger and more highly developed nations and, in the case of Venezuela, Peru and Chile, has led to legislation which requires advertising agencies to have at least 80 per cent local ownership. Faced with these sorts of constraints, there is an obvious need for the international marketer from a highly developed nation to consider carefully the role that advertising is expected to play.

Advertising and Economic Development

The more highly developed and complex a nation becomes, so the role and importance of the promotional activities, and of advertising in particular, becomes. There are several reasons for this, as Cundiff and Hilger point out:

> The importance of all promotional activities and of advertising in particular, tends to increase as the complexity of a society and the size of its population increase. As the physical and social distance between producers and their prospective customers widen, producers find it necessary to formalize communication efforts. Advertising is less important in simple societies because less sophisticated methods of communication, such as word-of-mouth, are effective in reaching the total market. In addition, in less developed countries the range of available advertising media is limited. Print media may reach only a portion of the population, as a result of widespread illiteracy. Television may be publicly owned and not available as an advertising medium; or if available, it may reach only the small portion of the population that can afford to buy a television receiver.[4]

The significance of this in marketing terms can be viewed from a variety of standpoints and has implications not just for the perceptions and level of acceptance of advertising, but also for the probable effectiveness of advertising and its potential role in the promotions mix. Thus, if a multinational firm adheres slavishly to the guidelines developed in the Western world, they are likely to overspend and overspend and over-advertise in a smaller and less sophisticated market where supplies of consumer goods are often in short supply and income levels are low. Despite this, global advertising expenditures are growing rapidly and from an estimate of $135 billion in 1983, are projected to increase to $780 billion by the end of the century. One increasingly evident consequence of this sort of growth is that an ever larger number of marketers are emulating American agency practices and that in many nations advertising expenditure as a proportion of the gross national product is growing substantially.

International Advertising Decisions

For many marketing managers, the international advertising programme is influenced by two sets of constraints: those that stem from factors internal to the company, including the managerial orientation to international business, and those that stem from the international marketing environment and which include the practicalities of coming to terms with the problems of language, cultural differences, the availability of media, the varying nature of competition, and so on. These constraints are then, in turn, reflected in the major decisions faced by the marketer concerning:

(i)   the nature of the international advertising objectives;
(ii)   the choice of an agency;
(iii) the determination of the promotions budget;
(iv)   the selection of the message and copy strategy;
(v)   the choice of advertising media;
(vi)   how to evaluate campaign effectiveness;
(vii) how to organise for international advertising.

The Nature of Advertising Objectives

In developing any promotional strategy, be it for domestic or international markets, the starting point must be the identification of objectives; in other words, what is it that the company is trying to achieve by means of its promotional campaign, how is it designed to interrelate with other aspects of the marketing mix, and over what time period is it designed to have an effect? However, although a statement of this nature might in many ways appear to be relatively straightforward, there are, in practice, a number of problems that need to be recognised. Prominent amongst these is the fact that in most cases it is difficult to say with any real degree of confidence what advertising has achieved without carrying out a considerable amount of research. For many companies operating internationally, this is often difficult largely because of the problems of conducting and co-ordinating a programme of research across a series of markets, many of which have only limited research facilities. It is, therefore, as Martin Mayer suggested in his book *Madison Avenue, U.S.A.*, 'Only the very brave or the very ignorant can say *exactly* what advertising does in the marketplace.'[5] As a consequence, a *precise* statement of the effect that advertising is expected to have upon sales or attitudes is likely to be meaningless. Nevertheless, an important starting point is a statement of the contribution that advertising is expected to make to the overall marketing programme and how this might realistically be measured in terms of, say, attitudes to the product. The role that advertising should be expected to play is, in turn, affected by the stage reached in the development of the market and hence the product's life cycle. Thus, in the early stages, the company needs to concentrate upon building awareness and knowledge of the product and its capabilities. Having achieved this, the emphasis within the promotional strategy needs to shift successively from encouraging a liking and subsequently a preference for the product, through conviction and finally to purchase.

There is, therefore, an obvious need for the marketing planner to pay close attention to the product life cycle when developing advertising strategy. This is particularly so in the case of international marketing, when the product may be in different stages of the life cycle in various markets. Thus it may be the case that the product is in the introductory stage in one market, the growth stage in a second, the maturity stage in a third and the decline stage in a fourth. Quite obviously, such a varied profile holds significant implications both for the overall marketing strategy and, more specifically, for the communication objectives and strategy. There is a need, therefore, for a detailed statement of what the advertising programme is meant to achieve both in terms of communication and sales levels.

Selection of an Agency

Although the majority of marketing tasks both domestically and internationally are performed in-house by company personnel, advertising is in many cases handled very largely by an outside agency. In the case of international advertising, the marketing planner is therefore faced with a choice between two major alternatives: either an international agency which has both domestic and international offices, or a series of local agencies in each of the markets in which he is operating. In practice, however, there are often several other options open to the marketer, such as a domestic agency which has foreign affiliates rather than branches, or local agencies which have grouped together to offer a degree of international coverage. For the purposes of our discussion here, we will however limit the analysis to the two major alternatives available.

Criteria for Choice

Although the most important single reason for a choice of agency is the extent to which it will be able to help the organisation achieve its marketing goals, this seemingly straightforward criterion is often difficult to apply. There are several reasons for this, although arguably the most significant is that the true nature and quality of an agency's work in a particular country only becomes apparent after the choice has been made. If the quality of advertising that then emerges is unsatisfactory, it is often both expensive and time-consuming to move the account elsewhere. With this in mind, the marketer needs to pay attention to a variety of other factors that might feasibly help in the process of choice. The starting point in this involves identifying the agencies that are capable of handling the account in each of the firm's markets and determining whether they hold competitive or conflicting accounts. Having done this, agencies can then be evaluated by means of the following criteria:

(i)   The degree of market coverage that they are able to offer.

(ii) The quality of their work in each of these markets.

(iii) The range of marketing services in the fields of public relations, market research, and so on, that each is able to offer.

(iv) The relative roles of the company's advertising department and the advertising agency. In the case of a company with a large advertising department, it may well be that a significant proportion of the work can be done in-house, with the agency taking its direction from this. By way of contrast, if the company's advertising resources are limited, the agency will be expected to perform a far broader role.

(v)   The degree of international co-ordination. Is it the intention to tailor the advertising to each market, or does the company want the advertising to be co-ordinated across the markets?

(vi)   Does the company want to develop a national or an international image? If it is the former, then there is a good case for choosing local agencies.

(vii)   The nature of company organisation. In the case of companies that are essentially decentralised, the choice of an agency is more likely to be left to the local subsidiary.

(viii)   The volume of international business. For firms with a relatively small amount of international business and low levels of advertising expenditure, the funds available may need to be aggregated on a regional basis in order to achieve an acceptable minimum level of service and attract an agency.

(ix)   The type of entry strategy used. Firms that have entered a market by using a joint-venture or licensing arrangement often find either that the decision on the choice of agency has already been made for them by the local partner, or that he has a distinct preference for a particular firm which acts as the determining factor.

For many firms, however, these sorts of criteria are of little real meaning since their desire to operate with a geocentric or global philosophy precludes making use of all but a relatively small number of agencies that are able to offer a global service. When this is the case, the choice of agency is more often than not determined by the way in which the firm operates in its domestic markets.

The Growth of International Agencies

The last ten years has seen a dramatic growth in the number of truly international advertising agencies, particularly in Britain and the United States. There are several reasons for their growth, although for many firms their attraction stems partly from the ways in which costs savings can be made by reducing the amount of duplication of the research and creative aspects involved in developing a campaign, and partly from the scope they offer for centralised advertising control. An additional attraction of an international agency is that greater opportunities exist for developing a broadly standardised approach across a series of markets. The potential benefits of this were recognised by Eastman Kodak when the Kodak Instamatic camera was launched globally at the same time that it was launched in the United States. A number of Kodak's overseas subsidiaries moved their account to J. Walter Thompson's local offices, and Thompson's account executive in the United States then took on the responsibility for co-ordinating the global advertising launch. A similar approach can be seen with many consumer goods for which a broadly similar appeal can be used in a wide variety of markets; the most notable examples of this include Pepsi-Cola and Coca-Cola.

The trend towards international agencies has also been encouraged by the rapid growth in world trade over the past fifteen years, and by a recognition on the part of advertising agencies that substantial profit opportunities exist by maintaining pace with their domestic clients as they establish an ever-larger presence overseas. The need for this is illustrated in part by the way in which the multinationals are increasingly targeting their advertising on a continental and/or international basis, rather than attacking one country at a time. In order to do this effectively, there is an obvious need for a multinational agency service. Recognition of this need is reflected in the way in which the volume of advertising business performed by multinational agencies grew from 13 per cent in 1976 to 21 per cent in 1983, and is estimated to be of the order of 34 per cent by 1990.

There is, of course, also a defensive reason for moving internationally as was illustrated quite dramatically in two notable cases:

The Volkswagen advertising in America was handled very successfully by Doyle Dane Bernbach. When this American agency opened an office in Germany, the Volkswagen company dropped its national agency there and gave the account in Germany to the German office of Doyle Dane Bernbach.
A case well remembered on Madison Avenue is that of the

giant Coca-Cola account. Once held by the D'Arcy agency, the account was lost to McCann-Erickson in the United States after McCann got its foot in the door abroad. Thereafter D'Arcy, too, moved into foreign markets.[6]

This trend towards international agencies should not, however, be seen by itself as evidence of truly global advertising. Instead, many agencies, having developed a basic advertising theme, then modify it to fit the specific needs of various markets.

The International Advertising Budget

Approaches to determining the size of the advertising budget vary enormously and have long been a source of controversy. At the heart of the problem is the difficulty of determining with any real degree of precision what advertising achieves and hence how cost-effective it is. In the case of international advertising, these problems are compounded both by the larger number of markets in which the company is operating, and by the often differing objectives being pursued from one market to another. Nevertheless, in theory at least, the question of how much money to spend is straightforward, with advocates of economic or marginal analysis arguing that money should be spent on advertising until the marginal profit from the marginal pound spent on advertising just equals the marginal profit which results from using that money in the most profitable non-advertising way. In practice, of course, the application of this principle is to all intents impossible, since it requires accurate measurement of the returns not just from advertising, but also from other marketing activities. Because of the obvious difficulty of doing this, a variety of infinitely more pragmatic approaches to advertising budgeting have been developed. In making use of these methods, the marketer should not, however, lose sight of the conceptual validity of the marginal approach, since advertising is not a solitary activity, but needs instead to be seen in terms of its contribution to the overall marketing process.

These more pragmatic approaches vary greatly both in terms of their complexity and the levels of analysis needed to make use of them. They include the *affordable approach* in which the firm spends what it can afford without any real reference either to market opportunities or threats; the *percentage of sales approach* which links advertising expenditure to either previous or forecast sales levels; *competitive parity* in which a competitor's expenditure is matched; and *the objective and task method* which requires a statement of objectives, the identification of the tasks needed to achieve the objectives, and an estimate of the costs of performing these tasks.

Although each of these methods has its advocates, their real value can vary greatly depending upon the type of firm and the competitive environment in which it is operating. Thus, whilst the percentage of sales approach has the advantage of simplicity and a seemingly strong rationale by linking advertising levels to sales, it suffers from the way in which it is the volume of sales that determines the level of advertising rather than the more logical opposite. Equally, one can argue that the percentage applied should vary from one market to another depending upon such factors as opportunities, objectives, the firm's market position, and the structure of competition. In practice, it tends to be the same in each market.

Similarly, competitive parity has the apparent attraction of resting upon the collective wisdom of the industry, but in reality fails to give sufficient recognition to the very different profiles and objectives of the various companies in the market. This is illustrated by the way in which in the cosmetics market Elizabeth Arden spends a considerable amount of money on advertising, whilst Avon relies almost wholly upon personal selling. In these circumstances, the obvious question is which of the two companies should provide the basis for parity. Equally, it is the case in many markets that the multinationals are the largest organisations operating and often have access to far greater funds and expertise. Typically, therefore, they adopt a proactive rather than a reactive stance which is the essence of the competitive parity approach.

Because of these sorts of limitations, the objective and task method has much to commend it, although if it is to be used effectively, the marketer needs a detailed market knowledge so that realistic objectives can be set. In practice, however, evidence suggests that particularly in the early stages of a firm's entry to a market, the sort of detailed knowledge that is needed is simply not there.

Although our discussion so far has concentrated upon the question of *how much* should be spent on advertising, it needs to be remembered that the effectiveness of an advertising campaign is influenced significantly both by the choice of media and the creative strategy that is pursued. In determining the size of the budget, the marketer should therefore also focus upon the scope that exists for improving the *quality* of the advertising appeal and ensure that the media used are as cost-effective as possible.

The Choice of Message

One of the most fundamental of the advertising problems faced by the international marketer is how best to develop advertising appeals for each market. The obvious difficulty that he faces is that each market is unique and there is, therefore, an argument to suggest that separate advertising appeals should be developed for each of the markets he is operating in. For a company that operates in more than a handful of markets, the cost implications of this are likely to be significant, particularly if national markets consist of segments with widely differing buying motives. This, in turn, brings us back to an issue raised at an earlier stage: should the company attempt to project a national or an international image? In practice, the answer to this will vary from one company to another, depending upon the nature of the company's products and of the markets in which they are operating, since in order to communicate effectively the message must be understood by the target group. Thus, although basic needs and desires do not differ between markets, consumers' expectations and the ways in which they are satisfied can vary significantly. Because of this, it is essential that the marketer gets advice from either the local subsidiary or from the advertising agency. At its extreme this is, of course, an argument in favour of decentralising the responsibility for advertising, something which the international marketer who is trying to optimise marketing at a global level may be reluctant to accept. Underlying this, however, is the fundamental issue of whether international advertising is in reality a meaningful concept.

Localised versus Standardised Advertising Appeals

Although the choice between a localised or a standardised advertising strategy might at first sight appear to be relatively straightforward, it is in practice a decision that is often made in the light of arguments based largely on self-interest and political expediency within the organisation. There are several reasons for this, although probably the most common is that in many firms there is a degree of friction and differences in perception between head office and subsidiary staff. In the case of advertising, these differences are often manifested in the way in which the subsidiary argues for a localised approach based upon its specialised local knowledge, whilst for a variety of reasons including cost and indeed his own role within the company, the international advertising manager argues the case for a far higher degree of standardisation. In the circumstances, the eventual choice often proves to be a compromise with the advertising strategy reflecting a broadly standardised approach within which scope exists for tailoring the appeal to local market conditions.

Amongst the other factors that should, however, be taken into account when choosing between localised or standardised appeals are the implications for costs. It is this point in particular which is pursued by the proponents of a standardised approach:

> Once an advertising concept is developed, it can be transferred to other nations with minor additional cost ... Related to this is the realisation of economies of scale, which the centralisation of worldwide advertising authority in the home office allows. In addition, standardisation permits full utilisation of home office advertising expertise hard won on the field. It also prevents the generation of disparate messages in different nations which eventually may blur the established image of the product ... and ensures proper concern for corporate-wide objectives in promoting the product. Finally, similarities in the usage of media among specific segments across nations justify a standardised approach.[7]

These sorts of advantages have long been recognised by many multinationals and are reflected by the way in which American companies in particular have transferred their successful advertisements both to Europe and the Middle East,[8] and by the findings of Donnelly and Ryans that 90 per cent of a sample of Fortune 500 companies made at least some use of their domestic advertising appeals in overseas markets.[9]

Opponents of a standardised approach point, however, to the substantial cultural differences that exist between markets and to the ways in which many attempts to standardise advertising campaigns have in practice failed to match expectations.[10] The possible reasons for this have been pointed to by Hornik who suggests:

> Product (need) universality cannot imply global message appeal ... (Israeli and American women) might manifest the same need for cosmetics (i.e. preservation of beauty), but this certainly does not mean that an Israeli woman perceives the American cosmetic ad the same way it is perceived by the American. Therefore, understanding consumer wants, needs, motives, and behavior is a necessary condition to the development of an effective promotional program.[11]

This theme has in turn been developed by Jain:

> Briefly, product-related attributes influence buyer behavior differently around the globe. Thus, a standard approach to advertising may not be practical. For example, General Motors' Nova car did not do well in Latin America since *no va* translated into Spanish meant 'doesn't go'. Emphasis on 'whiteness' from a laundry detergent will not work in Brazil because Brazilians do not wear white clothes. Chileans buy their coffee strictly on the basis of price. Kentucky Fried Chicken is viewed as an ordinary meal in the United States while the Japanese consider it to be a treat. A television candy commercial for South Africa with a circus elephant had to be changed since the animal is sacred to the Venda people, the segment to which the ad was directed. Besides, the royal title of the wife of the king of neighboring Swaziland is 'she-elephant', and it was feared the ad might offend that country. Students of West African culture recommend against printing an advertisement on white paper there. In West Africa, white is associated with death and it might be perceived as a death notice. Grammatical errors in copy annoy the French. The macho image of a model wearing a hard hat does not excite Latin Americans. They prefer their macho men in suits suitable for executives. Testimonial advertising is considered 'pushy' and 'phony' among the Japanese.[12]

Nevertheless, many companies such as McDonalds, Pepsi Cola, Coca-Cola, 3M and Esso have pursued a standardised approach with considerable success. In the case of Esso, for example, the

'Put a Tiger in Your Tank' campaign travelled around the world with only minor modifications and language changes. Amongst the slogans used were:

Put a tiger in your tank
Putt en tiger pa tanken
Ponga un tigre en su tanque
Kom en tiger i tanken
Metti um tigre nel motore
Tu den tiger in den tank
Pankaa tiikeri tankum
Mettez un tigre dans votre moteur.

Insofar as it is possible, therefore, to identify broad guidelines on the scope that exists for standardisation, it appears that the most important factors are the ways in which the product is used and the role that it plays in the consumption system. Thus, if the product meets the same needs across markets, then the idea of using similar appeals is more feasible. The success achieved by Coca-Cola and McDonalds, for example, suggests that the products satisfy broadly similar needs wherever they are sold. Equally:

> The same product may be purchased for a mixture of functional, convenience, and status reasons, but with a different combination of motivations in each country. The more alike buying motives are, the more desirable the use of common appeals. This is often the case with industrial goods but is less common with consumer durables.[13]

Nevertheless, even where broadly similar buying motives emerge, global advertising may not always work. In the case of 3M, for example, their move towards a global marketing strategy began in 1985 and was based on a worldwide advertising theme stressing the quality and durability of their Scotch video and audio cassettes, and their computer diskettes. In the United Kingdom, their success in the early 1980s was, in turn, helped very substantially by their use of a lifetime guarantee which within two years had pushed their share of the videocassette market from 7 per cent to market leadership with 29 per cent. The same tactic was subsequently used in the United States and then worldwide. Quite deliberately, however, Edoardo Pieruzzi, the worldwide head of 3M's magnetic audio/video division, whilst recognising the scope for a global product strategy, has dismissed the possibility of global advertising because of the idiosyncratic nature of the different markets in which they have a presence, and makes use of several advertising agencies.[14]

In an attempt to put these arguments into some sort of perspective, McCann-Erickson have developed a series of broad guidelines designed to illustrate the circumstances in which marketing and advertising standardisation is most likely to be effective (see Figure 8.1).

The Choice of Media

The growth of the advertising industry throughout the world is to a very large extent related to the development of mass media. The larger and the more complex the society, the greater is the choice available to the marketer. There are, however, substantial variations in the availability of media from one market to another as is illustrated by the way in which in 1980 India had some 992 daily newspapers but with a rather limited total circulation, whilst Great Britain's 125 daily papers achieved circulation figures of more than 25 million. Similarly, the availability of television varies enormously from one market to another with, in 1981, 609 sets per 1,000 population in the United States, 547 in Japan, 361 in the United Kingdom, 303 in France, 230 in Israel, but only 2 per 1,000 population in India. Equally, the number of magazines varies enormously with India having almost 15,000, the United States 10,000, France 7,000, the United Kingdom 3,000, Japan 430, and Saudi Arabia only 7.[15] Thus, although the principles of media selection are by now well-established, their application is likely to vary greatly from one country to another.

The primary objective in media selection is, of course, to reach the target market in the most cost-effective manner. It needs to be remembered, however, that cultural differences between markets are often significant and that one consequence of this is that the nature and degree of influence upon the purchasing decision that is exerted by, say, the husband and wife can vary markedly from country to country. There is a strong argument, therefore, for passing much of the responsibility for media selection to the local advertising agency or to the company's staff in the area. Indeed, as

Figure 8.1: Guidelines for Effective Marketing and Advertising Standardisation

Marketing standardisation works least well . . .	Marketing standardisation works best . . .	Advertising centralisation (one campaign) works best when the campaign . . .
• When the brand is established, national, or ethnic.	• When the brand is contemporary, international, fashion-orientated.	• Has a strong creative idea.
• Has differing price-value connotations.	• Is marketed at similar price levels to similar audiences.	• Is image orientated.
• Has a different consumption pattern.	• Has similar consumption patterns.	• Or product performance orientated.
• Appeals to older consumers.	• Is younger, or youth orientated.	• Is not dependent on price or promotion.
• Is a basic product (like food).	• Is an indulgence product, rather than a necessity.	• Avoids local personalities, models or slogans.
		• Has a strong central 'brand property'.

Reproduced with the permission of McCann-Erickson.

Wills discovered in a study of 28 multinationals, the greatest role of subsidiaries in advertising was in the area of media selection.[16] This is not to say, however, that the international advertising manager should not have some involvement in the task. By virtue of his position, he is often able both to provide an extra level of expertise in terms of media selction and to co-ordinate the local campaign with any international campaign thus is being run concurrently. His position is, however, complicated both by the ways in which media availability differs so greatly from one market to another, and by the often very different legal constraints that are placed upon the amount and type of advertising allowed.

An additional complication in many cases stems from the lack of reliable information on circulation and audience characteristics. Although in Great Britain and the United States advertisers have access to a considerable amount of information on the size of audiences and their socio-economic characteristics, few other markets offer such detailed profiles and all too often the advertiser is faced with either an almost total lack of audience data or unaudited figures provided by the media themselves. The effects of this lack of accurate information are felt in a number of ways and affect not only the media selection decisions, but also the methods used subsequently to assess the effectiveness of the advertising campaign.

Measuring Advertising Effectiveness

Approaches to measuring the effectiveness of advertising vary enormously in their complexity and sophistication and range from the occasional *ad hoc* assessment of whether advertising *appears* to be working, through to the use of mathematical models incorporating economic and competitive variables. Perhaps surprisingly, however, relatively few multinationals appear to pursue a consistent or sustained policy of assessing advertising's sales performance. There are several apparent reasons for this, including pressure upon budgets which places a higher priority upon other marketing activities; the relative lack of expertise in this area amongst subsidiary staff; the possible lack of marketing research facilities; and, in many smaller markets, a feeling that the exercise is simply not worthwhile. Nevertheless, there are several ways in which advertising effectiveness can be measured — in broad terms at least

— at a relatively low cost both before and after the advertisements have been run. They include opinion and attitude ratings, laboratory tests, measures of recognition and recall, and sales card enquiries. All too often, however, the distance and communications gap between the head office and subsidiary staff together with the often relatively lower levels of advertising in all but a few international markets, leads firms to ignoring the need for assessing advertising's effectiveness.

Organisational Issues

In organising for international advertising, three major alternatives are open to the company: (1) to centralise the decision-making at head office; (2) to decentralise the decision-making to the subsidiaries; or (3) to develop a mixture of the two. In practice, of course, the decision cannot be viewed in isolation but will instead be influenced by the firm's overall international structure and by the levels of expertise available at head office and subsidiary level. The question of how best to organise the firm as a whole is discussed in Chapter 10 and at this stage, therefore, we will limit ourselves to a rather broader treatment of the sorts of factors that are of particular relevance to advertising.

Centralisation. The implication of centralisation, which in practice is rarely total, is that the decisions concerning the development of the campaign, determination of the advertising budget, and the choice both of agency and media are all made at headquarters level. The obvious appeal of this for many managers is the degree of control that it provides them with. For it to be a feasible or a realistic alternative does, however, depend upon a number of conditions being present. Perhaps the most important of these are that the company is working with an international agency with branches or subsidiaries that cover all of its markets, and that headquarters staff know the foreign markets sufficiently well to make valid decisions. In addition, the channels of communication that exist must be sufficiently well developed both for control to be exerted and for information to flow back.

The argument advanced most frequently to justify such an approach is that it leads to economies of scale both in staffing and administration. At the same time, however, it needs to be recognised that it can also lead to a degree of rigidity and a failure to recognise and adapt to local market needs which in the end may well prove to be counter-productive.

Decentralisation. As an alternative to centralising its advertising decision-making, the company may choose to go for almost total decentralisation in which each national operating unit is made responsible for its own advertising. The circumstances in which this is likely to be a realistic alternative are very broadly when the company is attempting to develop a national rather than an international image; when the company has a high degree of confidence in the locally based staff; and possibly when communications between the headquarters and national operations make centralisation an unrealistic proposition.

The most obvious advantages of a decentralised approach are that it should lead to higher levels of motivation at the local level and result in more specifically tailored advertising programmes. The major disadvantages are that the parent company is heavily dependent upon the skills of the staff at the local level and that in smaller markets in particular, the cost-effectiveness of advertising campaigns is likely to be low.

A Mixture of the Two. In practice, few companies opt for either total centralisation or total decentralisation, and attempt instead to reach a happy medium that makes use of the best aspects of each, whilst avoiding the sort of shortcomings to which each is prone. The result is a system to which each contributes his particular strengths. Sometimes referred to as 'co-ordinated decentralisation', it typically involves the international advertising manager in developing the advertising policy, overseeing the basic creative work (including the selection of an advertising theme), and establishing standardised operation procedures for all subsidiaries. The staff at the national level then have responsibility for selecting media, modifying the advertising appeal to meet the specific demands of the local market, and generally implementing the corporate guidelines. In this way, the company achieves a degree of conformity at the international level, whilst at the same time benefiting from local inputs and expertise.

Image, Reputation and Country of Origin

Image and reputation are essential elements of long-term marketing success and, as many companies have found to their cost, are often affected by factors outside the firm's control. For companies operating internationally, image takes on an added importance and is influenced not just by the company's behaviour and marketing mix, but also by the image of the home country. It is the case therefore that:

> The increasing internationalisation of managers means that, even without direct experience of a particular company, individual managers are increasingly aware of, and making judgements about, the characteristics of companies throughout the world ... if British companies have a general reputation for trustworthiness, then a buyer will be influenced by this when considering and forming an opinion about a particular British supplier company. Thus, the generalised reputation of a country will affect the ability of all companies of that country to win export business.[17]

The significance of this has been illustrated in a number of cases, including the often poor reputation for quality of British cars in the North American market, and by the generally favourable reaction throughout the world to products originating from Germany and Japan.

Given the very obvious marketing implications of a country's general reputation, Turnbull, in a study of 416 purchasing executives in France, Germany, Sweden, Italy and the United Kingdom, examined the attitudes of buyers in Europe to Britain, together with their perceptions of British marketing competence. By adopting a comparative approach, he was able to illustrate the relative perceptions of each country and arrive at an overall measure of image. His findings revealed that, on balance, the image and reputation of British suppliers throughout Europe when measured in terms of their customer orientation, technical and commercial competence, delivery performance, after-sales service, new product technology, and product quality, lagged behind German, Swedish and French suppliers by a considerable margin, and were on par with the image and reputation of Italian firms. The particular areas of weakness amongst British companies proved to be in the areas of product quality and delivery. German firms, by way of contrast, scored very highly on all of these dimensions, and particularly in the areas of product quality, and technical and commercial competence, and in their analysis of customer needs, willingness to adapt the product to fit specific requirements, their understanding of customer problems and methods of operation, and in their sensitivity to complaints.

German firms also performed extremely well when compared with British firms in the general area of customer service, a phrase which is used to include after-sales follow-up, the availability of information, the provision of information in a foreign language, and in ensuring that customers are kept up-to-date with the latest technical and product developments. The significance of these findings was emphasised by Turnbull in a concluding comment:

> Foreign buyers are less than enthusiastic about British suppliers and it is disturbing to note that between one-fifth and a third of foreign buyers are unhappy about having to buy from the UK. One can surmise that many such buyers were only buying from the UK because of the lower prices of British products at the time of the study, or because no alternative source of supply was available. If this is so, then loyalty to suppliers must be low and buyers will switch to other sources of supply as they become available and/or are competitively priced.[18]

On the positive side, however, Turnbull found that the British have a very 'personal' style of marketing characterised by an emphasis upon personal contacts and face-to-face meetings, an approach which the Swedish in particular responded to favourably. At the same time, however, he also discovered evidence of a considerable cultural gap between the British and the French which, from the French side, led to a degree of reluctance to conduct business with British firms.

Summary

For many companies, international advertising decisions pose considerable problems. To a very large extent, these stem from the cultural and language differences that exist between markets, although they are in turn exacerbated by such factors as the very different levels of media availability and possible conflicts between head office and subsidiary staff. A number of significant trends have become apparent in recent years, including the growth of international agencies and a greater emphasis upon global advertising. In many cases, however, advertising decisions are still made on either a local or a regional basis, with the firm's international advertising manager acting as the co-ordinator across a series of markets.

References

1. D. Ricks, M.Y.C. Fu and J.C. Arpan, (1982), *International Business Blunders*, revised edn (Columbus Grid Inc, 1982).
2. 'Anti Advertising Movement Worldwide, I.A.A. Head Says', *Advertising Age*, 43, 25 September 1972, p. 68.
3. See V. Terpstra, *International Marketing* (The Dryden Press, 1978), pp. 438-9.
4. E.W. Cundiff and M.T. Hilger, *Marketing in the International Environment* (Prentice Hall, 1984), p. 327.
5. M. Mayer, *Madison Avenue, U.S.A.* (Harper and Row, 1958).
6. Terpstra, *International Marketing*, p. 399.
7. S.C. Jain, *International Marketing Management* (Kent Publishing Co. 1984), p. 462.
8. M. Colvin, R. Heeler and J. Thorpe, 'Developing International Advertising Strategy', *Journal of Marketing*, Autumn (1980), pp. 73-9.
9. J.H. Donnelly and J.K. Ryans, 'Standardised Global Advertising', *Journal of Marketing*, April (1969), pp. 57-69.
10. See, e.g. J. Killough, 'Improved Payoffs from Transnational Advertising', *Harvard Business Review*, July-August (1978), p. 103.
11. J. Hornik, 'Comparative Evaluation of International versus National Advertising Strategies', *Columbia Journal of World Business*, Spring (1980), p. 43.
12. Jain, *International Marketing Management*, p. 464.
13. Terpstra, *International Marketing*, p. 405.
14. *Marketing*, 20 June 1985.
15. *World Advertising Expenditures* (New York, International Advertising Association, 1981) pp. 44-5.
17. J.R. Wills, *The Role of Headquarters Management in Non-Domestic Advertising Decisions*, unpublished (1976).
18. P. W. Turnbull, 'The Image and Reputation of British Suppliers in Western Europe', *European Journal of Marketing*, vol. 19, no. 6 (1985), p. 39.

Further Reading

For an interesting treatment of the arguments for and against global advertising strategies, see 'Global Marketing and Global Agencies: Papers from a Seminar', in *Admap*, September (1985), pp. 419-39, and S. Winram, 'The Opportunity for World Brands', *International Journal of Advertising*, vol. 3, no. 1 (1984), pp. 17-26.

9 INTERNATIONAL DISTRIBUTION AND LOGISTICAL DECISIONS

In an earlier chapter, we examined the ways in which companies might enter foreign markets and discussed how the choice of entry influences the risks, costs and level of commitment of the international marketing process. Within this chapter, we turn our attention to the ways in which firms select their channels of distribution *within* the market and subsequently how they go about the process of physical distribution.

International Channels of Distribution

The choice of channels of distribution is one of the most fundamental and far-reaching decisions faced by the domestic marketer. In the case of international marketing, the decision is made far more complex by virtue of the greater number of markets in which the company is operating, their physical distance, its distributive peculiarities, and the marketer's probable unfamiliarity with the market and its particular legal, cultural and political characteristics. Nevertheless, it needs to be remembered that a poor choice of distribution channels is likely to spell commercial disaster for even the best product. In making a choice, therefore, there is a need for a detailed analysis of the alternatives that are open to the company and of the ways in which they might best be exploited.

In examining how international companies have developed their distribution channels, a number of commentators have observed that two major approaches can be identified. The first of these tends to be pursued by companies with a manufacturing or production orientation for which the major criterion when selecting channels appears to be the logistical aspects. Thus, it is the location of the firm's *manufacturing* capacity which influences the choice of markets and channels. The second approach, by way of contrast, reflects a very different philosophy and involves identifying marketing opportunities, determining the patterns of distribution, and subsequently recommending where manufacturing should be located so that the marketing objectives are served most effectively. Referred to as *market logistics*, this approach begins with the marketplace and works backwards to the factory.

The Channel Decision

The significance of the channel decision stems from two main factors: firstly, the way in which the choice of channel influences every other marketing decision, and secondly, that it involves the organisation in what is normally a long-term commitment from which it is often both difficult and expensive to escape. There is, therefore, a substantial degree of inertia that, within marketing, is peculiar to channel arrangements. In choosing channels, particularly in international markets, the marketer must therefore attempt to determine not only what is appropriate for today's market, but also how market conditions — and hence distribution demands — are likely to change over time.

In approaching the channel decision, possibly one of the greatest problems faced by the international marketer stems from any preconceived notions and preferences that he has. The channels of distribution available in any particular country emerge as the result of culture and tradition, and are likely to vary considerably even between neighbouring countries. In Japan, for example, there is often a myriad of channels involved in the distribution of a product, and channel structures lack the degree of consolidation and ease of access that is often the case in European markets. It is this which has led many international marketers to level the criticism that, despite the fact that Japan is one of the largest economic powers in the world today, its system of distribution is complex, cumbersome, outmoded and highly inefficient. This is illustrated by the way in which many products move through three or more wholesalers and then a sales company before reaching a retail outlet. An additional source of complexity and inefficiency with which the marketer has to cope is that the wholesale networks are for the most part highly product specific.

For the international marketer, the barriers to entry that the Japanese have long imposed are often sufficient obstacles by themselves; the added complications and intricacies of Japanese channels of distribution simply make access to the market more expensive and far less attractive. Equally, channels in the developing countries tend to be scattered, limited in scope, inefficient and often insufficient. By way of contrast, Finland has what is arguably one of the most highly concentrated large-scale wholesaling operations in the world with just four large wholesaling groups accounting for most of the country's wholesale trade. Indeed, the largest of these, Kesko (The Wholesale Company of Finnish Retailers), has a market share of more than 20 per cent and services some 12,000 retailers throughout the country. Any system of international distribution must of necessity, therefore, be developed within the general constraints of each individual country's established patterns and practices, with innovations being introduced only slowly.

Approaches to Managing Foreign Distribution

By referring back to Chapter 4 in which we considered the various market entry strategies open to a company, it should be evident that the problems of managing foreign distribution will vary considerably depending upon whether the firm opts for indirect or direct methods of international marketing. For those companies that opt for the former by selling through trading companies or export management companies, the patterns of distribution offered by the foreign distributor generally give little scope for change. It is generally the case, therefore, that the pattern of distribution acts as a constraint within which the company has to operate in the most effective manner that it can identify. For companies that opt for one or other forms of *direct* international marketing, the situation facing them does, however, differ considerably in that the firm is in the position of having to establish or modify a pattern of distribution that not only satisfies their short- and long-term marketing objectives, but which is also capable of fitting into the distributive infrastructures that already exist within each of the target markets. The ways in which this can be done depends to a large extent upon the firm's profile and resources, as well as the method chosen to establish any foreign subsidiaries. Thus, where it is the case that the subsidiary is a joint venture, the freedom to establish particular patterns of distribution may well be influenced by the objectives and previous methods of operation of the national partner. Similarly, where the subsidiary is the result of an acquisition, the firm will find that, in the short term at least, its distribution options are limited by the previous practices that have been inherited. It is, therefore, only when the firm is starting from scratch that it can be said that there is any real degree of latitude in establishing an international distribution network. However, even in these circumstances, the apparent freedom may well prove to be misleading in that the market's existing distributive infrastructure offers little opportunity for radical change. The strategic decisions that face the international marketer are therefore:

1. Should the firm extend its domestic distribution approach uniformly to foreign markets or adapt its distribution strategy to each national market?
2. Should the firm use direct or indirect channels in foreign markets?
3. Should the firm use selective or widespread distribution?
4. How can the firm manage the channel?
5. How can the firm keep its distribution strategy up-to-date?[1]

In practice many firms attempt to ease their market entry and channel problems by making use of export and import middlemen who will take on the responsibility for distributing the product. In doing this, however, the firm may well find that its distribution alternatives are limited significantly.

Types of Channel in International Marketing

The availability of distribution channels varies significantly from market to market, even within the industrialised world. Figures 9.1 and 9.2 however, illustrate the various types of channel that a marketing manager might reasonably expect to find existing in developed markets. It needs to be recognised, however, that the figure is illustrative and that not every form of distribution will exist in every market. Nevertheless, the channels illustrated can be characterised according to the number of levels that exist, with each of the institutions that carries out some part of the task of taking the product from the manufacturer to the final user being seen as a channel level; the fewer the number of intermediaries, the shorter the channel is said to be. However, in entering a market and emerging with a distribution network, it is, as we have observed, that all too often the manufacturer has to reconcile what is available and what is ideal.

Figure 9.1: International Channel Alternatives for Consumer Products

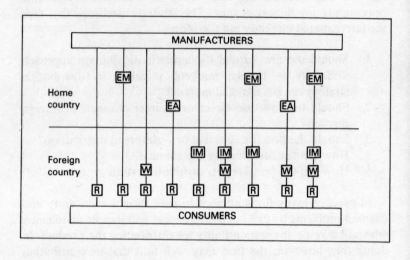

Figure 9.2: International Channel Alternatives for Industrial Products

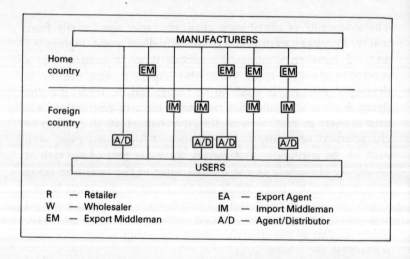

R	— Retailer	EA	— Export Agent
W	— Wholesaler	IM	— Import Middleman
EM	— Export Middleman	A/D	— Agent/Distributor

Factors in Channel Selection

In choosing between the channel alternatives that exist, the marketer can not afford to lose sight of the fact that distribution choices generally represent long-term commitments from which it is difficult to escape if they subsequently prove to be less than appropriate. The choice of a distribution pattern is also significant and far-reaching in that it has long-term implications both for the company's ability to exploit a particular market and for the other elements of the marketing mix.

With regard to the first of these, the significance of the decision stems in part from the way in which legislation differs from one country to another. Thus, it may well be the case that the firm enters into an agreement with distributors when it first enters a market, and then for one or more of a wide variety of reasons, decides at a later stage to change its strategy. Altering or cancelling its earlier commitments to suppliers who fail to fit neatly into the new programmes is likely to prove both costly and time-consuming. It is therefore essential that the full implications of any long-term arrangements that the firm enters into are recognised from the outset. Because of this, the marketer needs to take account of five main issues before making his choice. They are:

(i)   the firm's international objectives;
(ii) the nature and availability of channels;
(iii) the financial and marketing implications of each of the alternatives;
(iv) the characteristics of the market;
(v)   the product.

Together, these fit into a tripartite framework of economic, control and adaptive selection criteria. Thus, in establishing the network, the marketer needs to identify the costs and likely returns from each of the alternatives open to him at various levels of sales. This can be illustrated by comparing the use of the company's own sales force with that of sales agents. The marketer recognises from the outset that employing his own sales force will be expensive, but that at the same time he will have a far higher degree of control over their call patterns and level of commitment. This in turn should lead to higher levels of sales. Nevertheless, using sales agents can often prove advantageous insofar as they offer greater flexibility and lower intitial costs. They may also have the added advantage of providing more immediate contact with the market. The costs and benefits of these two approaches can be compared with a straightforward break-even chart as illustrated in Figure 9.3. In these circumstances the marketer may decide that a sales level of X_1 is unlikely to be achieved and that in the short term at least, using sales agents would be more economical than employing his own sales force. At the same time, however, he cannot afford to lose sight of the control and adaptive implications of the decision, since sales agents often pose considerable problems of control. The reason for this is that sales agents are independent firms with their own profit objectives. They may well therefore concentrate upon other products they handle offering greater and possibly easier sales and profit levels.

It is because of this, together with the dynamic nature of many markets which can quickly invalidate existing distribution arrangements, that thought also needs to be given to the scope that exists for adapting or modifying the distributive network. We have already made the observation that distribution represents a long-

Figure 9.3: Break-Even Chart for a Comparison of a Company Sales Force and a Sales Agency

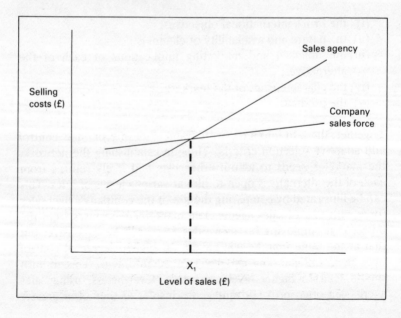

term commitment; whenever possible, therefore, the marketer needs to maximise the degree of flexibility and scope for alteration if he is to be able to cope effectively with changing market conditions.

It is in the light of this general framework that the marketer can then begin to evaluate the rather more specific issues that influence distribution choice.

The Firm's International Objectives.   Although the importance of establishing objectives has already been referred to at several earlier points in the text, we make no apology for returning to it here. A distribution policy cannot be determined until the firm's overall international objectives have been clearly established. The significance of this can perhaps be illustrated by considering the various objectives that a firm might pursue and how these influence the attractiveness of distribution alternatives. Thus it may be the case that the company wishes to restrict its investment in any one country to less than £2 million. Alternatively, it may be that the international marketing objective is to operate only in those markets which are capable of producing sales of, say, £5 million within four years of entry. Similarly, it may be that the firm has market share goals that can only be achieved in countries with a particular competitive profile, or that the company wishes to minimise risk by operating only in those parts of the world which have a very stable political environment. In each case, there are several implications for the choice of channels. In the case of the firm which wishes to limit its investment, sales agents may well prove to be the only realistic option. By way of contrast, if the firm has an objective of achieving a high market profile, it is likely that it will opt for its own sales force and support services.

Nevertheless, regardless of what the objectives are, it is clearly important that they are established at an early stage and that they are then taken into account when evaluating alternatives.

The Nature and Availability of Channels.   Having established the firm's overall objectives, the marketer needs then to turn his attention to the nature and availability of channels in each of the markets. It is almost inevitable that the marketer will approach a new market with certain preconceived notions and have a preference for particular patterns of distribution. However, as we observed in the introduction to this chapter, the distributive infrastructure of each country differs and, simply because one country has a particular form of distribution, there is no guarantee that this will be duplicated elsewhere, even in a neighbouring country. Because of this, there is a need for a marketing profile analysis which, in the light of the firm's objectives and product range, highlights the advantages and disadvantages of the channel alternatives.

But as well as giving consideration to the nature of each market's distributive infrastructure, there is also a need to focus upon their availability. It may well be that a company would like to make use of a particular form of distribution but that this is made difficult either because a competitor has already established himself within it and left little or no room for anyone else, or that the chosen distributor simply does not want to handle the firm's product. These sorts of problems were faced by Timex in the early stages of the company's development when it experienced difficulties in persuading jewellers to stock its watches. Because of this, the company opted for a different distribution network completely by going into mass-merchandising markets such as supermarkets and chemists. In retrospect, the jewellers' reluctance can be seen as a mistake, albeit an understandable one, since it was Timex that pioneered low-cost watches and opened up what subsequently proved to be a very sizeable market segment. Once the size and value of this market began to become apparent, jewellers changed their policy rapidly.

This lack of willingness on the part of a distribution network to handle a product is, for obvious reasons, most likely to be encountered in the early stages of a firm's entry to the market, particularly if the company is not able to offer a demonstrably significant marketing advantage such as superior product performance or high levels of advertising.

The availability of channels will also be influenced by the company itself, its size and its reputation. Thus, the well-known and well-established companies with a high profile consumer franchise such as IBM, McDonalds, Philips, Colgate-Palmolive, and Procter and Gamble, have little trouble recruiting middlemen. By way of contrast, many medium-sized firms, particularly in the industrial sector, experience significant difficulties in attracting distributors with the necessary expertise, a factor which in turn has implications for the terms of agreement between the two sides.

Nevertheless, regardless of whether the company finds it easy or difficult to recruit middlemen, attention needs to be paid to such factors as the number of years for which they have been in business, the other product lines carried, the growth and profit records, their co-operativeness and reputation, and the back-up support that they are able to provide.

Financial Implications. An analysis of the financial aspects of the distribution alternatives open to the company needs to take account of two factors: firstly, the relative costs of each of the various channels, and secondly, the consequences for the subsequent patterns of cash flow. The starting point for such an analysis can be the sort of break-even evaluation that we referred to briefly at an earlier stage, since the results can be used as a means of narrowing the field of choice and hence reduce the number requiring a detailed analysis.

In comparing in detail the *relative costs* of each channel, it needs to be remembered that non-recurring start-up costs are likely to vary significantly and that it is the long-term picture which is of greater significance. The analysis also needs to take account of the levels of performance and the returns that might realistically be expected. Thus, it might be the case that the costs associated with direct marketing are low when compared with the costs of setting up a sales force. If, however, the marketer goes on to forecast the returns that might feasibly be expected from each, it is possible that the extra sales volume that would be generated by the sales force would, *in the long term*, more than compensate for the difference. It is, therefore, both the total costs and the total returns to the business over a pre-determined time period that need to be identified and taken into account in the analysis.

The second major financial dimension that is of importance is *the pattern of cash flow* that emerges from each of the alternatives. By using wholesalers and retailers, cash flow problems are likely to be eased considerably, largely because of the cushion that middlemen provide by holding and paying for stock. By way of contrast, in a direct channel, the stock is held by the manufacturer with consequent implications both for cash flow and capital.

In examining the capital implications of distribution choice, the marketer needs to consider such points as whether finance can be raised locally; whether foreign companies are subject to special borrowing restrictions; the stability of the local currency; whether foreign firms are eligible for grants; and whether earnings and capital can be taken out of the country. If restrictions do exist, there is an obvious need to limit the level of direct investment as far as possible.

Characteristics of the Market.   A further factor for consideration in this process of evaluation is the market itself, the nature of its needs, its stage of development, and its future prospects. Thus, account needs to be taken of:

(i)   the size of the market;
(ii)   levels of disposable income;
(iii) patterns of income distribution within the population;
(iv)   the economic wealth of the country;
(v)   the potential for market growth;
(vi)   purchasing patterns and habits of consumers;
(vii) the existence of trade associations and cartels;
(viii) government attitudes to foreign competition.

The Product.   The final factor of importance in this process of channel evaluation is the product itself, since this quite obviously will have a significant influence upon the appropriateness of any particular channel alternative. Thus, *perishable* products require more direct channels because of the dangers associated with repeated handling and delays in delivery. Products that are *bulky* relative to their value, such as building materials and some food-stuffs, generally call for channels that keep the shipping distance and number of handlings to a minimum. *Unstandardised* products such as custom-built machine tools are generally sold on a direct basis because of the difficulties that are usually encountered in finding middlemen with the necessary product knowledge. Similarly, products that require installation or maintenance *services* are often best sold and maintained by the company or by a limited number of franchised dealers. Finally, products which have a *high unit value* are generally sold through a company sales force rather than through middlemen.

Other Corporate Issues

So far, our discussion of the factors that influence the choice of distribution channels has focused upon some of the rather more obvious elements in the evaluation process, such as financial considerations and the nature and availability of the channel alternatives. These do, however, need to be viewed against the general background of any constraints within the organisation itself, but particularly managerial resources and expertise, the company's image, the existing organisational structure, and existing patterns of distribution for the firm's products.

Managing and Motivating Channel Middlemen

Having evaluated the distribution alternatives available and decided upon the pattern that is to be used, the marketer needs then to consider how best to manage and motivate the middlemen involved, since the success of the firm's international operation is inextricably linked to their attitude and performance. In deciding how best to do this, there are several major areas to which attention should be paid, including:

(i)   the creation of distributor loyalty;
(ii) ensuring levels of remuneration are adequate and appropriate;
(iii) developing a training programme for distributor and his staff;
(iv) setting and evaluating levels of performance;
(v)   developing a system of communication between distributors.

In attempting to build up distributor loyalty, it is essential that emphasis is placed upon the relationship being a long-term one, since without this there is little real incentive for the distributor to do anything more than the minimum. There are several ways in which loyalty can be developed, but at the heart of all of these is the creation of a feeling of belonging to the organisation. This can be achieved by building effective channels of commnication between the parent company and the distributor by means of house magazines, a regular programme of visits by headquarters staff to the distributor, arranging periodic visits to headquarters for the distributor and his senior staff, discussion of sales targets and long-term objectives, and by sales competitions. Nevertheless, many companies use relatively unsophisticated approaches to motivation. These approaches have been labelled by a number of commentators as the carrot-and-stick approach, since the motivators alternate between positive elements such as high margins, special deals, advertising allowances, and sales contests, and negative sanctions such as slowing down delivery schedules and threatening to terminate the relationship. In discussing this somewhat crude stimulus–response approach to management, McCammon has said that 'many manufacturers' incentives programmes consist of hastily improvised trade deals, uninspired dealer contests, and unexamined discount structures'.[2]

A far better and potentially more fruitful approach is based upon recognising that the relationship is a partnership from which both can benefit. In this way the marketer can develop a far clearer understanding of what it wants from its distribution network and then develop an agreement with its distributors that maximises the likelihood of achieving it. Referred to as 'distribution programming', Kotler defines this as:

> building a planned, professionally managed, vertically integrated marketing system that incorporates the needs of both the manufacturer and the distributor. The manufacturer establishes a department within the marketing department called distributor relations planning and its job is to identify the distributors' needs and build up merchandising programmes to help each distributor operate as optimally as possible. This department and the distributor jointly plan the merchandising goals, inventory levels, space and visual merchandising plans, sales training requirements and advertising and promotional plans. The aim is to convert the distributors from thinking that they make their money primarily on the buying side (through an adversarial relation with the suppliers) to seeing that they make their money on the selling side by being part of a sophisticated vertical marketing system.[3]

An important part of this, of course, is the whole issue of *remuneration*. It has long been recognised that money alone is a poor motivator, although equally a distributor is unlikely to commit his own organisation unless it is financially worthwhile. In developing a remuneration package for middlemen, particularly on an international scale, there are few hard and fast rules, although generally the package would be made up of commission, a contribution towards promotional costs, prompt payment discounts, and periodic financial incentives to reach special seasonal targets.

Nevertheless, although there are few hard and fast rules, care needs to be taken to ensure that the total package neither under- nor over-remunerates the distributor, since the former will lead to an obvious lack of motivation, whilst the latter will adversely affect profit as well as subsequently creating possible difficulties between markets as the company learns from its mistakes and imposes a more realistic package in a new market.

The objective that should therefore be borne in mind is the creation of a package that will reward the distributor adequately for his efforts, whilst at the same time ensuring that inequalities between markets do not develop.

The third aspect of managing channel middlemen is the *development of a training programme.* In establishing such a programme, several objectives need to be pursued. The first and perhaps the most obvious of these involves ensuring that levels of product knowledge are fully developed. In addition, however, training sessions can contribute significantly to feelings of loyalty, as well as providing an ideal platform for an exchange of views between distributors and between the distribution network and the parent company.

In setting *performance standards* for distributors the inter- national marketer needs to aim for a target that is both realistic and achievable, since if it is too high there will be little incentive for the distributor to aim for it, whilst if it is too low it is likely that substantial market potential will not be realised. Arguably the best way in which to set the performance standards, therefore, is by the distributor and the parent company jointly agreeing upon the targets that are to be pursued (at this stage it is worth referring back to Chapter 5 in which we discuss approaches to planning in detail). The performance standards agreed upon should not, however, simply be limited to sales, but should also embrace a variety of other areas including advertising and publicity. A suit- able checklist might therefore include targets relative to:

- sales volume
- market share
- market growth
- new accounts
- prices and margins
- advertising and publicity
- the firm's image

- the amount of floor space relative to competitors' products
- new product introductions

Having established these performance standards, the international marketer needs subsequently *to measure and evaluate the performance* that is actually achieved. In carrying out this exercise it is imperative that the distributor sees it as a means of identifying any weaknesses that exist so that corrective action can be taken at an early stage, rather than as a punitive or futile bureaucratic exercise by head office. It should also be recognised, however, that if the targets have been agreed jointly and are realistic, but that the distributor consistently fails to meet them without good reason, this is a basis for withdrawing the distributor's franchise.

A final way in which distributor loyalty can be encouraged is by means of strong advertising support. International firms often have an advantage over national firms in this respect in that they are generally likely to have access to greater financial resources, as well as to greater expertise. It has been said of Procter and Gamble, for example, that the company is able to enter any Western European country and 'buy' 15 per cent share of a market almost immediately, simply on the strength of its advertising. Although this is a somewhat extreme and possibly apocryphal example of how advertising support can play a role in motivating channel members, it does illustrate how the resources of the international company can be used to build confidence and relationships within the channel.

The Terms and Responsibilities of Middlemen

In arriving at an agreement with middlemen, the marketer needs to specify in detail the responsibilities of each of the channel members. Typically, these responsibilities cover the major elements of the 'trade relations mix', and include pricing policies, the conditions of sale, territorial coverage, and the specific services that each is required to carry out.

Although in some markets, distributors are given considerable freedom to price the product as they wish, a more conventional arrangement involves the producer in establishing a *pricing policy* in the form of a list price and series of discounts for different target groups and for different quantities purchased. The *conditions of sale* refer to payment terms and to guarantees that come into play. Thus, it is likely that the distributors would be eligible for such things as prompt payment discounts, and that any faulty products would be replaced free of charge. The third element in any agreement is that of *territorial coverage and rights*. Most distributors require some form of assurance that other distributors will not intrude upon their territory and that the area for which they are responsible offers sufficient scope for a worthwhile level of sales. The fourth and final major aspect of the trade relations mix relates to the *services* that the producer and distributor are each responsible for. Most frequently, this covers levels of advertising support for the product, appearances at trade shows, and achieving a certain level of publicity.

The Evolution of International Channels

In Chapter 4 we commented that many companies begin their international operations either by straightforward exporting or licensing and that over time they gradually move towards more complex approaches involving greater expertise, commitment and expense. One consequence of this, of course, is that channel arrangements made in the early stages of a firm's international operations may prove to be less than ideal at a later stage. When this occurs, the international marketer needs to determine whether the existing channels can be modified sufficiently to cope with the new and changed demands, or whether totally new channels should be developed. This process of evolution has a number of important consequences and because of the long-term nature and importance of distribution decisions, the question of *when* and *how* to change needs to be considered carefully. In part, the need for change can be minimised by selecting distributors carefully in the early stages and by placing emphasis upon their flexibility and capability for growth.

If, however, having established itself in a particular market the firm then recognises a need for change, it should ensure that the possible repercussions of the change are handled smoothly. Prominent amongst the sorts of problems that firms typically encounter is a degree of antagonism and insecurity from other distributors who, seeing change elsewhere, feel threatened themselves. In some countries, particularly in the developing world, changes made to existing and perhaps well-established distribution arrangements can also lead to a certain amount of government reaction. It is essential, therefore, that in making changes, full consideration is given to all of the possible consequences.

A further factor that should be borne in mind by the international marketer is that in certain countries the distributor who has invested time and money in building up sales for a foreign firm is eligible for compensation if the arrangements are subsequently changed.

Because of these potential problems, the marketer should attempt to build in a degree of flexibility from the outset, possibly by means of a clause in the distributor's contract which spells out the circumstances in which the contract may be terminated. The contract should then go on to specify the nature of any financial compensation that is payable.

Overall, therefore, altering distribution arrangements is a complex and potentially risky activity which, if handled badly, is likely to have serious and financially significant consequences for the firm.

Physical Distribution in International Markets

Having selected the channels that are to be used, the international marketer is then faced with the task of developing and organising the logistical or physical distribution system that will ensure the right product is in the right place at the right time. It is only if this system is developed effectively that the objectives of the international marketing task will be achieved. Nevertheless, despite the crucial importance of physical distribution, it is an aspect of the marketing task that often fails to receive the attention it deserves. The result is that the entire marketing system suffers. In commenting upon this, Majaro has said:

> It is often forgotten that physical distribution represents a significant cost area and any savings can amount to important amounts and profit improvement. In primary metals, chemicals and petroleum products physical distribution can amount to as much as 25 per cent of the sales revenue. In the food manufacturing industry it often amounts to as much as 30 per cent.[4]

Similar sentiments have been expressed by many other commentators, with physical distribution being referred to as 'the last frontier for cost economies' and 'marketing's economic dark continent'.

Despite this, the physical distribution function rarely receives the same degree of attention as other functional areas of business with the result that, not only is cost control often far poorer than it should or could be, but that it also tends not to be viewed or indeed managed in a strategic way. Quite obviously, the consequences of this in a domestic market can be significant. In a series of geographically distant overseas markets a poorly formulated and badly managed physical distribution system is likely to be catastrophic. For these reasons, physical distribution, particularly on an international scale, should be seen as part of the overall marketing task and managed accordingly.

Using this as our starting point, we can then say that the marketer should recognise the *total* costs of distributing the product. These include both the direct costs of moving the product from one location to another, and the indirect costs which might feasibly include the costs of stock-outs because of the possibly long lead times between ordering and delivery, the effects on cash flow of fast delivery, the warehousing costs, and so on. The significance of a stock-out was illustrated in a quite dramatic way in 1976 when Kodak began a national advertising campaign in the United States for a new instant camera before sufficient cameras had been delivered to retail outlets. Many customers, who found that the product was simply not available, bought a Polaroid instead.

Approaches to Physical Distribution

In planning patterns of physical distribution on an international scale, it is possible to identify three basic models of operation and distribution, each of which has widely differing implications for the physical distribution task.[5] These three models are illustrated in Figure 9.4. In the first of these, the company has one manufacturing base from which it supplies each of its markets. In this situation, the process of physical distribution is organised and managed centrally and has as one of its principal roles the task of ensuring that the product reaches each of the markets in the most economical way and that inventory levels ensure that stock-outs do not occur. An obvious advantage of this approach is that the size of the operation ensures that economies of scale are likely to be achieved in transporting the goods. At the same time, however, it is possible

— particularly with bulky items — that overall costs are likely to be high.

As an alternative to this, many companies in recent years have established or acquired subsidiaries with manufacturing and marketing capabilities in each of the markets in which they operate. In these circumstances the international physical distribution problem simply does not arise, since such a highly decentralised approach means that physical distribution is relegated to a purely domestic management task. The parent company can, of course, provide general advice and possibly training facilities, but little more. The economies of scale referred to above are unlikely to come into play and little or no interplay between operating units

Figure 9.4: Three Models of Physical Distribution

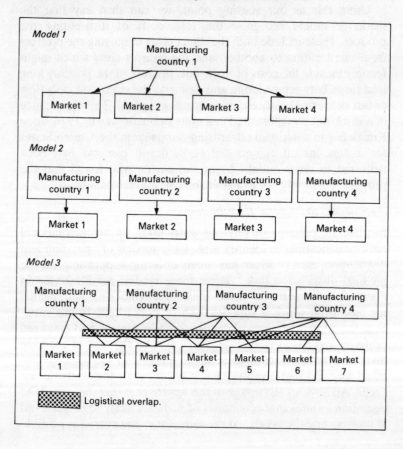

Logistical overlap.

is possible.

In the third of the models outlined, the company operates with a small number of plants which, in turn, service a larger number of markets. Of the three models, it is this form which is by far the most common, particularly amongst large companies which have been operating internationally from any length of time. The system of distribution is complex and requires a clear definition of responsibilities, as well as a highly developed planning system. The rationale underlying the system, which is often referred to as the *total logistics concept*, is that the costs of distributing the product need to be looked at from the overall corporate point of view rather than for any narrower and more insular level. In this way, it is argued, the company should be able to locate plants and warehouses more economically with the result that the firm's capital resources are used more effectively. However, if such a system is to work properly, it is imperative that it is supported by a management information system that incorporates data on each major segment of the distribution system, and that the level of expertise within the distribution function is sufficiently well developed to make full use of the information generated. The skills needed to manage this sort of system effectively are far greater than those needed for purely domestic distribution patterns, as indeed are the financial consequences if mistakes are made.

One further consequence of implementing such a system is that there is a need for a centralised planning body to co-ordinate activities and exercise overall control. Without this, the system is likely to degenerate so that distribution once again becomes more of a domestic issue. This is not, however, to make a case for total centralisation, but rather it is giving recognition to the fact that the levels of expertise needed for such a system are a scarce and expensive resource that simply cannot be made available to each operating unit within the organisation. The need for a central distribution planning authority is also a reflection of the fact that because of the ways in which interrelationships exist between the various manufacturing units and the markets being supplied, many logistical decisions simply cannot be taken at the operational level without significant dysfunctional consequences being felt elsewhere in the firm. The two major decision areas to which the marketer should therefore pay attention are, firstly, the relationships between one market and another, and secondly, inventory control. By focusing upon these two areas, it is likely that he will begin to recognise in greater detail the scope that exists for optimising the management of physical distribution costs, and minimise the potentially catastrophic consequences of stock-outs occurring.

Summary

When entering a foreign market, the choice of a pattern of distribution is likely to be an important determinant of the firm's success. The marketer may well, however, experience difficulties in developing the distribution network that he wants. There are many reasons for this, but most notably that competitive action or middleman inertia provides a barrier that is hard to overcome. The marketer does, however, need to exercise considerable care when making a choice, since typically he will find it difficult to alter the arrangements at a subsequent stage.

Physical distribution is also a major problem in international markets with transportation and inventory decisions often being made at a considerable distance from the market. Nevertheless, unless the logistics of the international firm operate smoothly and consistently, it is probable that the whole of the marketing effort will suffer.

References

1. V. Terpstra, *International Marketing* (The Dryden Press, 1978), p. 368.
2. B.C. McCammon, 'Perspectives for Distribution Programming', in L.P. Bucklin (ed.), *Vertical Marketing Systems* (Scott Foreman & Co., 1970), pp. 32-51.
3. P. Kotler, *Marketing Management: Analysis, Planning and Control*, (Prentice Hall, 1984), p. 546.
4. S. Majaro, *International Marketing: A Strategic Approach to World Markets* (George Allen & Unwin, 1978), p. 157.
5. Ibid., p. 160.

Further Reading

For a detailed discussion of the peculiarities of Japanese distribution channels, see K. Kobayashi, 'Marketing in Japan: Distribution Channels', *Tradepia International*, Winter (1980); and K. Ohmae, 'Myths and Realities of Japanese Corporations', *The McKinsey Quarterly*, Summer (1982).

10 ORGANISING FOR INTERNATIONAL MARKETING

Handled effectively, a firm's international operations offer considerable opportunities for expansion and growth. In practice, however, the extent to which advantage is taken of these opportunities will depend upon two factors: firstly, the nature and suitability of the marketing strategies pursued, and secondly, the appropriateness of the firm's international organisational structure. For many firms, organisational issues represent a significant challenge which, in practice, is often either only partially recognised or inadequately met. There are several reasons for this, including the frequently under-estimated difficulties of organising and co-ordinating operating units of varying size, type and complexity, which are staffed by people of differing abilities in geographically separate markets. In an attempt to come to terms with these difficulties, many international companies in recent years have gone through the process of re-structuring. The range of organisational options open to international companies is, however, extremely broad. There are no 'right' structures as such, although certain structures are likely to involve a better 'fit' with the company's objectives, strategies, and culture than others. The problems of identifying and subsequently implementing this structure are, however, compounded both by the ways in which the international marketing environment is changing at an ever-accelerating pace, and by the conflicting demands of globalism and the pressures of the national governments in the countries in which subsidiaries are located. But just as firms must arrive at strategies to resolve these conflicts, so they must organise operations to take account of the varying interests and lobby groups that exist within their environment. In doing this many companies have, in recent years, opted for substantial and rapid structural change, whilst others have pursued a rather slower evolutionary approach. At the same time, some firms have chosen to emphasise geographical factors in their structure, whilst others have focused upon either product divisions or developed matrix structures that attempt to give equal emphasis to a number of relevant dimensions. Equally, some companies have insisted upon a uniform structure worldwide, whilst others have been quite content to permit variations at a regional or national level. It is to these sorts of issues that we turn our attention within this chapter.

The Unique Problems of International Organisation

Few firms that operate internationally fail at one time or another to encounter significant organisational difficulties. Perhaps the biggest and most frequently encountered problem stems from the difficulties of maintaining a reasonable and adequate level of control, with the result that decisions are made either too slowly or in the absence of less than well-developed criteria. At the subsidiary level, probably the most common problem stems from the pressures from head office for a constant stream of reports on the market and the subsidiaries' activities. The net effect of these problems is that far too often there is a degree of suspicion that develops with corporate management believing that the subsidiary is failing to exploit market opportunities fully, whilst local management views corporate objectives and expectations with scepticism on the grounds that they do not fully understand local market conditions. These problems have been pointed to by various writers, including Wiechmann and Pringle who, in a study of US and European multinationals and their subsidiaries, found that it is not the political, legal, competitive and social complexities of foreign markets that cause the major problems in international marketing, but rather it is the friction, suspicion and mistrust that often builds up between head office and local staff that causes difficulties. In particular, the sorts of problems that are manifested most frequently stem from:

(i)   a lack of strategic thinking and long range planning within the subsidiary;

(ii) a lack of marketing expertise within the subsidiary;

(iii) a lack of marketing expertise locally;

(iv) inadequate patterns of communication;

(v)   insufficient use being made of head office expertise and resources;

(vi) inadequate *or* excessive head office control procedures;

(vii) unrealistic and excessive financial and marketing constraints;

(viii) an inadequate recognition at head office level of local market differences;

(ix)   a shortage of useful information from headquarters; and

(x)   a lack of a multinational orientation within corporate management.[1]

Although these sorts of problems can for the most part be overcome relatively easily, there is, as Wiechmann and Pringle argue, a fundamental need for management both at the headquarters and subsidiary levels to recognise fully the firm's objectives, the ways in which both sides might best contribute to their achievement, and the very real problems of international organisation and control.

In commenting upon these, Cundiff and Hilger suggest that:

> The job of organising marketing responsibilities, never an easy one, is still more difficult in a company engaged in international marketing. Size, in itself, presents a problem: the larger the organisation, the more complex is the job of charting the organisational relationships among the people within it. Many international marketing organisations are multinational corporations, larger than average ones. But in addition to size complexities, there are a number of specific problems unique to the international marketing environment that makes organisational planning more complex.[2]

For Cundiff and Hilger, these unique international dimensions include:

(i) *Communication Problems.* Communication across national boundaries is generally slower, more erratic and less reliable than in domestic markets, and increases the difficulties of achieving high levels of co-ordination. In addition, communication costs are often considerably higher and greater scope exists for misinterpretation and ambiguities. Equally, face-to-face communication between headquarters and subsidiary staff is generally time-consuming and adds considerably to the costs of international operations.

(ii) *Government Regulations.*   In many countries, government

regulations cause considerable difficulties for the international firm by limiting their freedom of choice. This is
particularly the case in the developing world where governments have introduced legislation requiring a minimum
percentage of local ownership, a minimum percentage of
indigenous labour, and restrictions on the repatriation of
funds. The implications of this sort of legislation can be
considerable, since it is generally designed to ensure that
multinational operations within the country take the form
of a corporate subsidiary, rather than that of the far simpler
and lower cost local branch office. This, in turn, has major
consequences not just for the method of organisational
structuring, but also for staffing and development.

(iii) *The Movement of Human Resources.*   As many commentators have observed, experienced marketing personnel are a
scarce resource in domestic marketing. At the international
level, they are an even rarer commodity and, in cost terms,
are often available only at a substantial premium. The
implications for the organisation are, therefore, once again
significant since the company has to make a choice between
exporting domestic managers who are familiar with the
company, its products and culture, but not the individual
market, or recruiting managers locally and then training
them, often at a high cost. Whichever course of action is
taken has advantages and drawbacks and, in practice, many
firms try to strike a balance of expediency. Thus, in certain
markets it is almost inevitable that a foreign manager will
experience extreme difficulties in integration and will rarely,
if ever, be accepted by the local business community. In
these circumstances, there is little real alternative to local
recruitment. In other markets, such problems are rarely if
ever encountered and offer the firm a far higher degree of
organisational flexibility. In yet other markets, the solution
has proved to lie in hiring nationals from a third country
(for example, using Danish personnel to operate in other
Scandinavian markets).

(iv) *The Effect of Foreign Sales Volume.*   An additional influence on organisational structure is the proportion of sales
volume that is imported. Thus, in some cases the majority,

if not all, of the products sold are manufactured in other countries and simply brought in via a small sales office. In other cases, the level of manufacturing capacity is far higher and may involve a proportion of the output being exported in turn to other markets. The organisational consequences of each of these varies significantly and needs both to reflect the existing pattern of operation and offer scope for further development.

(v) *The Effect of Product Line Size.* In international marketing, a relatively straightforward and uncontroversial axiom that has long been accepted is that simple product lines can be marketed with simpler marketing organisations; complex product lines need complex marketing organisations to support them. Thus, for a company with a relatively small number of technologically straightforward products that are sold into established distribution channels, organisational arrangements can be developed in an uncomplicated way. For companies which, by way of contrast, operate with a large and diverse product range, which is manufactured in a combination of local and foreign plants, the organisational structure that is needed to support and co-ordinate marketing activities will, of necessity, be far longer and more complex.

(vi) *The Nature of Market Demands.* The final major complexity of international business that needs to be reflected in the organisational structure is the extent to which the needs of buyers are similar. Thus, in many markets for products such as machine tools, office equipment and computers, the products sold are broadly similar and allow for a reasonably high degree of centralisation of activities. In a majority of consumer goods markets, however, the nature of buyers' needs differ considerably from one market to another and, of necessity, the marketing strategy has to reflect these differences. In these circumstances, the opportunities for centralisation are reduced considerably and as companies such as British Leyland, Nestlé and Unilever have found, call for a far higher proportion of marketing decisions to be made locally.

These sorts of organisational issues have, in turn, been elaborated upon by others, including Picard who focused upon:

(i)   The relatively poor quality of management in many markets which has the effect of inhibiting any real possibilities of decentralisation.

(ii) The breadth and interrelationships of the product line and its influence upon the scope for centralisation or decentralisation.

(iii) The size of the firm. Firms which are dependent upon foreign markets for a substantial proportion of their business generally move away from a divisional structure and towards a product or geographic structure in order to encourage growth.

(iv) The location and characteristics of the subsidiary operations. For a firm with subsidiaries which exhibit similar characteristics to the domestic operation, there is little real incentive to use geographic structures, since these are far more appropriate to markets which have very different features. Instead, a structure emphasising standardisation is likely to be more effective.

(v)   Economic blocs. Companies operating within a trading bloc tend to use an integrated approach within the bloc in order to cope most effectively with trade barriers.[3]

In the light of these comments, it can be seen that the major determinants of the international structure are, therefore, the degree of centralisation or decentralisation that is feasible; the evolutionary stage reached in the corporate culture; the nature and size of the business; the significance of the international marketing effort; the skills of the employees in the various operating divisions; and, perhaps most importantly of all, the international orientation of corporate management.

This international orientation can be seen to embrace a variety of factors, but refers particularly to corporate management attitudes towards the overseas environment and its willingness to invest in overseas markets, and adapt its strategies and practices to the needs of international perspectives. In discussing this, Perlmutter has identified three major international orientations amongst marketing executives: ethnocentric (home country oriented); polycentric (host country oriented); and geocentric (world oriented).[4]

The essence of the ethnocentric view is that domestic employees are both more trustworthy and more reliable than foreign nationals and that as a consequence, the perspectives and methods of operation of the domestic operation should be the basis of operating overseas. A polycentric orientation, by way of contrast, gives recognition to the different attitudes of the host country and acknowledges that foreign operations should be given the opportunity to develop a local identity. The geocentric perspective involves viewing domestic and foreign markets on a largely equal basis, with the result that foreign operations are viewed as integral elements of the overall organisation rather than as mere satellites. Emphasis is placed upon an integration of activities as far as possible with each part of the organisation being expected to maximise its contribution on the basis of its particular strengths. The organisational implications of each of these perspectives are illustrated in Table 10.1.

Issues of Centralisation versus Decentralisation

Although few organisations are either totally centralised or totally decentralised, most executives exhibit a distinct preference for one or other organisational forms. In essence, the choice between centralised and decentralised networks, particularly at the international level, is the choice between control and delegation. In practice, identifying the optimal balance between the two is often difficult to determine, but is influenced by such factors as the size and importance of the overseas operations, the location of headquarters staff and their proximity or distance from each individual market, managerial preferences of a particular style of management, their perceptions of the overseas operations (at this stage, it is worth referring back to our discussion of ethnocentric, polycentric and geocentric perspectives), and the type of decisions being made.

This final factor has been examined in some detail both by Aylmer, and Brandt and Hulbert. Aylmer's study, which focused upon the Western European activities of US-based consumer durables companies, revealed that local managers were responsible for 86 per cent of advertising decisions, 74 per cent of pricing

Table 10.1: Three Types of Headquarters Orientation towards Subsidiaries in an International Enterprise

Organisation design	Ethnocentric	Polycentric	Geocentric
Complexity of organisation	Complex in home country, simple in subsidiaries	Varied and independent	Increasingly complex and interdependent
Authority; decision-making	High in headquarters	Relatively low in headquarters	Aim for a collaborative approach between headquarters and subsidiaries
Evaluation and control	Home standards applied for persons and performance	Determined locally	Find standards which are universal and local
Rewards and punishments; incentives	High in headquarters, low in subsidiaries	Wide variation; can be high or low rewards for subsidiary performance	International and local executives rewarded for reaching local and worldwide objectives
Communication; information flow	High volume to subsidiaries' orders, commands, advice	Little to and from head-quarters. Little between subsidiaries	Both ways and between subsidiaries. Heads of subsidiaries part of management team
Identification	Nationality of owner	Nationality of host country	Truly international company but identifying with national interests
Perpetuation (recruiting, staffing, development)	Recruit and develop people of home country for key positions everywhere in in the world	Develop people of local nationality for key positions in their own country	Develop best people everywhere in the world for key positions everywhere in the world

Source: H.V. Perlmutter, 'The Tortuous Evolution of the Multinational Corporation', *Columbia Journal of World Business*, January–February (1969), p. 12.

decisions, and 61 per cent of the channel and logistical decisions. In the case of product decisions, however, strategies were in virtually every case determined by corporate staff.[5]

Brandt and Hulbert's work, which was carried out amongst 63 US, Japanese, Canadian, and European subsidiaries in Brazil, revealed broadly similar patterns, with product decisions being heavily influenced by head office, whilst pricing and promotional decisions were left largely to local management. The apparent rationale for this was the recognition that local staff often have a far better insight to the market, although at a corporate level, the search for economies of scale requires management to centralise R & D facilities and to standardise product specifications as far as possible.[6]

Criteria for Choice

Although the effectiveness of an organisational structure can ultimately only be determined by its ability to meet the organisation's goals, there are several factors to which the marketer should pay particular attention when deciding how best to develop the international structure. The most important of these are the lines of authority and responsibility, the patterns of communication, and the scope that exists for co-operation of international activities.

The complexity of many international structures offers considerable scope for confusion and doubt as to who is responsible for what, and unless particular care is taken to ensure that patterns of authority are well-delineated, the structure of the entire international operation is likely to be weakened. Equally, truly effective co-ordination can only be achieved if these lines of authority and responsibility allow for a high level of communication between the various parts of organisation.

In practice, however, the criteria for choice that are used are often far less specific and many organisations have developed largely on the basis of expediency with communication and co-ordination gaps being filled as they become evident.

The Evolution of International Structures

In order to understand how and why international organisational structures have developed in the way in which they have, we need to begin by examining the organisational life cycle through which many international corporations appear to progress.

When companies first begin the process of international marketing, the activity tends to be largely ad hoc in nature with a limited number of products being introduced into a small number of markets by means of either a home-based export programme or a licensing agreement. At this stage, control poses relatively few problems and the existing headquarters staff generally take full responsibility for overseeing the international operation. In time, this leads to the creation of a specialised export department designed to give more structure and impetus to overseas activities.

As the volume of international business grows, companies tend to adopt an increasingly strategic perspective involving a series of decisions about the nature and scale of international activity. One result of this is often the emergence of a more autonomous international division with its own divisional board to develop and co-ordinate wholly or partly owned companies with their own manufacturing and marketing capability in foreign markets.

If the range and size of international activity then continues to grow, evidence suggests that, in many companies, the scale of operations simply becomes too great for a home-based international division to manage. There seems then to be two common structural reactions. The first of these involves the creation of worldwide product divisions. The second reaction, which may be consonant with the retention of the international division, leads to the development of regional headquarters with the responsibility for developing and co-ordinating plans on a regional basis. In terms of their suitability, product divisions have generally proved to be appropriate for companies with unrelated product lines, whereas an emphasis upon a regional structure has been favoured by companies with a limited and inter-linked product mix.

In the late 1970s, however, many international companies found that a specific emphasis on either product or geography was becoming increasingly unsatisfactory, and attempts were made to accommodate both elements by developing matrix structures. More recently, the emphasis upon globalism has led some international companies, and particularly the largest, to declare that they are global companies with an organisational structure that makes no distinction between domestic and international operations. Whether this is indeed the case is, however, arguable since even the very largest multinationals have a country of origin which is often where their corporate management is still located. This, in turn, leads to a particular managerial philosophy and culture emanating from corporate headquarters and pervading throughout the organisation. It is also to the corporate staff that the rest of the organisation ultimately looks for direction and control, and from where vetoes emerge.

In practice, however, the extent to which international firms have moved through this organisational life cycle varies enormously, and has proved to be more true of American than European multinationals. Many European multinationals, for example, omitted an international division stage and moved directly from 'Mother–Daughter' structures to worldwide product divisions or global operations. By the same token, some American multinationals have simply remained at the international division stage, and appended product divisions and/or regional head-quarters to the international division. The rationale of the model is, however, straightforward and suggests that international structures need to change in order to cope with changing environmental pressures. The pressures that create change and the reactions to those pressures by international companies are complex and varied. However, it would not be overly simplistic to conclude that the fundamental issue often revolves around the need to reconcile the urge on the part of the company to integrate its operations globally with the need to take note of national differences both in terms of consumer needs and tastes, and political pressures from national governments for the international firms to conform to their needs and requirements. This fundamental issue has an impact upon key organisational debates surrounding individual subsidiary autonomy, regional or subsidiary decentralisation, headquarters centralisation of decision-making and pressures for global strate-gies. In commenting on this, Yves Doz concludes that, in essence, companies are faced with three choices:

(1) *To adopt a worldwide integration strategy* in which the economic imperative for a global strategy dominates. The activities of national subsidiaries are integrated and centrally managed. To illustrate this, he cites Ford as an obvious example.

(2) *To adopt a national responsiveness strategy* whereby companies give subsidiaries much greater autonomy and leeway to respond to local political pressures and local consumer demand.

(3) *To adopt an administrative coordination strategy* which, whilst allowing for genuine strategic planning, involves the company in making every strategic decision *on its own merits*. In essence, there is no predominant mode of decision-making nor a consistent structure in terms of the location of decision-making.

Doz suggests that (1) will predominate in free world trade situations and (2) in industries where the political imperative is likely to prevail. In reality, a large number of companies operate in markets where both economic and political imperatives have some influence and are therefore organised along the lines of administrative co-ordination.[7]

A Framework for Change

Even within the constraints imposed by economic and political imperative, technology, scale, and the competitive environment, companies have a choice with regard to the rate at which they change their organisational structure. Work by Bartlett, for example, has indicated that whereas some companies choose to restructure radically and rapidly (he cites Westinghouse in 1979), many companies concentrate upon developing successful multi-dimensional decision-making processes without necessarily resorting to major changes in their formal organisations. Bartlett illustrated this by means of a study of five health care companies whose task complexity involved: 'The need to be simultaneously responsive at the national level yet efficient globally; the need to develop multiple functional expertise at multiple organisational levels; and the need to be flexible in the way all these demands were managed.'

Rather than implement immediate major structural changes the companies in the sample tended to concentrate upon the management of a gradual evolutionary process. The process involved interlinked phases consisting of:

(1) The gradual development of new management perspectives and skills. Essentially this centred upon an attempt to strengthen the influence of product and functional managers who had previously been less influential than country managers. As part of this process, it was hoped that country managers would accept the growing influence of product and functional managers and would work together to enhance decision-making.

(2) Subtle and incremental changes in structure. Reflecting the philosophy expressed in (1), regional offices were established, divisional level staff groups were strengthened in quality and size, and the information and control systems were developed.

(3) Senior management worked on the 'organisational climate' to institutionalise the changes outlined above. The target climate was one of broadened managerial perception, flexible decision-making and multiple channels of communication.

By adopting this sort of phased approach, it is likely that many of the stresses that companies face in restructuring can be minimised. This has been emphasised by a number of writers in recent years, including Doyle who has suggested that much organisational restructuring in the 1970s was influenced by fashion and by the influence of companies and, as a consequence, in some cases misdirected. With a changing international environment requiring further structural change, companies should therefore be careful before beginning the process of change and pay attention to each issue as:

(i)   ensuring that the key problem/issue is an organisational one;

(ii) keep the modification as simple as it can be whilst fulfilling the need for change;

(iii) do not automatically attempt a unitary solution;

(iv) continually monitor the strategic goals of the company to ensure that the new structure will facilitate attainment of those goals;

(v)   link the structural changes to the planning and control function;

(vi) avoid too radical a move along the centralisation/decentralisation spectrum;

(vii) ensure that key managers' duties are clearly delineated;

(viii) involve key personnel in the new design;

integrate the structure with the information systems of the company;

(x)   review constantly; and

(xi) study the problems faced by other international companies when changing their structure.

The Organisational Alternatives

Although there are in practice many ways in which the multinational firm can be organised, the approaches adopted by a majority of firms can be examined within a framework of five distinct structural patterns:

(i)   international subsidiary structures;
(ii)   international division structures;
(iii) geographic structures;
(iv)   product structures;
(v)   matrix structures.

A sixth type, the functional structure, could feasibly be added to this list, although a study by Stopford and Wells of 170 multinationals concluded that because of its emphasis upon centralisation, few, if any, firms now use this approach.[8]

International Subsidiary Structure

As we have already observed, when companies are in the very early stages of international marketing, the activity tends to be managed within the existing domestic structure. The first organisational change is likely to occur when the company formally establishes overseas subsidiary companies and the home country headquarters needs to develop a communication structure for these subsidiary operations. Typically, this is done by creating a series of subsidiary boards with responsibility for the development of overseas markets, and reporting directly to the main board of the parent company (see Figure 10.1). Whilst this is a relatively straightforward and low-cost approach to international organisation, there are several advantages to this, including the way in which it provides a counter pressure to dominance by product division and headquarters staff; the greater potential that it provides for national market targeting; the increased career opportunities it offers for local nationals; and the way in which it leads to a greater awareness of local market needs. Insofar as there are disadvantages, they stem from its possible encouragement of parochial thinking on the part of local managers; the pressure that it puts on headquarters senior management as the number of subsidiaries increases; and its inhibiting influence upon proper international integration. Nevertheless, it is a form of organisation which, in the early days of international operations at least, has been found by many companies to be an attractive and effective structure.

Figure 10.1: International Subsidiary Structure

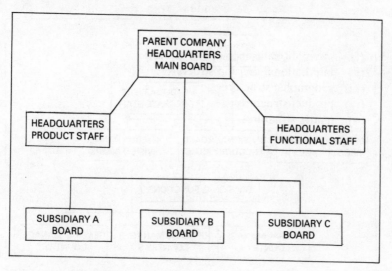

The International Division Structure

Having begun with a series of international subsidiaries, many firms as they grow move towards an international division structure in which the firm's activities are rather more formally separated on the basis of domestic and international operations. The rationale for this is to provide a more obvious and direct focus for international development and is normally achieved by giving a senior headquarters manager line authority and direct responsibility for the international division's profitability. GEC operate with an Overseas Division that manufactures and markets a large proportion of the output of domestically based divisions such as Power Engineering, Industrial Products, Components, Cables and Wires. By doing this the organisation begins to develop greater international expertise and provides an authoritative and more substantial lobby group within the company to champion the cause of international business (see Figure 10.2). Insofar as there are limitations to this structure, they tend to emerge as the organisation grows and the business simply becomes too diverse for truly effective co-ordination. In these circumstances, corporate planning of two largely autonomous units — domestic and international — becomes increasingly difficult and conflicts begin to emerge in such areas as research and development and product policy. In

Figure 10.2: International Division Structure

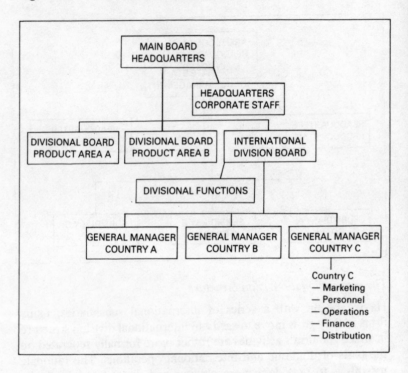

commenting on this, Jain has observed, 'that R & D cannot be easily decentralised and, therefore, it tends to be domestically oriented. With the basic research domestically centred, R & D for overseas is usually diminished to only product modification.'[9]

Geographic Structures

Because of the sorts of problems that are typically experienced with international divisions, many multinationals eventually move towards a worldwide geographic structure in which domestic and foreign functional activities are integrated, whilst markets are separated into geographic regions (see Figure 10.3). Day-to-day responsibility is passed to area line managers with headquarters staff having overall responsibility for planning and control. In 1977 Cadbury-Schweppes adopted a structure based on five world regions: the United Kingdom, America, Europe, Australia and Other. Each region had product divisions. In addition there was a

Figure 10.3: Geographic Structure

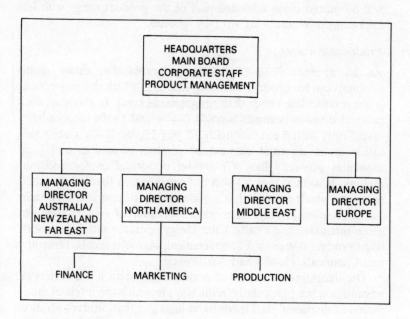

Health and Hygiene Division with worldwide responsibilities. Headquarters' functions of Finance, Marketing, Technical and Personnel were invested with worldwide responsibilities.

In discussing a regional organisation, Phatak suggests that the structure has proved to be most appropriate for multinationals which exhibit certain characteristics, including:

(i)   diverse product lines;
(ii) relatively short channels of distribution;
(iii) products are adapted to match local needs.[10]

The advantages of geographic organisation can be considerable, since the delegation of authority and responsibility is both logical and clear-cut. The opportunities for co-ordination of production and marketing is increased and the organisation has the opportunity to develop far higher levels of international expertise than previously. Insofar as drawbacks do exist, they lie in the fact that the system is heavily dependent upon highly competent managers if it is to run effectively, and that unless product managers are introduced into the system, there is a danger that over-emphasis will be placed upon a limited part of the product range with less important products being virtually ignored.

Product Structures

As an alternative to organising geographically, many multi-nationals opt for product-based structures in which the major focus is the product line rather than geographical areas. In this way, each product division becomes a profit centre and profit responsibility rests firmly with the divisional head (see Figure 10.4). Decentralisation is an essential element of product structures and local managers generally have far greater opportunities for decision-making. It is, therefore, a system of organisation that is best suited to a firm which not only has a wide variety of end users, but also has diversified product lines which, because of cost factors, are often manufactured locally. Ciba-Geigy operates with four world-wide product divisions: Pharmaceutical, Agrochemicals, Dyestuffs and Chemicals, Plastics and Additives.

The decentralisation that underlies this system has a variety of advantages, but particularly in the ways in which the levels of motivation of divisional staff tends to be high and that product addition

Figure 10.4: Product Structure

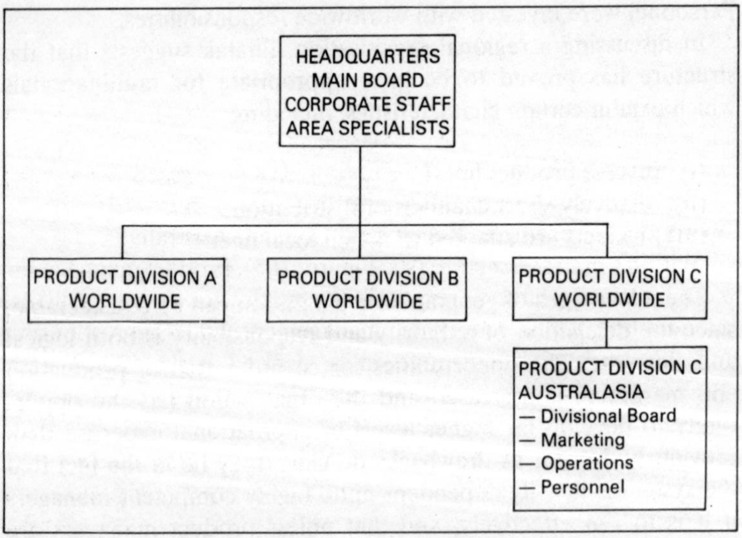

and deletion decisions can often be made relatively easily. The disadvantages of product structures are, by way of contrast, relatively limited and manageable, and stem from the possible problems of co-ordination *across* product divisions, and the way in which minor product areas may be overlooked in certain parts of the world. In an attempt to overcome this latter problem, attention in recent years has been paid to making use of area specialists with specific responsibility for ensuring that this does not happen.[11]

Matrix Structures

As multinationals have grown ever larger, the single-line-of-command structures that we have discussed so far have, in practice, proved to be increasingly inadequate. Because of this, the very large multinationals in particular have begun to pay greater attention to matrix organisations in which certain staff report to two bosses rather than to one. The major advantage of this dual chain of command is most evident when the firm needs to respond quickly to changes in more than one dimension of the environment (for example, products and geography); where there is a high level of environmental uncertainty and change; and when resource constraints exist.[12] Thus, matrix structures provide an obvious solution to the need faced by many multinationals to respond effectively to differing economic, political and competitive environments, since they can incorporate elements of product management and geographic management. The Reckitt and Colman group employ a fairly complex matrix structure with executive directors responsible on a regional basis to the Chief Executive. However each product division (Food and Wine, Household and Toiletries, Pharmaceutical, and Leisure) has worldwide responsibilities. In addition certain overseas companies attain almost complete autonomy because of the scale of their operation, for example, Reckitt and Colman, Australia.

Within a matrix structure (see Figure 10.5), product management would typically have a responsibility worldwide for a particular product line, whilst geographic management would be responsible for the total product range in a defined geographical area. The overlaps that then emerge are then used as the basis for decision-making in the sense that geographic managers are expected to argue the case for overall efficiency and competitiveness. Underpinning this in the majority of matrix organisations is a system of dual budgeting, together with twin accounting systems

Figure 10.5: Matrix Structures

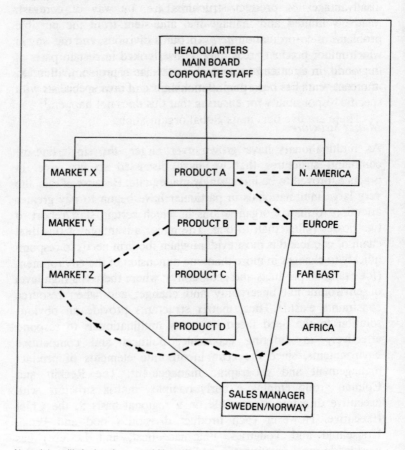

HEADQUARTERS
MAIN BOARD
CORPORATE STAFF

MARKET X   PRODUCT A ‑ ‑ ‑ ‑ N. AMERICA

MARKET Y   PRODUCT B ‑ ‑ ‑ ‑ EUROPE

MARKET Z   PRODUCT C   FAR EAST

PRODUCT D   AFRICA

SALES MANAGER
SWEDEN/NORWAY

Note: It is unlikely that there would be a direct reporting relationship on market lines.

designed to provide independent measures of performance.

The obvious complexities of matrix structures have in practice led to some multinationals experiencing a variety of problems in their implementation, including lengthy power struggles which have on occasions led to an imbalance between the two arms of the matrix. Nevertheless, many others have found the system to be an extremely effective way of responding to a rapidly changing environment and this, in turn, has led to some organisations developing the system further. The majority of matrices are, however, as we have shown, two-dimensional, balancing product and regional emphases. However, some firms such as Philips and Ciba-Geigy, have experimented with three-dimensional matrices in which individual markets are also incorporated, seemingly with reasonable degrees of success. In the case of Philips, the Dutch electronics giant, for example, a matrix structure incorporating regional, product and functional inputs has emerged. Within this there are multiple reporting relationships and responsibilities.

There are five tiers in its global organisation:

1. The Board of Management — the president and two vice-presidents — reports to the Board of Directors.
2. Fourteen product divisions with global responsibility for development, manufacture, and marketing of their products.
3. Operating service departments at Eindhoven (head-quarters). Staff services available both to product divisions and national subsidiaries.
4. Regional bureaus represent national subsidiaries in a region, performing an 'ambassadorial' function in the area and facilitating communications between Eindhoven and subsidiaries.
5. National organizations (subsidiaries). Have a dotted line relation with regional bureaus but actually report to the Board of Management. Of course, product divisions have a voice in their operations too.[13]

Organisation in Practice

Because of the ways in which multinationals generally develop and operate, it is difficult to conceive of a situation where a company can make a considered and objective decision regarding the choice of a future international organisational structure. Instead, the structures adopted by companies tend to be a reflection of their history, their past and present culture, managerial preferences, and expediency. This, in turn, has led to different patterns of development amongst European and American multinationals and, in many cases, to a hybrid system emerging in which there is a mixture of matrix, product, geographic and international divisional structures. This has been pointed to by a variety of writers, includ-

ing Holmen who revealed that in the case of large American multinationals, the majority appear to have developed matrix structures
with geographic and product/market elements on the two axes.
Regional Offices or international divisions then act as an inter-
mediate step between managers at the corporate and national
levels. The major advantage of this from the viewpoint of corporate management is that it no longer has the problem of constantly
having to come to terms with individual market peculiarities.
Equally, national management benefits because of the way in
which the international division can interpret corporate policy and
act as a conduit for information.[14]

Implementing Organisational Change

Although very few firms would claim to have the ideal international structure, considerable evidence exists to suggest that
many companies go through a regular process of review and
structural change. The sort of criteria to which attention should be
paid were identified by Widing and subsequently incorporated into
a framework for an evaluation of the various alternatives that exist
(see Table 10.2).[15]

The motives for change can, quite obviously, vary considerably
and include an attempt to cope with issues such as sales growth,
increased competitive pressures, new product development acquisitions, and a growing awareness of the inadequacies of existing
structural arrangements. Clearly, however, the structure chosen
must fulfil such criteria as:

(i)   the creation of a clear and comprehensive system of
      power, authority and decision-making;
(ii) facilitate effective communication between the various
      parts of the organisation;
(iii) provide for effective co-ordination of global activities;
(iv) facilitate a concentration of company resources upon key
      markets, products and regions;
(v)   ensure effective global new product development;
(vi) ensure that managers are not demotivated by structural
      elements that create impediments to action.

Table 10.2: The Appropriateness of Multinational Organisational Structures to Corporate Concerns

Area of corporate concern	International division	Level of suitability		
		Worldwide product division	Area division	Matrix
Rapid growth	Medium	High	Medium	High
Diversity of products	Low	High	Low	High
High technology	Medium	High	Low	High
Few experienced managers	High	Medium	Low	Low
Close corporate control	Medium	High	Low	High
Close government relations	Medium	Low	High	Medium
Resource allocation:				
Product considerations should dominate	Low	High	Low	Medium
Geographical considerations should dominate	Medium	Low	High	Medium
Functional considerations should dominate	Low	Medium	Low	High
Relative cost	Medium	Medium	Low	High

Source: J. William Widing, Jr., 'Reorganising your Worldwide Business', *Harvard Business Review*, May/June (1973), p. 149.

In addition, the structure must be consistent with future international objectives and product/market strategies.

European and American Multinational Structures

Although some observers have argued that all multinationals are broadly similar in terms of their objectives and outlook, there is little or no evidence to suggest this is really so, particularly when comparisons are made between, say, European, American and Japanese firms. In the case of European and American multinationals, for example, there are considerable differences between their patterns of development in terms of the scale of operations, growth rates, relative importance of domestic and overseas markets, strategies and objectives, and in their organisational structures.

The Historical Development of European MNCs

One of the most extensive historical accounts of the development of European multinationals remains that of Franko. Some of the key historical strands outlined in his work include:

(1) The predominance in the pre-1971 period of the 'mother–daughter' structure in which close links exist between the president of the subsidiary and the president and board of the parent company. Franko estimated that, in 1971, 25 of the 70 companies he studied had such a structure (see Figure 10.6). By way of contrast, US experiences suggested that such a pattern had disappeared many years previously.

(2) In many cases, the European mother–daughter structure was used by companies with relatively narrow product-lines.

(3) In the post-war period, European multinationals were faced with a high level of geographical dispersion of their operations worldwide. Their markets were often very separated and this led to a certain logic underpinning the mother–daughter structure.

(4) The European multinationals lagged behind US companies in recognising the communication benefits that could evolve from a genuine supranational structure.

(5) The move away from a mother–daughter structure was led

Figure 10.6: The 'Mother–Daughter' Structure

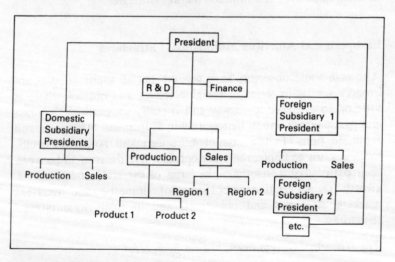

Source: L. Franko, *The European Multinationals* (London, Harper and Row 1976), p. 187.

by companies with large operations in the USA such as Ciba-Geigy, Philips and Nestlé.

(6) Linked to (4) and (5), a major incentive for change appeared to be the need within some European companies for authentic international communications. This need was particularly highlighted in industries facing US company competition within European markets.

(7) The pattern of structural change of European companies followed a different sequence to that experienced by American companies:

    (i) many European companies missed out the international division phase;

    (ii) some European companies experienced concurrent home and international reorganisation.

(8) Some companies with large home markets did opt for an International Division structure.

(9) Along with international restructuring, more formalised management procedures were introduced.[16]

In a subsequent article that was published in 1974, Franko provided further insights to the structural development of European companies. In particular, he highlighted an apparent move amongst a number of European companies towards a multi-divisional structure that appeared to be prompted both by an increase in the competitive environment (in many cases from US multinationals), and by a breakdown in the negotiating environment that existed prior to the formation of the EEC. In addition, he concluded that structural evolution appeared to be moving at an ever-increasing pace in companies that were based in European countries in which there is a high level of US penetration. Thus, restructuring activity was intense in the UK and Benelux countries, but much slower and more leisurely in France and Spain.

In the light of these comments, a question that then arises is what is likely to happen in organisational terms during the remaining part of the century. On the basis of current trends, it seems likely that the market environment will be equally turbulent, although evidence suggests that there will be greater emphasis upon organisational evolution than upon revolution in order to cope with this. Achieving satisfactory organisational structures will not, however, be helped by the frenetic merger and acquisition activity that has characterised the 1980s, particularly in Europe.

Nevertheless, it seems likely that further mergers amongst European firms will be necessary simply to withstand increasing Japanese competition. Mergers aside, the key issue that appears likely to dominate the structural debate is still the degree of autonomy that is to be granted to regional and national subsidiaries.

Future Organisational Scenarios

During the final part of the century, the organisational structures adopted by companies operating in international markets will be continually subjected to change as competitive pressures increase and conflicts between economic and political imperatives increasingly come to dominate the thinking of international managers. Within this, the move towards global strategies and products will undoubtedly exert a significant influence, as will the mergers and acquisitions that will occur as the weaker competitors find that their international viability is eroded. In addition, there will be even greater pressure upon headquarters to cope with an array of challenges and it is likely that increased autonomy will be devolved to the regions. Simple shifts of decision-making may not, however, be adequate to meet the challenges. The world environment is changing so fast that companies may need to give consideration to a general move from essentially bureaucratic structures towards structures that are more able to cope with change, structures that Minzberg would classify as 'adhocratic'.

Some reorientations that are already apparent and which seem likely to feature in 'new' international structures include:

(i) decentralised matrix structures in which companies rely not on a global matrix structure, but upon regional/product matrices;

(ii) more frequent relocation of divisions in order to take advantage of tax incentives offered by potential host countries;

(iii) greater emphasis upon a federalised approach to global management, with a top management group consisting of representatives of fairly autonomous regional/local operations;

(iv) more adhocratic structures in which temporary task forces and project teams designed to cope with change operate within a more traditional framework.

Against this background, it is also possible to identify a number of trends that appear to have specific relevance for European companies:

(1) *Convergence.* In the late 1970s and early 1980s, a number of studies of multinational companies and their operations overseas concluded that European companies allowed greater autonomy to subsidiary operations than did American companies. European companies were alleged to be more informal in style, demanded less headquarters consultation and allowed for greater autonomy in decision-making. There is, however, growing evidence of convergence as American companies allow greater autonomy in certain areas whilst the European companies have tended to move in some measure to greater headquarter control.

(2) *European Companies Operating in the USA.* It would appear that European companies have in the past, and will continue in the future, to give a greater level of autonomy to their subsidiaries operating in the USA (and other key markets) than is their normal practice. It seems likely that the predominant view is that such autonomy is necessary to facilitate effective competitive strategies.

(3) *Structural Similarities.* Linked to the issue of greater convergence, American and European structures are much closer in terms of similarity than they were a decade ago. Many European and American companies are still experimenting with structures that are essentially matrix in nature. Overall there appears to be a move to strengthening regional orientations. However this appears to be more marked in American companies. Some European companies have been experimenting with product divisions. Other European companies have a structure that reflects a history of regional product/area matrices and are building up this legacy in their international structures. Indeed, it has been predicted that such structures will become the dominant international organisational form of the future.

Summary

The question of how best to structure international operations can only be answered with extreme care. The consequences of an inadequate organisational structure are significant and can have a major impact upon the firm's performance in the market place. Many organisations begin their international activities by adopting a relatively straightforward approach in which a high level of control rests with corporate management, and then only over time more towards more complex and decentralised structures. The criteria for organisational choice are in one sense relatively straightforward, although in practice their interpretation is often complicated by the preconceived attitudes of management, resource constraints, and by the lack of managerial skill available in subsidiary operations.

References

1. U.E. Wiechmann and L.G. Pringle, 'Problems that Plague Multinational Marketers', *Harvard Business Review*, July-August (1979), pp. 188-24.

2. E.W. Cundiff and M.T. Hilger, *Marketing in the International Environment*, Prentice Hall (1984), p. 222.

3. J. Picard, 'Determinants of Centralisation of Marketing Decision Making in Multinational Corporations', in *Marketing in the 80's* (American Marketing Association, 1980), pp. 259-61.

4. H.U. Perlmutter, 'The Tortuous Evolution of the Multinational Corporation, *Columbia Journal of World Business*, January-February (1969), p. 12.

5. R.J. Aylmer, 'Who Makes Marketing Decisions in the Multinational Firm', *Journal of Marketing*, October (1970), pp. 25-30.

6. W.K. Brandt and J.M. Hulbert, 'Headquarters Guidance in Marketing Strategy in the Multinational Subsidiary', *Columbia Journal of World Business*, Winter (1977), pp. 7-14.

7. Y. Doz, 'Strategic Management in Multinational Companies', *Sloan Management Review*, Winter (1980).

8. J.M. Stopford and L.T. Wells, *Managing the Multinational Enterprise* (Basic Books, New York, 1983). Also see Douglas Dickson, 'Case of the Reluctant Multinational', *Harvard Business Review*, January-February 1972, p. 6.

9. S.C. Jain, *International Marketing Management*, (Kent Publishing Company, 1984), p. 630.

10. A.V. Phatak, *International Dimensions of Management* (Kent Publishing Company, 1983), pp. 65-89.

11. W.H. Davidson and P. Haspeslagh, 'Shaping a Global Product Organisation', *Harvard Business Review*, July-August (1982), pp. 125-32.

12. See, e.g. W.C. Goggin, 'How the Multinational Structure Works at Dow Corning', *Harvard Business Review*, January-February (1974), pp. 64-5.

13. V. Terpstra, *International Marketing* (The Dryden Press, 1978), p. 572.

14. M.G. Holmen, 'Organisation and Staffing of Foreign Operations of

Multinational Corporations', Paper presented to the Academy of International Business, New Orleans, October (1980).

15. J.W. Widing, 'Reorganising Your Worldwide Business', *Harvard Business Review*, May-June (1975), p. 159.

16. L. Franko, 'The European Multinationals' (London, Harper and Row, 1976), Ch. 8.

Appendix 10.1 Case: Reckitt and Colman PLC

In the mid 1980s Reckitt and Colman PLC had sales worldwide worth £1,124.40 million. Reckitt and Son was first registered as a public company in 1888, J. and J. Colman in 1898. In 1913 a joint company, Atlantis Ltd was formed by the two companies to trade in South America, with profits being pooled. In 1938 Reckitt and Colman was formed to manage all business outside the United Kingdom. In 1953 Reckitt and Colman merged within the United Kingdom to be formally joined by Chiswick Products in 1954.

Today Reckitt and Colman has a portfolio of brands ranging from ethical pharmaceuticals to wine. The company has manufacturing facilities in 37 countries and sales in over 120. The company's portfolio is divided into six divisions:

Division	Brand Examples
Food and Wine	Colman's Mustard, Robinsons Drinks, Gale's Honey
Household and Toiletry	Mr Sheen, Swish, Windolene
Pharmaceutical	Dettol, Solmin, Disprin, Gaviscon
Colours	Reckitts Blue
Industrial Cleaning	—
Leisure	Winsor and Newton paints

Approximately 72 per cent of the company's sales were outside the United Kingdom in 1984 and 34,800 employees were engaged in company activity worldwide. Profit before tax was £106 million. In the first six months of 1985 world sales were £663 million and profit before tax £58 million. In December 1984 Reckitt and Colman purchased the Airwick Division of Ciba-Geigy. Reckitt and Colman Chief Executive, John West, argued that the purchase enhanced the company's world operations 'through synergy both in product terms and geographical spread, its main units being in those countries in which we needed to be considerably stronger in the household product category'.[1]

An interesting global structure has emerged at Reckitt and Colman which can be best described as matrix in nature. There are main board directors with Group responsibilities for the following world regions:

The Americas
U.K. and Europe
Australasia, Africa and Asia.

In addition product divisions, headed by managing directors, have worldwide responsibility for the products within their divisions. To ensure effective global co-ordination specific main board directors also have oversight of nominated product divisions.

Reference

1. Company Annual Report, 1985.

INDEX